To Mary Lee
A beautiful woman —
Much love,
Connie Morgan

STAND, WALK
RUN FREE

Overcoming Expectations of a Perfect Life

CONSTANCE MORGAN

SHALLOW
CREEK

TABLE OF CONTENTS

Foreword
Prologue

Epilogue
Acknowledgments
Book Order Form

FOREWORD

The birth of your first child is a moment in time that you, as a parent, vividly remember. In that child you see reflections of yourself and aspirations for your future. When you realize your child has a disability, your dreams are shattered, your future is altered.

As a young mother, Connie confronted her sadness and overwhelming fear without the benefits of experience and maturity that come with parenting. Instead she armed herself with love and determination to face a challenge that was enormous and awe-inspiring.

This is a compelling book that bares a parent's most painful thoughts and candidly conveys soul-wrenching decisions. We hope that Connie's honesty will help other parents who are learning to live with a disability or suffer any kind of painful situation.

From birth to adulthood, we never know what life may bring. But we at *United Cerebral Palsy* know that with compassion and a willingness to give joy and purpose to each individual life, children and adults like Chris can return this joy and a sense of fulfillment to all of us. We can learn from them and are privileged to be included in their circle of family and the universe of caring. May that universe be ever expanding.

Ronald S. Cohen
Executive Director & CEO United Cerebral Palsy
Serving Los Angeles, Ventura, and Santa Barbara Counties

Prologue

The Beginning of My Journey

Dear Reader,

The writing of this book was not preceded by extensive research or a structured concept. That all came later. First, I had to place myself physically, mentally, and emotionally into each and every incident. After the details were documented, countless years of work and spiritual guidance created the master plan. There is no scholarly pretense about this work nor an attempt to target any specific person, group, or incident, but rather an earnest desire to help others along their journey.

My childhood took place during the early forties, after the Depression and during World War II. My parents, Larry and Isabel Morgan, persevered with faith and hard work to turn barren, sun-parched plains into a beautiful ranch on the Smoky Hill River in western Kansas, an environment that gave me unlimited opportunity for adventure and creativity.

A typical day on the ranch started with a hearty breakfast and ended with family dinner around the table. On Sunday, I attended church with my parents, my younger sister, and brother. Once a month, after services, we dined at the historic Waters Hotel with its simple elegance of hardwood floors, crisp white linens, and fresh flowers. During the twelve-mile drive home against a background of Kansas skies, golden wheat fields, grazing cattle, and an occasional windmill, I watched with fascination as Dad smoked a cigar and created perfect smoke rings.

During those early years, I learned that my parents' tenacity and courage helped them overcome hardship and adversity. While Dad exercised his independent ideas and leadership skills in community service, his agriculture interests and ranching experience led to banking positions of agricultural loan officer and bank director. Mother, with her analytical nature and artistic abilities, was dedicated to the domestic scene and a shared role in coordinating ranch activities.

My education began in a one-room schoolhouse four miles from home, then continued with grade school and high school in Goodland, Kansas, and graduation in 1960 from Kansas State University. Growing up in a community of 5,000 people, I was active in local and state 4-H activities, cheerleading, baton twirling, and national organizations. These activities, as much as I enjoyed them, were always overshadowed by a curious and inquiring mind that caused me to suspect there was more to my world than what I knew.

It wasn't until my expectations of a *perfect life* were shattered by painful and heartbreaking events that I discovered what was missing. Through my experiences with my disabled son, Chris, I realized the true purpose of living.

In the long process of learning to deal with Chris' cerebral palsy, I joined with one hundred forty-eight members of the Mothers' Auxiliary to create better services and more stimulating activities for our disabled children. During that same time, I became a primary participant in fund-raising for a five-acre site in Chatsworth, California, a model residential facility where Chris became a resident.

Later, after my divorce, I returned to school and earned a Master's Degree in Education from the University of Denver. As Social Services Coordinator for Hope Center, I supervised financial and educational services for sixty-eight developmentally disabled students and their families. I served on the Board of Directors of Denver Developmental Services, which focused on residential alternatives. I participated in parent education groups, community workshops, and a brother-sister group.

I wrote articles for the *National Camp Fire Leader Magazine: What Is Mental Retardation; Understanding the Mentally Retarded Person; Activities for Children with Disability; Everyone Needs a Friend.*

Other educational writings include: *WHERE IS THE LIFE THAT WAS LOST IN LIVING? Sociological Aspects of Culture and Marriage: The Construction of Reality in Relation to the Adjustment Process Faced by Parents of Handicapped Children; Contrasting Existentialism with the Nature of Human Society As Seen By George Herbert Mead and Implications on Education.*

A tragedy, such as a disabled child, an incurable disease, or a major loss is an opportunity to realize the true meaning of *suffering*, and to become fully engaged with life. That is when suffering ceases to be suffering.

In this book, I am reaching out to women, men, parents, teachers, counselors, clergy, and even adult children who are not only seeking to better understand themselves, but ultimately discover more effective ways in which to contribute to the lives of others. I hope my story will help you find the truth in your own experiences and discover possibilities you never imagined.

Constance Morgan
MA - University of Denver

Although I have made every attempt to be accurate and fair while writing this book, the credibility of STAND, WALK, RUN FREE *is based on professional research, carefully documented events, and my perceptions of the experience. The story is presented in a spirit of love and gratitude to significant people in my life – both past and present.*

In sections of the book I have taken minor liberties with chronology to enhance the flow of the story. Some of the names in the book have been changed, but where names are authentically used, it is with the intention of honoring their role in the story and their contribution to my journey.

CM

1

ROSEBUD ON THE ALTAR

Phil drove up the winding mountain road toward the General's home. Glimpses of the famous Hudson River were visible through the trees that lined the water's edge just beyond a large grassy area below us. The gentle summer breeze moved across my face through the open window, as Phil exclaimed, "We're almost there!" It seemed so perfect I hardly knew what to say. The mountain road curved and we could see the General's home up ahead, an ivy-covered stone mansion overlooking the Hudson, surrounded by lush vegetation. Tall, majestic trees gave it a splendid sense of history.

I was awestruck by the stately reflection of wealth and power as the private, unpaved road led us directly to the front entrance of the mansion. As Phil opened my door I nervously stepped onto a cushion of bark and pine needles, barely noticing the eerie silence that accompanied the shadowy rays of the late afternoon sun filtering through the foliage.

We approached the mansion's ornately carved front door and were greeted by the housekeeper. Smiling, she said, "You must be Connie and Phil. The General's wife is expecting you."

Inside, dark hardwood floors provided a rich, warm background for fine oriental rugs and handsome period furnishings. Architectural treasures and art from around the world enhanced the classic elegance and appealed to my longing for dignity and prestige.

A country girl from Kansas, I felt I had just entered a palace and was in the presence of royalty. I took in every detail of an antique mahogany desk and a Queen Anne chair upholstered in a rich crimson. I observed the opulence of other pieces and

Connie's mother, **Isabel Porter-Morgan**, in her country kitchen.
Goodland, Kansas - 1940

felt a passion that simmered just beneath the surface. At that moment, I could imagine only the best for my life.

It seems like yesterday when Mother stood in the kitchen telling me the history of my early childhood. I can still hear the fluttering of the nasty miller moths against the windows as they were drawn to the light, and the banging of the screen door as our dog wandered onto the back porch.

"Connie," she said, "You were only two years old and your sister was barely one when we moved out to the ranch. A narrow dirt trail led to a house that was a colossal mess. When I first saw the house there was no running water or bathroom, not even a kitchen sink or cupboards. The only heat was a gas stove in the living room. Outside, the land was pretty bare. It was a bad drought in those years—awful, awful dry. People thought we were crazy to move twelve miles from town to this God-forsaken place, willing to risk everything for our dream.

"After you girls went to bed, Dad and I spent the evenings painting the walls. We also put layers of varnish on the pine board floors. I sent rags to a company that made braided rugs for the living room. I hung Venetian blinds on the long, narrow windows and made my first set of draperies. When the owner's wife, Mrs. Lorenz, came out from Ohio, she said the house looked like it should be in *Better Homes and Gardens*. It did look pretty good!"

It was impossible back then to comprehend my parents' broad vision and appreciate the tenacious pursuit of their ideas. I only knew that, as years went by, the ranch was a haven for adventure, as well as an outdoor canvas where I stood in wonder of magnificent rainbows painted across the sky, and beautiful sunsets woven into the fading landscape. Memories of young calves frozen in a desolate snowstorm, remains of sheep ravaged by coyotes, and ripened wheat leveled by hail-stones made lasting impressions. But these harsh realities were softened by the warm nuzzle of my horse against my body. We would stand quietly in the barn as I brushed his coat to a sleek finish and he eagerly munched on oats in his feed box, or while

Connie's father, **Larry Morgan**, with daughters, **Brenda** and **Connie**.

Connie celebrates her second birthday outdoors on the ranch.

Brenda and **Connie** feeding their pet lamb from the bottle.

Connie scatters grain to the chickens on the ranch.

Homecoming Queen
Sherman Community High School - Goodland, Kansas - 1956

I cinched up the saddle to ready for a ride. I loved the sense of freedom we shared, galloping miles together across the pastures, feeling the wind against my face.

Though I often sensed that my life was a story of adventure that had already been written, I was amazed when I occasionally glimpsed my own uniqueness. During those times when I broke evergreen branches from our trees for a table centerpiece, or waded into the creek to cut cattails, I realized a consuming passion. It happened again when a friend and I built a log raft from fallen cottonwoods, and when I organized a hayrack ride and a scavenger hunt for my seventh-grade classmates. I was excited not only by my creative idea, but by the spirit of play as we bounced along on a country road twelve miles from town, laughing and singing under a star-studded sky.

I was drawn to the loveliness and artistry of nature, and quite certain there was a power greater than myself. While standing alone beneath the billowy white clouds that consumed the Kansas skies, I felt small, but very important, as if an invisible force hugged me, letting me know I was safe. Words weren't always available to describe my feelings, but I was sure of what I knew.

During the summer months that followed high school graduation I fretted, knowing my parents would be disappointed if I didn't attend their alma mater. Finally, in September of 1956, I conceded. Mother and Dad drove me to Manhattan to enroll at Kansas State University. Dad's goodbye words were, "Connie, we've taught you all we know. The rest is up to you." Mother's thoughts were evidenced by her tears.

That beginning year of college was a bit like going on stage for the first time. Even though I had received the Distinguished Achievement Award for courage, leadership, and scholarship, served as president of several organizations, and had been elected Homecoming Queen in high school, I still didn't feel prepared for this kind of production. It was a drastic change of props and scenery. I was certain the other

Leading the Kansas State University Band
Sue Mechesney, Lynn Mechesney, **Connie Morgan**, Mary Ann Simpson

girls had better study skills and could more easily compete scholastically. Most of them seemed to have the ability to attract friends from the more sophisticated city cultures. And with *that* came the wardrobes of matching cashmere sweaters and skirts, handsome wool coats, a broad assortment of shoes, and sometimes, their own cars.

I often felt disheartened when other students appeared to be more self-assured, their confidence superior to mine. My feeling of separateness from others, a fear of being unable to communicate with the opposite sex, and not knowing how to adapt to roommates added to my tension.

Yet amazingly, I was soon in the spotlight, representing Kansas State University, as well as my sorority, with beauty queen titles and other honors. Since high school days I had wanted to become a baton twirler in college, and when surprisingly, I was chosen as the fourth twirler for the university marching band, I was thrilled to know that my dream had come true. A variety of activities gave me an opportunity to develop my true charismatic nature — marching in parades and doing half-time shows in front of thousands of people,

Miss Football National Competition - Berkeley, California - 1957
Tina Ellero - University of Washington
Connie Morgan - Kansas State University
Mary Ann Mobley - University of Mississippi - Miss America 1959

competing in the freshman talent show, performing at the *All Women's Day* event with a twirling and tap-dance routine, and participating in an organ recital with Bach's Larghetto. That first year I was chosen as *Miss Football of Kansas State* and was a delegate to the national competition in Berkeley, California. I appeared on the NBC television show, *It Could Be You*, and was elected by students from the school of agriculture as *Barn Warmer Queen*. It was an honor to be a member of the *Angel Flight Drill Team, Homecoming Attendant,* and a finalist in the *Miss Kansas Beauty Pageant.*

Barn Warmer Queen
Elected by the School of Agriculture at Kansas State University
Connie participates in "Chore Day" - 1957

Connie is a guest on the television program **It Could Be You.**
Host Bill Leyden and Actor Tony Perkins

In many ways I had prepared for these events and yearned for a chance to further prove myself, to distinguish myself from others in the crowd. But the importance of being accepted generated constant pressure. When I fell short of achieving a particular grade-point average, getting a date from a particular fraternity, or even winning another contest, I endured disappointment. I was anxious to advance to a more permanent stage, but not just any stage would do. I was always looking for the place where I belonged. One thing was certain: If I didn't find a husband in college, I would undoubtedly become an old maid for life.

When I realized that my original major — home economics for high school students — was not my heart's desire, I changed to another curriculum and graduated early with a degree in elementary education and a high grade-point average. Even though I was confident I could be an excellent teacher, marriage pointed to a more secure future and was the most acceptable goal for every female graduate in those days.

Of course, marriage and the fairy tale life I had imagined would include finding the *prince* of my dreams, one who was not only good-looking, but also very accomplished. In due time, pages of my scrapbook reflected the achievements of my handsome college prince. He was a proud member of the *National Honor Society, Student Council,* and one of the more prestigious fraternities. Most important, he was an honorable man. His affinity for rules and discipline aligned with his position of *Wing Commander of the Air Force ROTC Program,* a distinguished position the other coeds especially admired. I felt lucky to catch him.

When my parents announced my engagement to *Air Force Lieutenant Phillip Wright,* I felt that love would surround and follow us all the days of our lives. The thought of spending the rest of my life making him happy was simply wonderful. Like most young women of the times, I believed a commitment of marriage would provide everything I would ever need, the assurance of being safe, happy, and cared for *till death do us part.*

A few months after our engagement, Phil called to ask his happy bride-to-be if I would like to honeymoon in Paris, pending official notice of his transfer. *Paris!! France!! Europe!!* I would be the envy of all my friends. Only weeks later, his expected tour of duty to Paris was canceled in favor of an immediate assignment to Pope Air Force Base just outside Fayetteville, North Carolina. The harsh reality of military orders forced us to schedule the wedding sooner than we planned.

On Saturday, June 10, 1960, the morning sun filtered through a soft haze over the campus of Kansas State University. It cast shadows from clusters of trees surrounding the native sandstone chapel as Dr. Samuel George, at the altar inside, presided over our wedding.

"Do you, Phillip Wright, take this woman...?"

"Do you, Constance Morgan, take this man...?"

Phil and **Connie** on their Wedding Day
Manhattan, Kansas - June 1960

Connie wears a Swiss embroidered gown for her wedding.

In my view, the pledge of love and devotion *for as long as we both shall live* was a vow of willing dependence on a man, as well as a commitment to rearing children. It was a belief that my life would be complete and that the tall, dark and handsome groom next to me would be a generous provider and a conscientious father.

We celebrated our marriage with a honeymoon to Western Hills Resort in Oklahoma, and with that came my trepidations of a young virgin bride on her wedding night. Visions of a French honeymoon gradually softened as we traveled across the Smoky Mountains to Fayetteville, North Carolina, to Phil's first assignment. A newly constructed brick duplex with hard-wood floors and a charming knotty pine kitchen was the perfect beginning. With the addition of some basic pieces of early American furniture and a board-and-brick bookshelf for stereo equipment, it was a warm and comfortable stage for domestic bliss. Like my mother, I learned how to make drap-eries for our living room, all the time recalling how much I despised sewing classes in high school.

Phil's frequent absences made for lonely times, especially for an insecure young bride with no involvements outside the home. Marriage and family were my sole interests. Bringing home a black poodle puppy eased feelings of loneliness, but I soon learned that our poodle, *Andre*, who had just won top honors at the Kennel Club Show, would not be the only source of comfort and joy. My doctor confirmed we were going to have a baby. Bouts of excitement shot through my changing body. Phil and I were ecstatic with the prospect of a child that would fill our lives with a new kind of loving

During our first year of marriage, we established a beauti-ful relationship with our landlords next door and looked to them as family. I vividly remember the spontaneous ex-change of dinners, new recipes, and chitchat with military friends, Margaret and Allen, and former college classmates, Mary Beth and Dick, who now lived only a few blocks away. Life looked good. But the safe and fun-filled world we had created began to crumble when Phil received notice of an

Phil and **Connie** at home with their poodle "Andre"
in Fayetteville, North Carolina.

immediate transfer to New York State. Within hours, he had orders to select a co-pilot and flight engineer for a classified mission. He would send for me when the time was appropriate. For now, he would report for his mission in New York and I would return to Kansas.

Just the idea of spending these early months of pregnancy away from my husband was disappointing and painful, but the comfort of living with family gave me a lift and appeased the situation. A short-term teaching position in a local elementary school also helped the time pass.

Our six-month separation happily ended when Phil called to say he had found the perfect place for us to live in New York, a renovated carriage house on a General's estate overlooking the Hudson River, just twelve miles from West Point Military Academy. I pictured a fairy tale cottage that seemed too good to be true. I anxiously marked off the days until we could be together again, excited that our baby might be born on my twenty-fourth birthday. As clear as any movie, pictures flashed through my mind—beautiful images of Phil and me celebrating the birth of our first child and tender scenes of our life as a family.

When renovations were complete, our carriage house, with five rooms, two fireplaces, and French doors that opened onto a grassy meadow, would reflect the romantic style of a quaint New England cottage. Until then, the third floor of the General's home would provide simple, yet private, living quarters.

Our residency in the mansion had a great impact on me, especially when the General's wife served us dinner in a library filled with charm and family history. During the extended absences of her husband, our intellectual conversations lasted into the night. As we talked, I observed a striking profile of a robust woman, probably in her forties, with graying black hair pulled back into a small bun. Even though the use of a wheelchair (from having had polio) somewhat curtailed her activities, she had a stateliness and unrivaled composure that added to her earnest and deep-rooted sense of belonging.

I was deeply affected by her investment in family, having devoted her primary energies to rearing six children. She appeared to be remarkably undisturbed by her own physical limitations and appeared almost oblivious to the handicap of her sixth child, a daughter with Down's syndrome.

The General's wife showered me with compassion. She empathized with my position as a displaced military wife and assured me that once I gave birth and shed the pounds of pregnancy, the focus on personal needs that now seemed so paramount would be of less importance. She insisted I hire a professional nanny to ensure a comfortable transition during the first critical weeks at home. Considering the great distance from our family and Phil's duties associated with his classified mission, having a nanny would relieve the pressures of being alone with a new baby. Even though it was contrary to the customs of our family, I reluctantly agreed to hire Frau Schmidt, a highly recommended nanny from New York City—the same one who had efficiently served the General's family for years. She would come to live in the second bedroom of the carriage house when the baby and I were discharged from the hospital.

The last several weeks of pregnancy dragged and were darkened by Phil's absence. He attempted to keep in touch, but my hopes of sharing the experience of childbirth with him waned. I felt a mixture of disappointment and gratitude when his sister, Jane, arrived in New York, none too soon.

One morning, while I was standing in the kitchen, a slight *pop* in my stomach alarmed me. Then immediately my water broke. Not knowing what was coming next, I felt strangely relieved when contractions followed with marked regularity. Jane and I knew it was time to head for West Point Hospital. As she cautiously swerved along the banks of the Hudson without the usual small talk, I folded my arms gently across my body. I could feel the quiet movements of a tiny human being, a soul ready to enter the world. In spite of great joy, the anxiety and fear of childbirth were amplified by my husband's absence.

Jane easily found the sign, UNITED STATES MILITARY ACADEMY AT WEST POINT, and headed in the direction of the hospital, quickly finding a parking spot near the entrance. Inside the hospital, I was directed to a small room midway down a sterile-looking hallway, and someone gave me a hospital gown. The nurse curtly ushered Jane out of the room while I was ordered to get undressed. Then I was taken to a small cubicle with a bench-like seat and a curtain pulled across the opening, much like a dressing area at the local gym. I worried about Jane. Was she driving back to the carriage house or was she waiting in the hospital lounge? If my husband couldn't be with me, why couldn't they give permission for another family member to stay with me?

I felt helpless in the atmosphere of authority that dominated the hospital-patient relationship at that time, especially in a military setting. Leaving me alone and ill-informed about the process of childbirth seemed harsh, even ruthless. While the ordeal of childbirth wasn't exactly life-threatening, I was appalled at the staff's insensitivity toward a first-time mother.

For what seemed like hours, I sat in that cell, the solitude broken only by rare check-ins by a nurse or aide. When I was finally given a bed behind another set of curtains I felt some relief, but was still cut off from nurturing support. I lay there defeated and ashamed at having forfeited my superwoman status, and abandoned all hope that Phil would arrive in time for the birth. The contractions intensified, as did the fear. Unable to separate the physical pain from the torment of uncertainty and aloneness, I kept wondering how it was possible for a baby to move out of such a small opening in my body, and how I would endure the pain. But now, faced with the reality of childbirth, I found little comfort in the doctor's words, assuring me that nature provides through the dilation of the birth canal and the flexibility of the tiny baby's body. Overwhelmed with pain, I was hastily wheeled off to the delivery room, where I barely remember being given an epidural. To this day I have almost no recall of the birth of our first child.

In what I assumed was an uncomplicated delivery, I gave birth to the most resplendent six-and-a-half pound baby boy. He appeared absolutely perfect, with a beautifully formed body, a marvelous head of dark hair, brown eyes, and radiant porcelain skin. I gave thanks to God for breathing life into this angelic being who would enhance every day of my life.

Nearly five hours later, Phil came dashing down the corridor with a dozen red roses. His handsome, suntanned face and dark hair provided a striking contrast to the white summer sport coat that hung open as he ran. When I first caught a glimpse of him I remembered the groom in his white dinner jacket standing at the altar, nearly a year and a half before. It seemed from Phil's glowing smile at the sight of his newborn son, Christian Alan Wright, that this gift delivered by a divine hand would not only give definition and purpose to our lives, but would surely alter the course.

For nine months, I had anticipated the birth of this child, not knowing whether it would be a boy or girl, whether he would look like Phil's side of the family or mine. I could never have dreamed of a child who would embody such pure loveliness, my joy and his father's pride. My ideal world of family and fulfillment as a woman began to beautifully unfold.

Soon it was time for us to take our baby home. The first couple of minutes standing outside the hospital passed in absolute silence. I felt such incredible closeness to Chris, warmly bundled in my arms. With my husband by my side, I walked carefully down the front steps of West Point Hospital. It was there I first met our German nanny. Frau Schmidt had short, graying hair and a stocky frame that looked neatly poured into a starched white uniform. She emitted an aura of professionalism combined with coldness. Even as Phil introduced us, her steady hands moved toward me and solidly commanded me to relinquish my son. It initiated an immediate battle of wills.

Momentarily, my thoughts were jumbled. I clutched Chris more tightly and stood frozen on the steps. I didn't know what to do. Was I obligated to let a hired nanny take my child? I didn't know! Authoritatively, the nanny continued reaching for Chris. Since childhood, I had dreamed of caressing the warm blanket that would wrap my firstborn. This was my radiant moment! But now, in the face of Frau Schmidt's intimidating tenacity, I felt helpless and weak. Those visions from the past eroded until, after what seemed like an eon, I relinquished our newborn son into the arms of a woman I had just met.

During the next two weeks, Frau Schmidt assumed complete responsibility for Chris, imposing specific ideas on how to hold him and feed him. "Mrs. Wright, even though my method is a more involved preparation, you must make the formula exactly as I tell you. When you feed your baby, hold him in your arms in such a way that you maintain eye contact. This gives him a feeling of security."

She further insisted, "You should feed Chris in the quietness of his room without distractions from the television or stereo. It's necessary that this time be completely quiet and relaxing for both of you."

Frau Schmidt's actions were deliberate, her tone of voice

harsh and abrupt. In her brisk German accent, she belted out instructions that left no doubt who was in charge. Her demeanor blunted any thought of disagreement or questions as to how other mothers might have done it.

The routine seemed strict and confining. Frau Schmidt's professional persona and standards of perfection demanded a strict application of her rules. My inexperience left me vulnerable to her demands, and caused a clash between us that was similar to the feelings I had during adolescence, when I learned not to be assertive, but rather sweet and selfless, and play a more feminine role. Now, years later, Frau Schmidt, a woman I hardly knew, conjured images of bad, and even forbidden, behaviors from my younger years. And, while I tried to understand Frau Schmidt's demanding ways, and empathize with the atmosphere from which I was unable to escape, these images instinctively replayed…over and over in my mind.

Churning inside with resentment, I finally capitulated to Frau Schmidt's routine, just to keep the peace. At the same time, I was certain that I was capable of making the correct decisions for my child, if only I could escape the fear of failure. Needing time to myself, I retreated to the bedroom, realizing how much I also wanted to shake the words *disloyalty* and *ingratitude,* words that were contrary to the virtues I learned in childhood, and weighted my mind with guilt.

A short time later, I walked up the hill toward the General's house. As I neared the mansion, I began to understand how authority figures such as Frau Schmidt might resort to rules and regulations just to disguise their own inner conflicts. But in spite of my insight, I felt the pain of her harsh words and a fear of my own fate.

Later that week, I received a letter from the Air Force chaplain informing us that the birth of our son had been officially announced at West Point Military Chapel. This gracious gesture not only added to our joyful beginning, but also enhanced the idea of a perfect family.

First Lieutenant and Mrs. Phillip A. Wright
778th Troop Carrier Squadron
Stewart AFB, New York

Dear Lieutenant and Mrs. Wright,
Congratulations on the birth of your son, Christian Alan,
on August 15, 1962. May we join with friends in extending
our sincere good wishes on the birth of Chris. It is a privilege
to join with God in the gift of bestowing life to a child. It is
a time when foresight is tender with dreams and aspirations
of a wonderful life as Chris matures under your parental
guidance.

Last Sunday we shared your good news with the families at
West Point by placing a rosebud on the altar during the
chapel service. We want you to have this rosebud as a
memento of the congregation's prayer, "that even as a rosebud
will unfold, your son's life will unfold into the full bloom of
manhood, growing in wisdom and in stature, in favor with
God and man."

Sincerely yours,

Ch, Major, USAF,   Ch, Captain, USAF   Ch, lst Lt., USAF
Base Chaplain

As my eyes scanned every word, they misted with the joy
of new birth, the tears of a mother who dared to ask for
everything that is good and beautiful for her child. The
tenderheartedness of the chaplain's message inspired a
certainty that our son would be a flawless symbol of love and
life, a beautiful gift to everyone who knew him.

Phil and **Connie** with their son, **Christian Alan**
at their carriage house on the Hudson River - August 1962.

2
A Sharp Twig

Chaplain Howell's extraordinary acknowledgment of the birth of our first child reinforced my childhood dream of being a loving mother with a strong and healthy baby. It was part of the romance of being married to a handsome man I dreamed would be the breadwinner, a conscientious father, and a compassionate and sensitive husband who would love me for the rest of my life.

The dream of a perfect home and family began when I was a little girl growing up on the ranch, playing house with my younger sister, Brenda, under a large cottonwood tree. We carefully drew the four rooms of our playhouse in the dirt with a sharp cottonwood twig. Occasionally our brother Lyn, eight years younger, was invited to a *make-believe lunch* in our dining room. Tea was served to imaginary guests in the living room, which had a view of the rock cliffs that overlooked the river to grassy hillsides beyond, dotted with herds of grazing cattle. Some days, Brenda and I took naps on a blanket in our *imaginary bedroom*. I can still remember lying there with the smell of newly mowed alfalfa from the field nearby, enhanced by the dry summer heat.

My new home in New York state overlooking the Hudson River had a feeling of tranquility similar to the playhouse on the ranch, except now, it included real people and real responsibilities.

Having had an uncomplicated delivery, at least according to the medical records, I thought my recovery period would be brief. But when I could barely walk around and had difficulty sitting down to put on my shoes, I wondered what the military doctors had not told me. Even Frau Schmidt showed a bit of compassion as she scolded me for not going to bed earlier and cautioned me against doing simple everyday chores. As for Chris, Phil and I had noticed the red marks on each side of his head, presumably evidence of forceps used to accelerate the birth, but we dismissed any significance.

A visit to the doctor would undoubtedly ease the anxiety over my delayed recovery, so I then called to schedule an appointment. Luckily, he arranged a time for the following day.

In the doctor's office before the examination, I asked why I had so much discomfort, why my body didn't seem to be mending as fast as I had anticipated. He told me that at least half of the women who give birth in the United States have an episiotomy, a procedure that usually occurs in the second stage of labor and includes an incision just below the vagina. The routine episiotomy enlarges the vaginal opening, thereby preventing tearing as the baby begins to emerge. The incision is sutured after delivery. He said that in my case, more than the usual incision had been necessary to speed the delivery.

Sensing the doctor's reluctance to divulge more information, I bravely asked, "How many incisions were needed during my delivery?"

He said, "The delivery process itself wasn't abnormal, but the procedure did require at least thirty sutures."

THIRTY SUTURES! FOR WHAT!! I silently questioned, realizing that at the time of delivery no one at the hospital ever told me what actually happened. As much as I wanted to trust my doctor's reassurance, my intuition told me that facts had been withheld and undocumented.

Unfortunately, during those first two weeks at home, Phil's schedule had taken him away for days at a time. In his absence, I tried to cope with Frau Schmidt's relentless demands. She gave orders on how to make coffee and suggested the right brand of shoe polish, a better furniture polish, and a more efficient laundry detergent.

Underneath the growing resentment of our capable, but oppressive, nanny lurked the realization that my body still wasn't recovering in the time my doctor had predicted. Having my husband in bed next to me, feeling nurtured by his presence, would have made the situation more tolerable. Instead, I clutched my pillow; the tears flowed, and loneliness intensified.

Nearly four weeks went by before I could move around well enough to manage household chores and single-handedly care for my son, as well as feeling self-assured and strong enough to dismiss our German nanny. It was then that I realized the enormous responsibility and awesome privilege of caring for a new life. Confident with the instructions and demonstrations given by the hospital nurses, I made Chris' formula according to their scientific *one-step method* rather than Frau Schmidt's *old-fashioned method*. It was simpler to mix water with the prepared formula, then pour the mixture into freshly washed bottles and place them into an electric sterilizer. This process left no room for error, though it did cause a *milk line* to form around the inside of the bottles, making them more difficult to wash.

Assured that I had mastered one of the important steps to caring for a new baby, I finally began to feel like Chris' mother. I was excited about taking him for short trips in the car to discover antique shops tucked away in the hills above the Hudson River. As I drove the narrow road that curved through the trees, I was awed by the solitude that enhanced the deep bond with my child. Indulging in the sheer joy of being alive, I felt a love for my baby that was greater than anything I had ever known.

Back at the carriage house, we strolled down the winding dirt road to the mailbox, stopping along the way so Chris could listen to the chorus of birds singing overhead. Later, as we lounged together on the patio, the August sun shedding its rays on my body, I could envision my son kicking a large rubber ball across the grassy area that stretched toward the river. It wouldn't be long before I could put him on the back of my bicycle to ride into the village with me. When he was older, the two of us could hike up the mountainside to pick wildflowers. He would know the coolness of the rain, the tantalizing feeling of mud between his toes, and the freedom of running with his face to the wind.

From the day Frau Schmidt left, a profound sense of love for my child grew within me as I meticulously washed his bottles, took the necessary steps in preparing the formula, handled all those dirty, smelly diapers, and tenderly bathed and fed him. But early on, my idealistic perception of our mother-and-son rapport began to be tested when Chris reacted in distinctive and disruptive ways at feeding time. He eagerly anticipated his bottle, but when I put it to his mouth, he immediately rejected it with piercing screams that stunned and rattled me. It seemed he was reacting to pain of some kind — somewhere in his tiny body.

I checked the temperature of the bottle. When I assured myself it was not too hot, I placed it back in his mouth, only to hear the same startling reaction. I adjusted the pin on his diaper. I held him in different positions. The wailing continued as I silently pleaded, *Chris, please don't cry. Everything will be okay.* But he cried and cried. Helplessness overwhelmed me. I could not determine the source of his pain nor give him relief.

Chris was already scheduled for his thirty-day checkup at West Point Hospital. My concern going into the appointment that day was his difficulty in eating, but when I asked about possible digestion problems, they glossed over the subject. Rather, in the examination, the pediatrician reassured me of Chris' neurological progression, stating that he was an alert, four-week-old baby who successfully measured up to the child development chart. According to the doctor, Chris had the proper responses to light and sound and appeared to have normal muscle reflexes. Even though I didn't know what caused the pain at feeding time, I went home with the encouragement that our son was *normal*, assuming the stomach pain and crying would gradually go away.

But it did not. I lay in bed night after night, unable to sleep. Instead of celebrating these early months, I suffered excruciating pain. Somehow, I had to resolve these questions: *Why does Chris have such difficulty taking his bottle? Why does he cry so much?*

Then, as abruptly as Phil had been notified one year ago of a classified mission in New York, he was told the mission was complete. We would soon leave New York and he would resume duties as a pilot at Pope Air Force Base in North Carolina.

We used the sudden news as an opportunity to explore the sights and sounds of New York City before returning to North Carolina. Our short trip into the city meant we had to find someone to care for Chris. The idea of having Frau Schmidt return to our home nagged at both of us, but reluctantly, we made the call.

When she arrived at the carriage house, she astutely observed what she called *formula lines* inside the newly sterilized bottles. "Mrs. Wright, are you making the formula the way I showed you?"

Just from the tone of her voice and the familiar stance of her body, I knew I would be reprimanded for making the mistake of doing things my way.

Nevertheless, daring to risk the pain of rejection, I finally answered, "No, Mrs. Schmidt. I'm using the simple *one-step method* taught by the nurses at the hospital."

"Hmph," she spouted. "Young mothers these days are always in a hurry." Shaking her head, she hurried into the kitchen to prepare lunch.

With Frau Schmidt back at the helm and Chris relatively quiet and comfortable, Phil and I slipped away and unhurriedly drove across the George Washington Bridge into New York City.

The skyscrapers and conglomerate masses were more than an ethnic melting pot. They represented wealth, poverty, artistry, competition, and eccentricity—a city of opportunity with fervor for creativity. Just driving through the elegant Manhattan theatre district, with its exquisite haute cuisine, Fifth Avenue shopping, and renowned museums, I was dazzled by the energy of it.

In the heart of Greenwich Village, I could feel the sharp contrast between the conservative middle-class views of my upbringing and the intense passion expressed by artists and musicians on the street corners. Their bizarre and sometimes freakish style of dress, and their unorthodox, but strangely beautiful sounds, were contrary to the icons with which I had grown up. Part of me wanted to be more like them, but their outrageous appearance and free-spirited behavior just didn't fit the model of appropriateness that had been instilled in me. In spite of an adventurous childhood, my instinct was to follow a pattern of how things *should* be done.

I wandered in and out of bookstores, lured by the many-colored jackets. I had always enjoyed the writing assignments for English classes and was thankful for unusual experiences that provided a wealth of material: the flood when my horse and her newborn colt nearly drowned, the prairie fire when neighbors came from miles around with wet gunny sacks and barrels of water, and the time when I rode my horse across the pastures to visit the thirty-year-old site of a one-room schoolhouse that was still standing. What I remembered most was the creative surge when I wrote about those adventurous times. It was an energy I couldn't quite define.

Ambling along the streets of the Village, absorbing everything around me, my spirit yearned to reach for something more than the challenges of my earlier years. It was as if Greenwich Village was my teacher, a stimulant to the artist within. As the inner tension eased, my self-image suddenly seemed more pliable. A part of me wanted to slough off the high school and college beauty queen titles, renounce the role and status of a lieutenant's wife, and shatter my ever-present compulsion to make conventional choices.

Driving back across George Washington Bridge, life felt wider and fuller. Phil leaned over and said, "Are you ready to go home?" I hesitated—"I guess so."

The road along the Hudson continued to twist and wind while scenes of the city grew dimmer with every curve. The diverging shades of foliage were part of an unspoiled landscape as a luminous haze opened up to reveal the river below. New and breathtaking scenes continued to inter-weave, one after another, around and through the trees. I gradually accepted going back to life as it really was rather than dwelling on the life that existed in my imagination. The last bend in the road brought us into view of the General's home sitting elegantly against the ridge, the carriage house discernible on down the road.

Eager to see our baby, Phil and I entered the carriage house through the Dutch doors that opened into the dining room. With one glimpse of the expression on Frau Schmidt's face, we knew something was out of order. Without warning, she lashed into me. "Mrs. Wright, you need to take time to make the baby's formula exactly the way I showed you. Your baby frets entirely too much. He is extremely nervous. You have made your baby sick because you're not making the formula the way I showed you."

A slow, numbing shock passed through my body, momen-tarily dulling my senses before new accusations were hurled. "And Mrs. Wright, that baby needs the exact number of blankets that I used when I was here before. Why aren't you using them?"

Weakened from the shock, my mind and body seemed frozen, unable to function. Panic gripped my soul at hearing the words, "You've made your baby sick." In spite of my having done everything as the nurses and doctors had told me, could Frau Schmidt be right? Could this be my fault? No! Of course not! But then, what was the problem? I stood in absolute silence, as if Frau Schmidt's words had put me on trial.

I was hardly aware of Phil standing behind me when Frau Schmidt launched another attack. "Furthermore, how can you expect us to stay warm in a house without heat?"

Phil suddenly stormed across the room, and in a deep military voice, demanded, "Nurse Schmidt, do you know how to regulate a thermostat?" She didn't answer. "Unless the control on the thermostat is turned up, there will be no heat." Pointing his finger at her, he continued, "I can't imagine a qualified nurse not knowing how to operate a thermostat."

"Well," she fired back, "I've never had young whipper-snappers like you talk to me that way. I'm not going to spend another night in this house!"

Defiantly, she strode toward the bedroom where Chris slept. Minutes later, she hastened out of the room carrying her bag and a lightweight sweater thrown over her shoulders. Before any of us could speak, she scurried through the French doors that led outside to the patio and plunked down in the lawn chair, determined to sit alone in the chilly October air.

Phil, shaking his head with disbelief, followed her to the door and in a frantic tone of voice, called, "Frau Schmidt, it's much too cold for you to spend the night out here. There isn't a bus back to New York City until tomorrow morning. Please come inside."

She retorted, "I'm not staying another night in a house where I am not respected. I'm never coming back here!"

The idea of the four of us being imprisoned together for the night was a desperate thought. Apparently, it was also something Phil was trying to avoid as he picked up the phone to call the nearest bus station.

"Uh-huh. Okay," I heard him mumble. Then, hurriedly placing the phone back on the wall, he bolted through the open French doors to the patio. He seized Frau Schmidt's arm with one hand and grabbed her bag with the other. "Come on, Nurse Schmidt, we're going for a ride!"

I barely had time to grab a blanket and lift our son from his crib before Phil was out the door with the nanny. Frau Schmidt, obviously perplexed, had no choice except to yield as Phil put her in the front seat of the car and fastened her seat belt. Chris and I rode in the back seat, watching Phil aggressively shave one curve after another down the narrow, winding road in the blackness of night. Frau Schmidt gripped the armrest with her right hand and the edge of her seat with the left. No one spoke.

The mountain road finally intersected the main highway. Phil slammed on the brakes and came to a screeching stop just as approaching lights appeared down the highway. He leaped out of the car, frantically waving both arms at the oncoming bus. Phil hustled Frau Schmidt from the car and, gripping her arm, he stood rigid by the edge of the highway, waiting for the bus to stop. His timing had been exact!!

When the door of the bus closed behind the nanny, I called it a victory of a lifetime, and sighed relief.

Back at the carriage house, I again took on the role of being Chris' loving caregiver. During the previous nine months, I had immersed myself in books on childcare, privately nursing the *ideal* of a giving and loving mother.

Now I devoted most of my time to my son, applying the principles outlined by the experts. When his outbursts of crying persisted, I was haunted by Frau Schmidt's charges of having made my baby sick.

When Chris was barely two months old, Mother flew to New York to visit her first grandchild, bringing her energetic spirit and humor. When she arrived, the air was filled with a sense of gaiety and lightheartedness. Chris' alert brown eyes gleamed in response to her affectionate words of praise. My mother's glowing smile at seeing her grandson lying on his stomach on a blanket — lifting his head and shoulders — was a gift my heart would always cherish. I was overjoyed to have her in New York, if only for a few days.

The next day, she watched as Chris lay on his back with his feet in the air. She noticed his feet pointed upward in a rigid position and gently tried to change the posture to a more relaxed position, but it didn't happen. Finally, with a little laugh, she commented, "Chris, with your stiff little toes, you're going to be a ballet dancer." Then, placing her finger in the palm of his hand, she checked his grasp reflex. "Come on, Chris," she coaxed. "You're supposed to take hold of my finger." He didn't.

As I watched my mother conduct her subtle, but diligent inspection of her grandson, a slow, agonizing fear moved through my body. But even after she returned to Kansas, we never spoke about her attempt to get Chris to grasp her finger, nor did we talk about whether his inability to do that could be an indication of a problem.

During this time, Phil was on a special assignment and was seldom at home. Unmistakably, I was in competition with the U.S. Air Force for the strong, dependable man I had married, but I had no recourse. I could only fantasize that his presence would lessen the weight of responsibility that consumed me during the day, and ease the emotional fatigue I felt at the end of the day. In truth, I felt very alone, and overwhelmed by questions and doubts. There was the issue of the baby's formula, and the question of whether I had done something during my pregnancy that could now cause our son to behave so abnormally. There was also a fear that Phil was too preoccupied to even be concerned about *my* condition. These doubts stood in the way of my appreciation of motherhood, causing me to think *this* role could be the most difficult of all.

Until our move back to North Carolina, I continued to take Chris to his regularly scheduled appointments at West Point Military Hospital. Each time, we saw a different pediatrician, someone who wasn't familiar with Chris' history of feeding problems. However, their evaluations were consistent, "Chris is a normal healthy baby. He seems to have occasional bouts of colic, not uncommon in the early months. Colic is often caused by excessive intake of air during feedings, which creates pain in the abdomen and causes severe irritability. It's nothing to be alarmed about."

At home, the feedings trailed into hours of pain-filled monotony and the frustration of getting nowhere, exacerbated by the attitude of indifference by medical professionals. The conflict between the doctors' observations and mine evolved into a question so compelling that my son's development and my own integrity hung in the balance.

I don't remember whose idea it was but, eventually,

someone suggested we have one of the pediatricians at the hospital monitor Chris' behavior during his feeding time.

On the morning of the appointment, I awakened early. After hurriedly getting dressed before Chris woke up, I sipped on coffee while stirring oatmeal and making toast. Unable to completely erase the opinions of various doctors regarding Chris' normalcy, I looked forward to having another military professional not only hear me describe Chris' behavior during feedings but observe, first-hand, the real happenings. I was determined this day was going to be a major turning point.

I pulled into a parking space outside the hospital. My heart pounded as I walked toward the building—so much for courage and confidence. As I slowly turned the knob on the door to the doctor's office, I stepped into another world. Holding Chris in my arms, I was fixed on finding the truth. The doctor, finally about to see evidence that wasn't documented on the chart, sat composed and attentive, with a studious but generally impassive face. Vigilantly, he observed as Chris' sucking motion began and continued at a steady pace. I closed my eyes and offered a short and sincere prayer of thanks for the answer I was sure would be forthcoming.

When I opened my eyes, Chris' calmness unnerved me. As I watched with utter amazement, I felt my body twinge. My blood ran hot. He was taking his bottle splendidly! Contrary to his inconsistent feeding patterns at home, there were no interruptions, no screaming, no reactions whatsoever.

The doctor glanced up. With perfect diction, giving each syllable equal treatment and confidence, he said, "Connie, I see absolutely no problems."

It was as if heavy mud just oozed into my ears, blocking out the faintest sound. I couldn't think straight. Angry and frustrated, I don't recall whether or not I acknowledged the doctor before leaving his office. I only remember driving Chris back toward our carriage house, oblivious to anything we passed along the way.

3
A Mother's Tears

Ready to return to military duties in North Carolina, Phil and I drove down the winding, unpaved mountain road for the last time and turned the corner where the mailbox stood. Words seemed inappropriate. As our fairy tale cottage on the Hudson and West Point Academy faded from view, a quiet reflection on sentimental images of the General and his wife, and even Frau Schmidt, stirred sadness. Before going to North Carolina, we headed westward to visit our extended families.

As we traveled through fading hues of autumn colors, we could feel the early chill of winter coming on. Chris was restless and cried a lot, which made our eight-hundred-mile trip an extremely long one. I prayed for patience as I tried to find ways to comfort him and deal with my feelings of inadequacy. The unanswered questions from the last four months, and his mysterious behavior patterns, placed a cloud of uncertainty over our trip back home.

I was more emotionally than physically exhausted when the last leg of our trip took us onto the country road, twelve miles from Goodland, that finally dead-ended at my parents' ranch in western Kansas. We turned into the long driveway flanked with shapely elm trees, and as we pulled up in front of the house, a barking collie welcomed us. When I saw Mother and Dad hurrying out to meet us, I knew they were filled with love and exhilaration, eager to share in the future of their first grandchild.

It wasn't surprising that on the first day home, Dad proudly displayed his new colt, with Chris smiling and obviously intrigued by this long-legged, wobbly animal. I swelled with pride as I anticipated my son riding the handsome beauty when they both came of age, galloping under a clear western Kansas sky as far as the eye could see. The next day, we jostled over creek beds in the Ford pickup, bumping across pastures of buffalo grass, checking water and hay for the cattle just as I had done in younger years. That evening, as I observed my parents' indulgence in their grandchild, I had no doubt in my mind that, through Chris, I was making a contribution to our family heritage.

Then we drove across the plains to southeastern Kansas to visit Phil's family. It was a long and arduous trip, but the tension eased when the familiar sweep of rolling hills indicated the end of our journey. Phil's parents had maintained a comfortable lifestyle on their farm with a sizable acreage of wheat just outside Lyons, a small community where the hankering to boast of one's grandchildren was commonplace among friends and neighbors. Soon after we pulled into their circle drive, we heard shrieks of joy and were once again embraced with passionate hugs and kisses.

The following day, in the machine shop where he worked, Phil's dad proudly showed off his technical skills as he welded pieces of farm equipment. He became excited as the conversation turned to how he and his grandson could restore the Model A Ford and ride in the local Centennial Parade. With Chris in the stroller, we walked over to the old sand pit that had long served as the family fishing hole, then strolled back past the house and on to the hangar where a four-passenger Cessna was parked. We were all excited by the idea that someday Chris would log a few hours.

Our brief layover in Kansas was a God-sent renewal of my spirits. As we headed in the direction of North Carolina, the early morning sun peered over the horizon, soon dominating a sky that was flawlessly clear except for a few puffs of clouds. My everyday concerns had over-shadowed any concerns about our red brick duplex that had been leased along with our furnishings during our twelve-month absence. As we crossed the Smoky Mountains, reminiscing about our honeymoon only a year and a half ago, clouds hung low over distant peaks. When we entered Fayetteville, the rain made tiny trickling streams on the windshield, and I began to anticipate the comforts of our cozy first home.

Within days of our return to *Pope Air Force Base*, old friends welcomed us with gifts for Chris. A college classmate, holding him in her arms, was tickled pink. She said, "Connie, he is such a beautiful baby. He has Phil's dark brown eyes and your gorgeous smile." Another friend, expecting her first child in four weeks, glowed with excitement. "Just looking at Chris makes me feel like a proud new mother."

Once again, I began to settle into a conventional military lifestyle, content with a few carefully chosen pieces of our own furniture. There was little time, however, to focus on any kind of lifestyle or to re-establish old friendships before Phil received orders for a transfer. As a new lieutenant, he was required to attend a three-month officer training school at *Maxwell Air Force Base* in Montgomery, Alabama.

Subleasing the duplex with our furnishings and leaving friends in North Carolina was difficult enough, but we were also moving to a city where the social and political upheaval over segregation, voter registration, and university enrollment was as intense as the Alabama summer heat and humidity.

When we arrived in Montgomery, it was easy to locate our military housing, which was a sparsely furnished two-story townhouse that served our short-term needs, but with disgusting brown tile floors, chalk-white walls, and minimal furnishings, our new living quarters seemed as cold and barren as a life without friends and family near.

My primary focus was to get to the cause of Chris' crying episodes, which had so far been interpreted as normal behavior. If indeed the West Point doctors were right that he was perfectly normal, I had to find ways to calm him and reduce my frustration and disappointment with his behavior. I tried everything: holding him, walking him in the stroller, long rides in the car. Nothing worked.

Phil and I had only recently observed slight jerking movements of Chris' head and arms, which added to our puzzle-ment. According to the books on childcare, a baby typically exhibits a startle reflex that appears at birth and generally disappears by the age of three months. Chris' jerking move-ments were happening at the age of six months and seemed to coincide with loud noises such as a telephone ringing or a door banging shut. With blind optimism, we rationalized that the movements were just natural reactions to jarring sounds.

We were concerned enough, however, that during our visits to the base hospital, we asked about the jerking movements. We were told repeatedly they were not frequent enough to be of any significance. In Chris' case, they were considered a *pro-longed startle reflex* that would eventually subside.

In spite of my efforts, I could no longer deny the deep despair and loneliness that became even more real when I re-cognized the intense emotions my child stirred in me. It was unbelievable how love, anger, rage, exhilaration, and guilt now seemed common and reasonable aspects of being a parent. In spite of having mastered an unlimited amount of tolerance, my biggest hurdle was conquering a sense of hope-lessness. I wanted to shake my baby until the noise stopped, but fortunately, I didn't.

The evenings, with hot temperatures and suffocating humidity without air conditioning, weighed heavily with my worst suspicions. Having Phil home for dinner became a comforting diversion from my solitary routine, but after a brief exchange (mostly news of the day), a quick kiss, and his inevitable return to the base library, I lapsed into my concerns and battled feelings of envy over the cool and comfortable environment where he spent most of his evenings.

One night when Phil was late getting home, and Chris' wailing seemed nearly intolerable, I placed a transistor radio in his crib. I left the room to try to get some rest. What seemed like hours later, Chris slowly gave in to his mysterious new companion. When I realized he was not crying anymore, I tiptoed into his room and found him sound asleep with his head on top of the blaring radio. *Oh, my GOD! Something worked.* The radio is the answer! I didn't dare risk lifting his head to remove the radio, fearing I would awaken him. I figured it was easier for Phil and me to listen to the radio all night than to Chris' tormenting wails. On subsequent evenings, we tried it again and again with continuing success, hoping it relieved him as much as it did us.

One day after breakfast, with increased energy and determination to focus my attention elsewhere, I decided to put Chris in his stroller and head for a new friend's house. I had met Amy briefly during one of my visits to the hospital. I knew she lived just a few blocks away and that her son was the same age as mine. As I sat bouncing Chris on my lap, while talking with Amy and her husband, I watched her son reaching for toys on the table in front of him, then grabbing his pacifier and putting it into his mouth. I thought to myself, *that child is really advanced for his age!* Suddenly overcome with embarrassment that Chris might be lagging behind children his age, I quickly found a reason to head back home.

As I pushed Chris in the stroller, I tried to disguise the discomfort of knowing that my child could not do the things that Amy's son did. Instead, I dwelled on the philosophy from my teaching days which emphasized that *a child progresses at his own speed.* I discounted the thought that my child could be slow. Undoubtedly the other child was advanced. After all, Chris' regularly scheduled pediatric examinations by military doctors had consistently indicated a normal progression of development.

But I was having a hard time convincing myself that my son was normal. By the time I got back to our townhouse and put Chris down for a nap, it was clear that I was not only envious, but fearful, after seeing behaviors in another child that were conspicuously missing in *my* son's development. As hard as I tried, however, I couldn't tell the truth about these feelings to myself or anyone else. In fact, I don't remember a time in those early months when even Phil and I sat down to discuss these concerns. It seemed easy for him to remain busy around the house or preoccupied with his studies, while my time was primarily consumed with caring for Chris and preparing meals.

During the next few weeks, when my emotional pain became unbearable, I said to Phil one evening, "I can't go on like this without some help!"

Empathetic with my concerns, he contacted his Squadron Commander, Colonel Brantley, and told him that in spite of numerous appointments with military doctors, it was obvious there was still a problem with our seven-month-old son.

In a matter of days, Phil was notified that Chris could be seen at the Special Pediatric Ward located at the base hospital. At long last, with help in sight, my days were more lively and the sleepless nights more tolerable. Anticipating our appointment, I kept a detailed record that included times and duration of Chris' feedings, his pattern of crying, and the frequency of jerking movements. A written account would leave nothing to speculation.

On the morning of the appointment, I moved quickly through the usual breakfast and dressing routine. Outside, hardly a leaf moved in the warm, humid air. I packed Chris and myself into the car and headed across town through traffic toward the base hospital. The parking lot, thankfully, was uncongested. I breathed a sigh of relief at knowing I was one step closer to discovering the truth. At the front desk, the receptionist acted a bit testy, but I patiently endured, knowing her job depended on qualifying us for special services. After completing the paperwork, she curtly gave directions to Dr. Bern's office, then pointed toward a long hallway.

The stark corridor appeared endless until I saw a small sign with Dr. Bern's name embossed on a metal plate.

I opened the door to the unoccupied waiting room and carefully placed Chris, sleeping in his infant seat, on the floor so as not to awaken him. A few moments of solitude were comforting. Beyond that, I have only vague recollections of the passing of time. The clock hung too high and the hands seemed not to move.

Suddenly, a deep voice in a white coat, unbuttoned

enough to reveal a shirt and tie, broke the silence with a gruff "Hello, Mrs. Wright." Something about his demeanor caused a squeamish feeling in the pit of my stomach, and created serious doubt as to whether he would appreciate the painstaking symptoms I had judiciously recorded. I prayed he would believe me.

Once inside the examining room, Dr. Bern and I exchanged quick, evasive glances. After he instructed me to undress my son, he buried himself in Chris' chart. It was obvious he didn't want any input from me. Without looking up, he began reading the chart aloud. *You had a normal full-term pregnancy, an epidural, and an uncomplicated delivery. Child breathed easily at birth, he cried spontaneously, birth weight was six pounds and six ounces. There was no oxygen or incubator required, and no evidence of jaundice or seizures.*

Focusing a soft light into Chris' eyes, Dr. Bern continued the examination while ostensibly showing no emotion or willingness to engage in verbal exchange. Testing for proper reflexes in Chris' arms and legs, he confirmed that muscle tone and motor control were completely normal. He did acknowledge that Chris had peculiar jerking movements that involved the head and upper body. However, in spite of his pensive expression which indicated concern, he classified the jerking movements as a nervous disorder.

A nervous disorder?!! That was Frau Schmidt's diagnosis! "Mrs. Wright, you have made your baby sick! He is much too nervous!"

Dr. Bern continued his evaluation then abruptly stated, "Mrs. Wright, in the future, please don't write down any problems pertaining to his feedings *or* his behavior patterns. By putting them on paper, the problem is simply magnified. Chris is your first child and he cries a lot. You had expected a baby that was easy to care for, and Chris isn't that baby."

The likelihood of encountering someone like Frau Schmidt, who was bent on contributing unfavorable and unfounded accusations, seemed remote. But, in a similar fashion, Dr. Bern launched yet another attack. "Mrs. Wright, are you happily married? Do you like where you're living?"

His questions knocked me for a loop. Too stunned to answer, I couldn't help but silently debate issues that, in my mind, seemed irrelevant. *Of course I'd like to see my husband more and my marriage is fine. No! I don't like military housing. Our townhouse is hot and humid with no air conditioning. My kitchen is small and antiquated. The brown tile floors are impossible to maintain, constantly showing dusty footprints. And now, my son's crying is a nervous disorder caused by my being an unhappy wife and a mother with unreal expectations.*

Choked with disbelief, I felt my trust in military professionals crumble. Angry and physically enervated, I wanted to leave the office as quickly as possible. To maintain self-control I proceeded to dress my son, then stuffed his bottle, pacifier, and toys into the diaper bag. Without further conversation with the doctor, I scurried out the door and down a long hallway to the nearest exit.

In the parking lot outside the building, I felt enraged and temporarily delusional, unable to find my car. Finally locating it, I drove toward the main gate. Within minutes, a screaming siren brought me to my senses. A revolving red light appeared in my rearview mirror and sent chills through my body.

As the patrolman stepped out of his car and came toward me, he appeared tentative. Then moving closer to the window, he politely asked, "Ma'am, do you know you just drove through a stop sign?"

"No," I replied, my words barely audible. "I just received some bad news about my son."

The officer leaned forward to see Chris sitting in his car seat next to me.

"I'm really sorry, ma'am. We would be happy to give you a military escort home."

"Thank you, officer, but I don't have far to go."

"Please drive carefully," he warned, and waited for me to drive away.

Back at our townhouse, the air stood still. The rooms were stifling. I turned on a fan to make Chris' bedroom more comfortable, and lingered until he fell asleep. Downstairs, I fell into my chair, barely able to hang onto my glass of iced tea. My mind whirled with thoughts of the last seven months, specifically all the military doctors with no answers, only rude behavior. What did I have to show for it all besides a signature on the sign-in sheet at Special Pediatrics? The worst crime was that in seven months, I hadn't felt brave enough to speak my mind and trust myself as a woman and a mother. Once more I had allowed myself to feel degraded and intimidated by authority. I secretly vowed not to depend on anyone else to validate my integrity.

Even though I felt vulnerable and discouraged, I was still open to suggestions. A few days later, a concerned babysitter gave me the name of a well-known civilian pediatrician in downtown Montgomery. Without consulting Phil, I daringly decided to get a non-military opinion.

My heart pounded as I made the phone call to Dr. Huttner's office. With all the past diagnoses that never led to a solution, but always seemed to point a guilty finger at me, it was difficult to be optimistic.

The following Wednesday came sooner than I anticipated. On that all-important morning, I was committed to only one thing: ridding my life of the debilitating confusion that had dominated the last seven months. I dressed in a pair of loose-fitting, comfortable slacks. Then I woke Chris and dressed him in one of his cutest outfits.

As we anxiously drove through lower downtown Montgomery and into the historic business section, I watched for an old red brick building with the address above the front door. A few private parking spaces made for an easy entrance. Waiting inside the reception area and trembling with fear, I strained to make sense of my thoughts as I held Chris on my lap. I prayed that this time I would get an answer.

As Dr. Huttner walked into the room to meet us, Chris fussed and cried. Dr. Huttner asked empathetically, "Do you have a pacifier?"

"Yes, of course," I sheepishly answered.

Once inside his office, with a delightful sense of humor, he said, "At our house, the pacifier has become known as the peace pipe. Little guys like Chris love to smoke their peace pipes." He laughed and added, "It does wonders for the mother as well."

This gentle and perceptive man, handsomely dressed in a brown herringbone sport coat and open-collared blue shirt, had earned my trust even before he graciously listened to my frustrating and often discouraging experiences.

While Chris sat on my lap, Dr. Huttner stood with his arms folded and quietly studied my baby's behavior, watching for any indication of a problem. With my heart in my throat, I wanted more than anything to erase the darkened cloud that cast a lingering shadow on the magnificent gift of a beautiful son.

During the examination, I felt proud I had opened up to this doctor who had engaged my trust. Then, not knowing whether he might find some discrepancy in my observations and criticize me as the others had, I suddenly felt sluggish and weak.

In those moments, all the insecurities from past to present flooded my mind. Once again I was a guilt-ridden little girl who was unable to crawl out from under the familiar pattern of self-blame. My sense of inadequacy was profound.

Then, through my mental haze, I heard Dr. Huttner speak the words I thought I would never hear from a physician. "Connie, Chris' behavior pattern definitely indicates a problem. There is something wrong, but I have to admit I don't know what it is."

I quickly realized that when the truth was stated, I felt more in control of the situation. As I gathered up my son and prepared to leave the office, I was further comforted by Dr. Huttner's parting words: "Connie, I support your attempt to find the cause of the problem. Please keep me informed about any other symptoms."

"I will! Thank you, Dr. Huttner." Oh, how I wanted to hug him!

Grateful for Dr. Huttner's willingness to embrace my

concerns, I waited only a couple of weeks before calling him again. He happily scheduled a second appointment. This time, he proposed a plan. "Connie, it's possible Chris might have an allergic reaction to milk, which is causing his upset. Let's try some alternative formulas, just in case. We'll start with the soybean formula, then I'll give you instructions for mixing the others.

Driving back to our apartment, having weathered another doctor's appointment alone, I sighed with relief that I had gone outside the military system to seek a solution. I was hopeful that the possibility of an allergic reaction and the use of new formulas would produce definitive results. At the same time, I couldn't help but wonder how Chris' behavior could be dramatically altered with something as simple as changing his formula. I prayed that Phil would be receptive to the new plan.

When Phil came home, he eagerly embraced the new feeding routine. Within weeks, I tried them all...a soybean formula, a meat based formula, and other non-dairy types. But when, in spite of drastic changes in his formula, Chris continued to cry sporadically, I was even more discouraged. It was one more failed attempt to obtain a conclusive answer, ruling out the possibility of an allergic reaction. But, knowing that I had the support of a pediatrician whose *civilian status* was as important as his compassionate and consoling attitude, I scheduled my third appointment with Dr. Huttner.

Driving across town to the doctor's office, I breathlessly anticipated another approach to the problem. After we discussed the use of various formulas and failed results, Dr. Huttner had to admit he had no other suggestions.

Back at our townhouse, tormented by some of the darkest moments I could remember, I realized how much I wanted this doctor to be my hero, and how desperate I was for answers. That afternoon I was surprised by a knock on my door. It was Eleanor, the only other military wife I had met since Phil's temporary assignment to Montgomery. She always appeared calm and relaxed. When my confidence was low, her poise and self-assurance created a discomfort in me, but her gentle way of honestly expressing herself was a gift.

Chris played on my lap as we sat talking. Then excitedly, I said, "Eleanor, this morning I visited with a civilian pediatrician who is willing to look at every possible cause of Chris' feeding problems and his pattern of persistent crying."

"Good...," her words barely audible as she continued to focus on Chris.

"Connie, how long has Chris been doing that?" she finally asked in a pensive voice.

"Doing what?"

"I've never seen a baby with jerking motions like that."

"Yeah, I haven't either, but when I took Chris to Special Pediatrics at the Air Force base, the doctor referred to them as a nervous disorder. He assured me it was nothing serious."

When Eleanor left, my repressed fear suddenly came out of hiding. I immediately picked up the phone. Even though Dr. Huttner had insisted I call with any new information, I waited nervously while the phone rang.

"Dr. Huttner, this is Connie Wright. I wanted to let you know a friend stopped by today and observed jerking motions associated with Chris' head and upper body. I noticed them a few weeks ago, but a specialist in pediatrics at the base hospital dismissed them as a nervous disorder."

"Connie, I know you and Chris were here just this morning, but can you come back to my office right away?"

"Yes, I can be there in fifteen minutes."

In his office, Dr. Huttner observed the same jerking movements Eleanor had witnessed. They were identical to the ones that had been labeled as a nervous disorder by the specialist at Maxwell Air Force Hospital just a few weeks ago.

Dr. Huttner's face tightened.

"Connie, I would like to refer you to a neurologist. Dr. Leslie Thomas is a civilian doctor like myself, and a good friend. His evaluation will be extremely helpful. Even though tomorrow is Saturday, could you possibly see him in the morning?"

Sensing the urgency in his voice, I said, "Yes, of course."

He immediately picked up the phone to schedule an appointment. While I waited, I couldn't imagine what my life would be like without the crushing responsibility of caring for my child. But by now, I was fully aware that the initiation to motherhood was going to include pain as well as pleasure.

After Dr. Huttner confirmed an appointment for Saturday morning and I got ready to leave, I realized that few conversations had been so encouraging and yet so final. It left me with an eerie sensation, but there was nothing more to do that night except to sleep...and wait for another evaluation.

4
VALLEY OF DESPAIR

Fallen branches from the previous night's storm cluttered the streets as Chris and I made our way through the light Saturday morning traffic. Thankfully, the parking lot outside the medical complex was nearly vacant. I managed to get Chris inside and found Dr. Thomas' office just in time for our ten o'clock appointment.

Relieved to see we were the only ones in the waiting room, I prayed Chris would give me a few quiet moments before we were called in...and he did. But my thoughts and emotions wavered between Dr. Huttner's encouraging recommendation of a neurologist and my memory of all those months when I sat in other waiting rooms—only to have my expectations dashed.

With my attention fixed on a desert landscape on the opposite wall, I hardly noticed a figure that quietly entered the room. Suddenly, my deep thoughts were interrupted by a man's voice. When I turned toward him, I was surprised to see such a handsome man about six feet tall, with a thick head of salt-and-pepper hair that curled slightly at the base of his neck. He appeared to be in his mid-fifties. Dr. Thomas and I shook hands like old friends. My clenched jaws, which had been part of my well-disguised but ever-present anxiety, began to relax.

In the examining room, it quickly became apparent that Dr. Thomas was warm-hearted, competent, thorough, and forthright. As he began to evaluate Chris, he noted that he had a strong sucking reflex, and a healthy cry when pinched. For a seven-month-old, he had appropriate weight gain and good muscular strength. It all sounded normal.

With his broad, sturdy hands, Dr. Thomas held Chris in a sitting position on the table and commented on how he could not maintain his balance without support. Next, he observed that Chris was unable to roll over. When he attempted to hold him in a standing position, it became clear that Chris could not put weight on his legs. Though remaining calm and gentle, the doctor's deep concern at what he saw became more evident as his demeanor suddenly changed.

As he thrust his fingers rapidly toward Chris' eyes, the motion didn't provoke even a blink. Dr. Thomas commented on how objects such as a toy or a pencil failed to attract his attention. Additionally, he observed that Chris' sounds were not those of learned speech patterns.

Finally, I heard the two words that would alter my life forever. When Dr. Thomas said, "It's possible that *cerebral damage* could be keeping Chris from responding normally to stimuli of sight and sound," my mind froze.

But the worst was yet to come. Dr. Thomas suddenly looked at me and asked, "Mrs. Wright, do you mean to tell me Chris is seven months old and he's not rolling over, he's not sitting up, he's not holding a cracker, or reaching for his bottle?"

Of course he didn't know what I had been through with numerous other physicians — all of whom were military doctors except for Dr. Huttner. His questions burned on my heart, renewing the old charges of my ineptitude. I wondered why countless other doctors who had examined Chris since birth had not questioned his development. Were they not accountable in some way? My anger sizzled as the truth of this examination began to cast a glaring light on all past examinations.

Before I could recover, I heard Dr. Thomas' urgent voice, "Mrs. Wright, can you locate your husband? I want him to be present while I do a brain wave recording, a procedure we commonly refer to as an EEG."

"Yes, he left me a number where he could be reached."

I was thankful when nearly half-an-hour later, I heard Phil's steps in the front foyer. As he joined me in the waiting area, his expression was strained and his eyes darted with intense curiosity. He followed me into a room where Dr. Thomas quietly prepared for the EEG. Tiny electrodes, somewhere between ten and twenty in number, were attached to Chris' head with a clay-like substance. The long wires running from the electrodes were connected to a machine that recorded brain waves. Dr. Thomas explained that it was necessary to do one recording while Chris was awake and another after he fell asleep.

After the first procedure, we waited for what seemed like an eternity before Chris dozed off with the wires still attached. I finally asked, "What exactly is an EEG?"

"An EEG is a recording of the electrical fluctuations of the brain. It allows a neurologist to read the tracing and know whether the activity is normal or abnormal within the four areas of the brain."

A hundred questions raced through my mind; a morbid fear shot through my body; I felt nauseated. Barely aware of my husband's presence, I watched as our baby slept with wires attached to his head. I was anxious about the significance of the lines on the monitor. Waiting silently while shivering in the air-conditioned room, listening to Dr. Thomas' pen as he jotted down notes, I found myself trying to believe that regardless of what we learned today, the events would move me beyond the smoke screen of past examinations. Confident we were now dealing with the real issues, I also hoped I could get beyond my guilt feelings about Chris' condition and not crumble under the pressure of uncertainty.

Chris was still sleeping when Dr. Thomas suggested we go to into his office. Phil and I, seated side by side, faced the doctor as he reviewed his paperwork behind a large desk. As we waited for him to speak, the warm wishes of friends and family from two-and-a-half years ago came flooding back: *"You will have a good life. We wish you the best."*

In many respects, we were like any other young married couple, bound together with dreams about the future, while unconsciously attempting to avoid pain and hardship along the way. Even though our journey of marriage and family had consisted of two years of indecision and crisis, I now envisioned the possibility of putting those times behind us.

Finally Dr. Thomas, in a calm and compassionate voice, said, "Mr. and Mrs. Wright, the EEG has shown conclusively that Chris is having seizures. The brain wave pattern is grossly abnormal. There is extensive brain damage, which appears to be generalized without focus on a specific area."

In my mind the doctor's voice became small and thin, piercing enough to shatter fine crystal. The meaning of his words floated through me rather than to register with any degree of cognition. A giant lump formed in my throat, strangling me and restricting my breathing. I wanted to cry out, but no sound came. The anguish, the pain, and the overwhelming disbelief cut to the depths of my soul.

I turned to Phil. He looked strained and disbelieving, splintered with grief. Neither of us spoke.

Dr. Thomas continued.

"Right now, it's difficult to tell how severely Chris might be impaired, mentally or physically. He could be a great football player with learning difficulties. He might be slightly hard of hearing or have poor coordination. But with seizures and a pattern of slow development in the first seven months, his condition does not look good."

Suddenly I panicked, but this time not for Chris. There was something very important I had not told Dr. Thomas.

I quietly uttered, "Doctor Thomas, what about my unborn child?"

"You're expecting?"

"Yes, I'm three months pregnant. What does that mean?"

With empathy in his voice, he responded, "Don't worry. The chances of having another brain-injured child are minimal. It probably wouldn't happen again in a hundred times."

His compassion gave us a brief respite from our startling news, but it was hardly a cure for the condition of our firstborn child. Since Chris was a beautifully formed baby who had not suffered any sort of illness, high fever, or injury, it was impossible to absorb any real understanding except that he wasn't going to be normal; he wouldn't be the child of our dreams.

Barely able to put one foot in front of the other, Phil and I followed Dr. Thomas to the room where the EEG had been given and where Chris now lay peacefully awake. He smiled in recognition as we walked toward him.

My voice cracking, and tears forging a steady stream down my cheeks, I managed a "Hello, sweetheart," and looked on while the doctor removed the wires from his head.

Dr. Thomas concluded our visit by urging us to return to the hospital at Maxwell Air Force Base for further tests. Financially, it was the only way for Chris to receive a comprehensive evaluation and biological work-up to determine the cause of the seizures. Dr. Thomas agreed to make the arrangements.

We left the building in a fog, finally knowing the name of the adversary we had lived with for the past seven months. Dr. Thomas called it *hypsarrhythmia*. It was a rare condition that was recognized by a particular seizure pattern, and characterized in medical terms as eyes rolling back and stiffening of the body, with leg extensions. According to Dr. Thomas, some children develop the symptoms of hypsar-rhythmia after contracting another illness. Some simply display the characteristic spasms without a known cause. Due to the fact that birth trauma had not been acknowledged and documented on Chris' medical records, only our suspicions remained.

Back at our townhouse, as I climbed the stairs to take Chris to his room for a nap, a dark presence invaded my life, shattering my heart and leaving my orderly ways in ruin. I was in shock. My stomach churned. My body ached all over. My mind and emotions protested. *It can't be! It just can't be!!* Images I had dreamed about since I was a child all collapsed.

That evening Phil and I tried to escape the loneliness by taking a long walk with our baby. There was nothing to say, nowhere to go; it was as if we were on a ship sailing out to sea without a captain, a ship propelled by some mysterious force on a voyage that would end in disaster.

Two days later, the three of us went to the Air Force hospital. Soon after checking in, Chris was carried off to a room for immediate evaluation. Still standing in the lobby, we were greeted by the memorable Dr. Bern from Special Pediatrics. He warmly shook hands with Phil. Then, with an obvious look of embarrassment, he glanced at me, undoubtedly recalling his previous meeting with this *overly concerned mother with a baby whose jerking movements indicated no real problem*. He was again meeting with the same mother whose child had, just two days ago, been diagnosed with extensive brain damage.

Unknown to Dr. Bern, I had been allowed to view my son's medical records, and I saw how the doctor had summarized his findings on Chris' chart: *Baby is fine. Mother has the problem!*

Now he attempted to salvage his professional status by saying, "Mrs. Wright, is Chris crying a lot more than when you last saw me?"

"No, Dr. Bern!"

"Have the jerking movements increased since you were in my office?"

"No!"

While I stood there, the good doctor, caught in a perplexing situation, quickly outlined the procedures for a comprehensive evaluation, and told us he would be taking charge of the case. Phil nodded with agreement, but immediately following our consultation, we requested a meeting with the hospital administrator. After relating our experience with Dr. Bern, we asked that he be replaced as the physician in charge of our son's case. Our request was granted immediately. Dr. Bern would remain on the team, but only as an assistant to the medical staff.

Soon after Chris was admitted to the hospital, the doctors prescribed injections of ACTH, a hormone produced by the pituitary gland and found to be effective in controlling seizures, especially in the treatment of hypsarrhythmia.

The following days were filled with medical tests, which we hoped would not only reveal the cause of his seizures, but would somehow make up for the treatment we had received. If the seizures were due to such deficiencies as blood sugar, calcium, or blood protein, it was possible that further brain damage could be stopped or moderated with medication or specialized nutrition. We anxiously anticipated the results; we were told they could be available as early as Friday.

During the several days of tests, Phil resumed his studies, while I barely existed in a deep, dark, indescribable void. I retraced my steps of the previous seven months so often that going back over those tracks became fruitless, even boring. I sat on the edge of my bed, terrified of having no purpose, of not being needed by anyone. Most of all, I was grasping for a will to overcome these awful realities.

Sometimes I wandered aimlessly up and down the streets near our residence, scarcely aware of the sounds of screeching tires, blaring automobile horns, and squirrels scampering among the trees that lined the median of the boulevard. I existed in a state of semi-consciousness, oblivious to the rest of the world.

The nights were worse than the days. As the sun went down and the shadows of evening crowded around me, I felt as if I had been sentenced to solitary confinement. To no avail, I tried to quiet the tumultuous noises in my head and reconcile the anxiety and guilt. When I tried to sleep, broken dreams kept me awake.

Then there were the inevitable conversations with God, whose presence had been so keenly felt during the earlier periods of my life. God had never spoken to *me*. It was always one way. I imagined he could speak to me directly if he wanted to, but I concluded he probably wouldn't.

On one particular night, however, I wearily slumped to the floor beside my bed, determined to get some answers. I prayed: *God, ever since I was a little girl, I've talked with you, especially when things got difficult or when I badly wanted something. But, I actually never felt worthy of having a give-and-take conversation with you. And I still don't feel worthy. However, I desperately need your help with my son and all the other imperfections that seem to keep popping up in my life. I'm willing to do whatever it takes for Chris to get well, for him to walk and talk like other children. This time I'd really like to hear your answer.*

I cannot describe the sound that followed except to say it was not audible or in any human language, but I heard what I needed to hear: *I am always with you, even when you draw away from me. Trust in my unfailing love and know that the miracle your soul is seeking will come.*

I wish I could say that wonders occurred and that I was at peace until God did exactly what I asked, but that was not the case. Since that day, however, knowing I could have a two-way dialogue with God has helped me through the worst of times.

As quieting as my conversations with God were, I still needed a human being who would listen to my questions and frustrations and communicate back to me. The numbness from shock that had initially cushioned me from the reality of the diagnosis, was no longer a way of escape. My body was wracked with pain, my heart breaking, my mind a mass of confusion. My soul was weighted with guilt. Was there anyone who understood what I was going through? Who could I talk with when my world was crumbling? Where could I go to learn how to handle these highly charged emotions? Unfortunately, since childhood I had felt unable to share spontaneous feelings with my family. It was part of having to maintain the appearance of being strong.

Phil had a two-week deadline for an aerospace research paper. He attended lectures during the day and studied after class. The combined pressures to finish the program with top marks and deal with Chris' problem at the same time were horrendous, yet he seemed to be managing fine. I envied his discipline, but also envied the diversion created by his studies, a diversion that seemed to allow him to suppress his emotions, perhaps even bury them.

When Phil kept his thoughts to himself, I wondered if he blamed me for Chris' condition. In a society in which sons are a reflected asset and seemingly the height of a man's achievement, how would he cope with an image that rested in a disabled son?

I boosted my fragile emotions by daring to dream that something would alter the dreadful diagnosis, that the findings of the tests would somehow diminish our despair.

While Chris was in the hospital, my foremost pleasure was visiting him and helping with his lunch, but it was also my most searing pain. Entering his room, I would see him lying in his tall, cage-like metal crib, staring at the bare walls. My eyes brimmed with tears when he looked at me as if I were just another face. In those moments, it was difficult to feel love for God, myself, or anyone else. I just wanted to be free of the agony and the blinding uncertainty.

Dr. Bern, in spite of his tarnished reputation, did manage to keep us informed of the medical evaluations being conducted by the new team of doctors.

Suddenly, it was Friday morning, the day the test results were to be announced. I awoke before dawn. While Phil was asleep, I quietly slipped out of bed and moved toward the window. The moon in the distance was fading, but it lingered on the horizon, seemingly to comfort me. Standing there alone, I felt the promise of a new day and envisioned a world that, even with all its ruin, would take on a different meaning.

After a light breakfast, we drove in anxious silence to the hospital. As we got out of the car, I tried to imagine the outcome of the test results, but without any information to go on, I quietly hoped for a miracle.

Inside, Phil and I stood in front of the admissions desk announcing our arrival for the conference. A friendly assistant said, "Come with me please," and ushered us down the hallway to a conference room appointed with a large steel-gray table with straight-back chairs on all sides.

While we waited for the *mastermind team* to appear, I methodically dug my nails into the palm of my hand. Since I'd been old enough to contemplate loss, I never once imagined such personal bereavement. Now, in the midst of exhausting silence, we waited. I don't know how long we sat there, perhaps thirty minutes, before the first of several doctors entered the room, followed by the others.

Once seated, one of them finally broke the suspense. "Mr. and Mrs. Wright, I am sure it's been a long and grueling week for you. However, I must tell you that all of us have fallen in love with your son. And, after a complex investigation, we have some good news. Chris is a perfectly healthy child with no need for medication or specialized diet. After just one week of using the ACTH hormone for seizures, his jerking movements have disappeared and the crying episodes have stopped."

Phil and I looked at each other with disbelief while the doctor continued. "We know that Chris has brain damage due to an unknown cause, but other than that, he is a perfectly healthy child. We advise the continuation of the ACTH hormone for his seizures with a strict follow-up program."

After Phil and I pressed for answers to every urgent question we could think of, the conference was over, leaving us wondering whether the brain damage would be corrected from the use of the ACTH.

The aftershock felt no less severe than the previous uncertainty. I wanted to leave my body to escape from the pain of unsettled issues. In spite of good news that the jerking movements and persistent crying had stopped, we had no indication there would be a cure for the brain damage, no prediction about whether it would get worse or get better, nor even a hint of the kind of life Chris would live.

While Chris had no biological deficiencies, such as blood protein, blood sugar, or other areas of chemical or nutritional imbalance, the doctors still had no explanation for the cause of brain damage. Back home, our baby no longer screamed during his feedings. He slept at night. He could travel in the car and go for walks in his stroller without disruption. For the first time in months, I felt relief, even though we still faced insurmountable obstacles. This strange and mysterious intruder, a rare disease called hypsarrhythmia, remained an elusive element in our lives.

It was time to inform our families. In keeping with his role as head of the house, Phil became the spokesperson. He called my parents first. "We have just learned the cause of

Chris' problems. He has finally been diagnosed as having generalized brain damage. We've been told that it's a rare condition called hypsarrhythmia. The cause of the brain damage is unknown. And we are expecting another child in six months."

It would have been nearly impossible for me to convey this news to my parents, aching for reassurance of their love while also trying to comfort them. I could only imagine their heartbreak, and, indeed, the heartbreak of Phil's parents, as both families were forced to confront their own unfulfilled expectations for their grandson.

Realistically, we weren't given a sociological structure—by doctors, our families, or society—through which we could create and maintain a meaningful existence under these circumstances. We only hoped that through our second child we could somehow transcend our pain and learn how to be happy from one tentative moment to the next.

As we became more secure with the assertion of our own quiet strength, we began to break the news about Chris to people outside our family, to a few neighbors and friends. When the babysitters admitted they had never heard a child cry so much, I was angry they had withheld their concerns, standing by while watching me question and suffer.

Meanwhile, my mother did some research on hypsarrhythmia. She found information about a young girl named Susie Gardner who had severe disabilities from the same relatively unknown condition. Susie's parents had been told their daughter would most likely die before the age of three, and if by chance she survived, she would be mentally retarded. Susie Gardner, like Chris, was placed on ACTH treatments.

Miraculously, her seizures greatly diminished. She became increasingly alert and responsive. Her mental development kept pace with her physical improvement. Eventually, her brain wave recording was normal.

I prayed the same kind of powerful weapon would work for my son.

5

COMING THROUGH
THE DARKNESS

As Chris slept peacefully in his crib, I stood listening to the whisper of every breath. The softness of his presence was an incentive to transform my worst habits. He gave me more than a word or a touch, something strangely separate from the material world. I wanted to run my fingers through his dark brown hair and trace his perfectly formed features. As I perceived the loveliness of his soul, pictures played over and over in my mind, a composite of hopes for my child and our life together.

Months before, when I joined other young mothers in the conscientious and painstaking journey of parenting, I never imagined I would soon be forced to step outside the mainstream of motherhood. While other women chatted about birth weights and their children's development, I tried to understand and handle exhaustive medical terms, a complicated diagnosis, negative emotions, and severely crippled communication with my husband.

Every waking hour, I relied on hope that the ACTH treatments would result in a miraculous change. But the most immediate and predictable thread of my existence was tied to the fact that, at any time, Phil could receive orders to move to another base.

And now, after only three months in Montgomery, we would be returning to Pope Air Force Base in North Carolina. However, our stay in Montgomery had been significant. A physician had finally answered the question, "What's wrong with Chris?" And now, the haunting words, *brain damage,* would travel with us and cast a spell on our future.

We headed east through the Alabama countryside on a sparsely traveled highway, past landmarks, deteriorating farmhouses, and vine-covered fences. As we traveled, we reminisced about our own childhoods growing up in the country.

On the second day, as the last evening of our journey faded into dusk, I longed for a full moon hanging above the open sky. The thought served as an alluring, but brief, respite to the agony and embarrassment of going back to our North Carolina friends with our *retarded* child. As we drove into Fayetteville, the air was moist and cool inside the car. Chris' gentle cry indicated that he was awake and, undoubtedly, squinting from the city lights. We headed in the direction of our red brick duplex. With mixed feelings, we anticipated reunion with old friends.

It didn't take long to unpack and return to as orderly a life as possible. As a way to make our circumstances easier and accommodate the amount of time our son would require, we purchased a portable dishwasher that, in those days, may have looked silly and unnecessary to others, but it made us feel good. It gave us a sense of accomplishment.

Somewhat reluctantly, we invited our friends to a potluck dinner. All of them had been told ahead of time that Chris had brain damage. After arriving at our duplex, they excitedly cooed over our son and delighted at seeing him respond warmly to their affections. Mary Beth held him in her arms, saying, "He is such a handsome child." Another friend remarked, "He seems so alert." Understandably, for those without specific knowledge of early childhood development, it was difficult to believe he had brain damage, except for the physical things he was not able to do. Nearing ten months of age, he could not hold his bottle, he did not crawl from room to room, he did not get into the kitchen cabinets. For the most part, he was satisfied to lie on a small mattress in the living room or sit in his musical swing.

However, with his seizures now under control, and a somewhat normal schedule established, my time pressures eased and tension in our home fell to a more tolerable level.

The week following our potluck dinner was jammed with appointments at the big stone hospital at Fort Bragg, about ten miles outside Fayetteville. A neurologist was scheduled to do another EEG. This was critical; it was the only way of determining the progress resulting from the ACTH injections. Prolonged use of the hormone could cause excessive weight gain or hair growth, but we were forced to risk the detrimental side effects, knowing that EEG testing was a way of controlling them.

As in Alabama, the tests were done in two sets: the first while Chris was awake, and the second while he was asleep. In preparation for each brain wave recording, technicians attached wires to Chris' head with the same clay-like substance as before. The first set of tests was usually quite simple but, more often than not, it was difficult to get him to fall asleep for the second set. The process spawned the most intense frustration for me and the medical staff. When Chris finally did fall asleep, he frequently woke up before all the wires were attached, which meant going home and coming back to try again. During the many long, monotonous drives home, I was challenged to find ways to keep Chris awake as long as possible so we could get complete and accurate results the next day. This routine went on for several months.

While all my *medical* hopes were pinned on the scientific expertise of the professionals, I also needed a modicum of emotional support from them. While their stoic self-control and detailed attention to technology and methodology were sometimes necessary, I yearned for enough empathy from them to allow, and even encourage, my questions without fear of being labeled *the one with the problem*. While frustrated with trying to distinguish between what I needed to know, and didn't need to know, I was appalled at how these *professionals* related to me. Even though I didn't expect to be one of the medical team, I expected to be more than a bystander. I wanted to be included as a human being whose observations and critical information might be important in my child's evaluation.

In looking back, I don't know how much the patriarchal culture that held sway in the early sixties, and the ever-enduring role of the male-physician authority figure, fueled my pent-up anger. But, it was clear to me that my mental anguish was substantially influenced by the sheer incompetence of military professionals. I knew I had to live with a kind of brutality until I found a cure, or was able to prove medical negligence at birth. By some extraordinary intervention, I could perhaps come to accept there was little I could do to improve Chris' condition.

When the test results were sufficiently clear, the team sent copies of Chris' brain wave recordings to the University of Kansas Medical Center and Duke University Medical Center. They both confirmed the diagnosis of hypsarrhythmia. After the Illinois State Pediatric Institute of Chicago reviewed the results, they wrote: *"Our consultants have concluded that there are no alternatives to the diagnosis."*

All other letters indicated the same: *"It would be well for you to remain in touch with a pediatrician within a university setting so you will have the advantage of new and available information. From time to time, new discoveries are made, explaining the cause and treatment of certain types of retardation."*

Every letter added to our despair, as did the fatigue of the nightly routines, the daily drives to the hospital, and the fear of what our baby would look like, and how he might feel as he grew up.

After four months of continued use of ACTH hormones, Chris did become an exceptionally chubby baby with puffy cheeks. But reality didn't set in until I looked at his one-year-old photograph. I saw how his likeness was dramatically (and embarrassingly) different from other children, and I wept.

With the uncertainty of our son's future, Phil requested a transfer to an Air Force Base anywhere in the United States where we could receive the best medical services.

A few months later, we received an assignment to Randolph Air Force Base just outside of San Antonio, Texas. It was close to Lackland Air Force Base, which had the largest military hospital in the country. This would be our sixth move in two years.

After I hung up the phone from having made arrangements for the moving van to load our furnishings, my thoughts went from one question to another. Was this madness part of some higher purpose? Or was it simply an opportunity to develop a quiet confidence in the midst of an uncertain future? Right now, I had to focus on our move and the final stages of my second pregnancy. I was thankful for the absence of morning sickness and any apparent complications.

On the road again, we drove through the picturesque terrain of North Carolina, then crossed national trails and historic battlefields of the South, driving past old mills and manufacturing plants rendered vacant by new technology.

Phil had made an earlier trip to San Antonio to investigate housing. We would be living temporarily in an apartment while anticipating completion of our new three-bedroom, ranch-style home located close to the base.

Our recent move, the scorching August heat, and the inconvenience of living in skimpy and confining temporary quarters, even for a month, added to the fatigue of the final weeks of pregnancy. Besides all that, I was worried about our unborn child, the recurrence of similar problems, even the same attitudes by medical professionals. Having gained only eight pounds, my imagination ran wild. Could there be complications I didn't know about?

I kept these concerns to myself until the first appointment with my new gynecologist. Quietly hysterical, I finally blurted, "Dr. Ellis, with a gain of only eight pounds, what is this baby going to look like?"

"Don't worry about the baby," he calmly responded. "He will take all he needs from you. You're the one who is losing weight."

My parents' generous offer to help us move from the apartment into our new home helped enormously. Even though living in a place of my own gave me a new glow of self-respect and personal satisfaction, I dared not think of how much time another baby would require. Instead, Phil and I geared up for the challenge as if we were preparing for twins. We purchased a double stroller, a second crib, another infant seat, a high chair, and a feeding table for Chris.

As I took Chris for his daily walks in the stroller, I could imagine my neighbors, most of whom I hadn't met, talking about my circumstances: *"She already has one child that's not walking. How is she going to manage with a second one?"*

By mid-September, the nursery was complete with turquoise-and-white gingham tied back at each of the full-length windows. With morning sunshine and an inspired use of color, the room was simple, yet dramatic. Already, I could imagine my new child toddling toward me with a toy in his hand and, months later, playfully running into my outstretched arms. He would be a strong, healthy baby with dark brown hair and brown eyes. He would be a happy, spontaneous child whose accomplishments could easily become the measure by which I valued myself. Or would he? I couldn't help wondering.

Late one afternoon, as I joyfully finished painting a wicker basket for the nursery, labor contractions took me by surprise. At first I tried to ignore them, but as the pain intensified, I knew they were real.

I called Phil, who was working outside. It would take forty-five minutes to drive to the hospital at nearby Lackland Air Force Base. We had no time to lose. It was easy to pick up the phone and call our new friends, who lived just two doors away. Mary Lou would be happy to come and stay with Chris.

After my harrowing experience of giving birth at West Point without my husband there, I was thrilled that this time, he could drive me to the hospital.

En route, we were still discussing names. I suggested we use my maiden name of Morgan for the baby's first name, or even his middle name, but our debate ended with Phil insisting that the baby didn't need to have a name right away.

I was furious. I was the one giving birth. Why couldn't the baby have my name, too?

As we pulled into the emergency parking area, I got a glimpse of the foreboding hospital, more commonly known as Wilford Hall. Outside, the temperature was still hot. Even at night it was in the eighties. In spite of the heat, the sky overhead burst with stars. Phil managed to ease me out of the car, into the hospital, and up to the main desk, where he urgently asked directions to the examining room. Down the hall, my *apparent* emergency got attention from a young male attendant who ushered me into an examining room, then summoned the nurse to assess my condition. It didn't take long to determine my fate. "Mrs. Wright, you will not deliver tonight. Go home and get a good night's rest," she told me.

Devastated by the delay, I worried during the drive home about the various ways in which a child could suffer brain injury and retardation. I knew from all the research I had done since Chris' birth that brain damage could range from infections involving the central nervous system to any kind of physical impact to the brain, occurring either before or after birth. An abnormal growth within the brain, or certain other prenatal conditions, could likewise cause defects in the brain or the skull. Damage to a seemingly normal brain could occur from a premature delivery, prolonged labor, or a breach delivery.

At home, I tried to focus on the excitement and wonder of childbirth. But persistent pains made sleep impossible and squelched my efforts to be upbeat. Moving restlessly from the bed to a chair, then to the bed again, I cursed the nurse who pronounced, "You can't possibly deliver tonight."

Within thirty minutes of arriving home again, I began pleading with Phil to call the hospital. After he earnestly appealed my case, the nurse reluctantly gave in, saying, "I guess you'd better come back."

The moon, after being undercover for several nights, decided to honor us with its presence, as if providing an escort. As we neared the hospital, those wondrous moonlit moments turned to panic. I feared another episiotomy and possible injury to the precious, vulnerable being I carried inside. Phil swerved into the emergency drive and, within minutes, we checked in at the front desk, then went upstairs on the elevator.

The looks on their faces told me the nurses understood the urgency of my return. They quickly hustled me into a pre-delivery room and lifted me onto a table. But my problems were just beginning. Unknown to me at the time, the epidural is usually injected into the lower area of the back while the expectant mother lies on her side. It normally takes effect in less than twenty minutes and is minimal enough to allow the mother to remain awake without suffering and to assist in pushing the baby out during the second stage of labor. The seemingly inexperienced anesthesiologist, who didn't know where to insert the long needle, forced me to lean forward in a sitting position during my labor pains while he, in exas-peration, finally thrust the needle in somewhere along the spine. I was assured the pain-relieving shot would take effect quickly.

Impersonal masked attendants wheeled me into another bleak room, which I presumed to be the delivery room. They hurriedly strapped me to the table. Nearly delirious with fear, I wondered why my husband couldn't be with me. After all, this was one of the most unforgettable moments of his life, not to mention it would be an opportunity to give his wife badly needed emotional support. While I knew my rage at strict military policy wasn't going to change anything, I hoped at least for compassion.

But when the birthing pains increased, and the nurses realized the pain-relieving spinal wasn't taking effect, they thrust a gas mask over my face. Terrified and overwhelmed by a sense of quickening suffocation, I grabbed for the mask and struggled to gain control. While the nurses forcibly re-strained me, I surrendered to the labor of childbirth.

Finally, to my great relief, the doctor came rushing into the delivery room. "How's she doing?"

Quickly realizing my distress, he instructed me to inhale deeply…in and out…in and out…keeping a steady rhythmic pattern. But in spite of his attempt to ease the situation, I was hysterical with pain and concern for my unborn child. Quite unexpectedly, leg cramps caused me to scream for help, for someone to loosen the confining straps which restrained my legs—as if I were going somewhere. The nurse replied, "Oh, what a faker this one is," and ignored my pleas. The experience of childbirth without epidural anesthesia, the unexpected muscle cramps, and being forced to breath through a gas mask lasted for ten or fifteen minutes. The epidural never did kick in.

Finally, the doctor announced, "It's a boy!" I offered a prayer of gratitude for the gift of another son. By now, Phil and I had agreed on a name—Thane Richard Wright. In those moments of sheer exhilaration, I knew that this child, with every step of his development, would make our hearts swell with pride. Even before his birth, he had given us the most exceptional gift of all: the courage to pursue the beauty and freshness of new life. A magnificent spirit, who was only three months old in the womb when we received the news about Chris, had bestowed love and compassion on two welcoming parents.

Shortly after six-thirty in the morning, my baby was shown to me for the first time. Suddenly, months of anticipation melted into icy fear. My son's unusually pointed head looked small compared to his large and protruding eyes. He had a jaundiced color. *Oh God, please let this baby be okay!*

I was groggy from the lack of sleep and a chaotic delivery. Also despondent, not knowing where Phil was. Had he stayed with me or had he returned home? It was all so confusing, a living nightmare. The only thing that really mattered now was that I was starving for a meal. A nurse finally arrived with a breakfast tray. She placed it on the table beside my bed and left the room. In spite of strict instructions to lie flat on my back to prevent unpleasant effects from the epidural, I was so hungry that I lifted my body to reach for my breakfast.

As the morning wore on, I suffered severe back pains and a throbbing headache from the spinal anesthesia that had never taken effect. When the nurse came into the room, I asked for pain medication. "I'm sorry," she said, "the person who is authorized to give your medication doesn't come on duty until ten o'clock." Ignoring my plea for relief, she routinely straightened the room, making sure I had Kleenex and fresh water.

Meanwhile, the conversation among my hospital room-mates centered on family reactions. One new mother said, "My six-year-old is excited about having a *real* baby to play house with, but I'm afraid her excitement will soon turn to jealousy when she sees how much attention the new baby gets." From across the room, another concerned mother spoke up, "My youngest son doesn't seem to share in the same happy feelings as the older children. I'm worried be-cause I have read that confused feelings in children can lead to stuttering or thumb sucking."

I slumped down in my bed, hoping they wouldn't ask how our new baby would be received. It was likely Chris wouldn't even notice he had a new baby brother.

My attitude grew worse when another nurse, who came in shortly thereafter, tossed piles of green sheets on the foot of our beds.

"Okay girls, everyone up to make your beds," she demanded.

I was still in so much pain there was no way I could consider getting up to make my bed. I lay there without relief until Phil arrived to take me home.

My mother-in-law, Lillie, came during my first week back home. She was absolutely thrilled to be a grandmother for the second time, and willingly used her loving and efficient ways to help me establish a routine for my two babies. This time, since I had made the decision to breastfeed, motherhood took on a whole new meaning. Reportedly, breastfeeding lowers the risk of infections and guards against colic. But nothing could begin to compare with the incredible closeness I felt with this tiny being snuggled next to my body, knowing he depended on me for his survival. It is a quiet place in a mother's mind where no one else can go.

When Thane was only a few weeks old, our family sat together in the living room, and with Chris on Phil's knee and Thane in my arms, we shared a moment I will always remember. As we showed Chris his new baby brother, Phil and I spoke in soft animated voices, not knowing whether he would understand that something wonderful had occurred. Surprisingly, he listened with great interest, then smiled his typical broad smile and squealed with delight. This kind of reaction always indicated he was happy. When I thought about it later, I was thrilled to know I had underestimated his perceptions.

During those first few weeks at home with our precious new son, we proudly took photos of the two boys to send to grandparents in Kansas and friends back in North Carolina. Naturally, I still had visions of normalcy for our family. But even with the birth of an apparently normal child, those images were shattered to bits when Thane began his own mysterious pattern of crying. They occurred about the same time as his feedings, causing me to panic. When I thought he was still hungry, I let him nurse on demand until I could no longer endure sore nipples. His crying increased at night, as well as during the day. Home alone with a new baby whose crying spells reminded me of Chris' earlier behavior, I thought I might break into pieces. *What am I doing wrong? Why is he crying so much?*

When I could no longer control my worries, I called my pediatrician at the clinic. He promptly scheduled an appointment for the following morning. That night, lying in bed alone while Phil was away on assignment, I longed for the warmth of companionship and prayed for the strength to get through another appointment alone. Somehow I would manage.

Sleepless hours later, with emotions steeled against all possible odds, I drove Thane to the clinic. Inside the typically austere-looking office, I held my son on my lap, grateful I had an appointment with a pediatrician whom I could see on a regular basis. He conscientiously listened to my concerns and then, after a careful examination, offered a surprising solution.

"Connie, I know you've been enthusiastic about breast-feeding, but it's possible that through nursing, your anxiety is being passed on to your baby. I think for his sake, as well as your own, it would be wise to discontinue the breastfeeding. That way you will know how much milk he's getting."

I was disappointed. I enjoyed the bonding process and didn't want to give it up. Besides, it was hard to believe that a mother's fear could be translated to her baby through the highly recommended practice of breastfeeding.

As I reluctantly changed to the new routine, the feedings became more predictable. Curiously, though, the crying continued. With depression knocking at my door, I returned to the clinic with more unanswered questions. This time, my appointment included several other pediatricians.

One doctor confidently asserted, "I believe Thane's particular pattern of crying is simply a case of the colic."

Another doctor countered, "But his crying pattern seems much too irregular for colic, especially considering that his worst periods fluctuate between late afternoon and evening. It doesn't appear to be a typical colic pattern."

They asked me to return to the waiting room so they could confer privately.

With frayed emotions, yet determined to get answers, I settled into my chair. Momentarily, the doctors returned with a new plan. "Mrs. Wright, considering the circumstances with your first child, we think it would be wise to do an EEG on your son, Thane."

"An EEG on Thane?"

"We merely want to confirm that a neurological problem does *not* exist. Can you take him to the hospital later this week?"

"Yes, of course."

On Thursday morning, after the forty-five minute drive to Milford Hall, the same place Thane was born, I parked in the nearest available space. I bundled my one-month-old son next to my tension-filled body, got out of the car, and walked across the crowded parking lot.

As we neared the hospital entrance, a kindly looking gentleman held the front door for us. I was too wrapped up in my thoughts to thank him. I kept walking, following the signs toward the neurology wing, all the time saying to myself, *I don't know how I would bear it if something were wrong with Thane. There just can't be!!*

Finally inside the neurologist's office, I was quickly ushered into the examining room. My heart pounded so hard I was certain it could be heard without a stethoscope. Once again, I watched the technician attach the electrodes, this time to Thane's tiny head. I knew all too well that an EEG tracing would show whether the brain activity was normal or abnormal. It could deliver devastating, or exhilarating, news. At times like this, I wished someone could invent courage and market it in neat foil packages, to be consumed whenever my fear seemed insurmountable.

After the tests, I waited alone outside the lab until the results were available. The long hallway tunneled endlessly as I searched for a friendly, consoling face. If only I could call my husband. At this moment, in the deepest pain I had known yet, I felt there was no way Phil could fathom how incredibly wonderful it would feel to have him hold me in his arms — just holding me tight.

A few disinterested nurses walked past me. One who seemed more sensitive than the others murmured hello as she turned into another room. I couldn't help thinking about people who led *normal* lives while I hung out in hospitals and doctors' offices waiting for EEG results.

I thought of friends who had tried to console me, telling

me how well I had coped with a child who required so much care, and now, more concerns. But my angry thoughts persisted: *I am no more prepared than any of you! It's just that I am the one who is in this trying situation.*

An hour passed. The doctor emerged from the neurology lab, then walked across the hall to hand a folder to one of the nurses. As he came toward me, I tried desperately to read his face. He had to know the agony that sat like a dead weight inside my body. Why couldn't he at least change expressions? Instead, he would undoubtedly have Greek and Latin words to share with me, words synonymous with heartbreak and despair. The English translation—*Be prepared to cry.*

The doctor finally spoke.

"Mrs. Wright, the EEG is normal."

As I rose from the wooden chair and clasped my hands together in relief, the fear and tension that had plagued my mind from the first moment I realized I was carrying my second child, vanished instantly.

6

PROMISES, PROMISES

In the past, I had learned to transform our small living spaces into warm, cozy rooms. Now with a larger home, minimal furnishings, and early-marriage collectibles, I not only had an outlet for my talent, but a place where I could escape from doctors and hospitals, and have a life of my own. Surrounding myself with beauty added a sense of optimism and allowed the creative images to flow. An open kitchen looked across the counter into our spacious family room with hardwood floors and vaulted ceiling. An expansive view, seen through panels of glass, extended beyond the patio and across the open backyard to a grassy hillside of scrub oaks and blue skies.

One cloudless summer morning, while sitting on our patio and soaking up rays, I closed my eyes and began drawing slow, deep breaths. As I settled comfortably into the chair, my mind got quiet and my thoughts began to drift. While my two babies took their morning naps, I reflected on the expectations I had for fulfilling the dreams of a life I had long imagined. At the age of twenty-five, I had earned a college degree, married my handsome prince, organized and managed four homes, and given birth to two children. But in spite of these accomplishments, my most nagging problem was that of believing in myself.

Suddenly, I was interrupted by the uplifting voice of my new friend Glenda, coming around the corner of the house. I had met her through Sunday morning services at the base chapel, and was grateful for at least one close friend with whom I could share intimate thoughts and feelings, an element missing in the relationship with my husband.

"Hi, Connie," she called, as she stepped onto the patio, her face radiating with excitement. "Listen. You won't believe this. I heard an educator speak at our church today. He claims that with a new break-through therapy he can help disabled children learn to walk and talk. I know you and Phil have seen many specialists, but this man's theories are so convincing. He's been to Philadelphia to study these new techniques. He's looking for parents with children like Chris who can benefit from this therapy."

I didn't want to be rude to a well-meaning friend, but I replied, "Glenda, I just don't see how that's possible."

"Connie, I really want you to speak with him."

Mentally reviewing all of Chris' diagnosis, I was convinced that the claims of this man defied logic. Medical science hadn't yet discovered how to rejuvenate injured brain cells or replace damaged cells with new cells. At the same time, I dared to wonder...*Could this possibly be the answer we've been hoping for? Could this be the reason we were sent to San Antonio? Could it be the miracle I'd prayed for only a few months ago?*

Reluctantly I told her I would give it some thought, adding, "If you hear anything else, let me know."

"I'll call you," she said, and waved goodbye.

After I had time to think about this educator and his claims, I was furious. It seemed like an attempt to extort money from parents like us who were in situations where any improvement seemed better than none. I knew what Phil's reaction would be. As a pilot, he dealt with precise procedures that left little to the imagination. His evaluations were based on facts and proven results. He would undoubtedly question how an educator could make such claims of *healing*.

It was difficult to let the idea slide, but my busy schedule crowded out further consideration. From morning to night, my days were full: feeding schedules, changing diapers, bathing two babies, structuring play times, preparing the meals, taking care of the house, washing and folding what seemed like hundreds of cloth diapers, and, when Phil was away, keeping our new lawn alive.

Fortunately, Chris and Thane had their own bedrooms, each with a crib and changing table. At mealtimes, I used two infant seats, one in each side of my double sink, so I could feed them at the same time. It worked great until Chris got too big and Thane too active. Thane eventually grew into a high chair, while Chris used a larger, more substantial feeding table. As often as possible, I took neighborhood walks with them in the double stroller. I actually enjoyed the curious remarks from my neighbors; "When did you have another baby?" "I didn't even know you were pregnant."

Even though I organized my days well, life was erratic, mainly because of all the doctors' appointments for Chris. In my recent visit to Lackland Air Force Hospital, doctors reaffirmed that the ACTH hormone had stopped the seizures but, unfortunately, it had not promoted further development. Their final suggestions were discouraging. "There is nothing more we can do for your son. Take him home, enjoy him, and see what happens."

A frightening sense of helplessness accompanied the painful truth. When my two-year-old son could do nothing more than roll over on one side, I felt powerless to ward off the familiar feelings of inadequacy.

A few weeks later, Glenda stopped by my house again. "Connie, Dr. Wesloh really seems to be getting results. Some of the parents are excited about improvements they've already seen in their children. I think you should talk with him about Chris."

Finally, I conceded. "Give me the man's name and phone number. I'll call him tomorrow."

When Phil came home, I gave him time to change out of his uniform and have dinner before I brought up the subject. After a hearty meal, I managed to convince him we had nothing to lose by scheduling an appointment.

In a diversion from our usual roles, I took matters into my own hands and picked up the phone to call the Institute for Human Potential.

"This is Connie Wright. We have a two-year-old son with

brain damage. We've heard about your program and would like more information."

"Yes, Mrs. Wright. It's important that we meet with you and your husband in person. We would be happy to schedule an appointment for you. When would you be available?"

Since Phil wasn't scheduled for a flight that week, I quickly agreed to an appointment two days later.

The clinic, located in downtown San Antonio, was easy enough to find on the map. As we drove through a residential neighborhood nearing the address, I became more excited. At last I spotted a wooden sign standing saliently beside a small frame house. In large black letters, it proudly proclaimed: *THE INSTITUTE FOR THE ACHIEVEMENT OF HUMAN POTENTIAL.*

With a mixture of reservation and hopeful anticipation, Phil parked the car, and then we walked up the curving sidewalk. We rang the bell as directed on the front door and went inside. After sitting in the waiting room for only a few minutes, we were enthusiastically welcomed by Dr. Wesloh, the director of the clinic. It no longer seemed important to prejudge the person we were about to see. We just wanted the truth

After we were seated in a small conference room, Dr. Wesloh said, "I'm sure you are wondering what my qualifications are. I have a Ph.D. in education and have worked with exceptional children who exhibit all types of disabilities. At the Institute for the Achievement of Human Potential in Philadelphia, I learned how to evaluate brain-injured children. I was given instruction on how to teach parents to carry out new methods of therapy. Glenn Doman and Carl Delacatto are the founding forces behind the theory of neurological organization. The central purpose of the Institute is to help children become normal."

Dr. Wesloh explained that during the 1940s a group of doctors, psychologists, and therapists had begun to question how they were treating brain-injured children. When they shared recorded results from massage treatments, whirlpool baths, braces, exercises, and electrical stimulation, they saw that their classical treatments had failed the brain-injured child. In fact, their treatments had been aimed at the *symptoms* of disability rather than the source of injury that existed in the brain.

Despite the good intentions of so many professionals, this bold revelation inspired two medical experts, Doman and Delacatto, to put together a team. These experts studied hundreds of brain-injured children as well as hundreds of normal children. From their research, they derived new theories about the development of a brain, speculating that normal patterns of brain development could be imposed on an injured brain, and concluded it was possible for the undamaged areas of the brain to assume functions that were normally performed by the damaged areas.

Just as neurological growth could be severely impaired by the lack of oxygen or physical injury to the brain, we were told that neurological development could likewise be speeded up by excessive stimulation to the central nervous system. This new theory of educating undamaged areas of the brain to take over the functions of damaged areas became known as the Doman-Delacatto Patterning Program.

Phil and I sat enthralled as we heard how thousands of parents were learning to produce a miracle for their children at the Institute for the Development of Human Potential in Philadelphia. It had become the world's largest treatment center for brain-injured children, as well as a center for helping children with their speech and reading problems. As positive results from this new technology became available to doctors and educators across the country, they set up clinics in major cities across the country.

The important factor was whether Chris would qualify for the program. Dr. Wesloh indicated we would need to know whether he was of the *brain-injured* type or the *brain-deficient* type. A *developmentally delayed* child is one who has a perfectly normal brain at the time of conception and suffers injury to the brain at a later time. That is different from a child whose brain is *genetically deficient* at the time of conception.

I was reminded from my earlier research of the many ways *a normal brain can become injured.* Something could happen *prior to birth,* or *during birth.* A number of things could cause brain damage *after birth*: a severe blow to the head, a near-drowning, childhood encephalitis, a bullet to the brain, head trauma resulting from a car accident, even a maternal blood clot during childbirth. The list seemed endless.

Dr. Wesloh thoroughly questioned Chris' history and concluded that his brain damage did not stem from a genetic reason, but rather from injury due to some external cause. Except for an abnormal number of incisions made to my body at the time of delivery, and our earlier suspicion of the use of forceps, the precipitating factor of Chris' brain injury remained undocumented. At this point, we could only speculate that the injury occurred during the birth process, most likely through negligence by the military doctor who performed the delivery. Regardless of the cause, Chris was believed to be among hundreds of children who could benefit from the Doman-Delacatto Patterning Program.

We soon learned that disabilities could not be grouped into a general category, but range from a *severely brain-injured child* who can't move or make a sound to a *moderately brain-injured child* who is unable to walk or talk, but can move and make sounds. *Neurological disability* could include a child with reading problems, hyperactivity, lack of coordination, or simply the inability to concentrate. Chris seemed to fall into the category of a *moderately brain-injured child,* one who was not walking or talking, but could move his arms and legs and make sounds.

Somehow, being able to identify his level of development removed some of the mystery. But after two days of exposure to compelling charts and one man's prophetic words of encouragement, we still had lingering doubts about the program. The final part of the presentation was a film titled, *Whatever Happened to Eight?* It was the story of an eight-year-old boy named David who was struck by a car on Halloween night and became completely paralyzed. Because of massive cerebral damage, he couldn't remember his eighth birthday. Neurosurgeons told David's parents that if their son lived he wouldn't be more than a vegetable; they were advised to put him in an institution.

The parents refused to accept the diagnosis. After hearing about the revolutionary method for treating brain-injured children, they found enough tenacity to persevere with the patterning program.

After three-and-a-half years of intensive therapy at the Institute in Philadelphia, David relearned how to crawl on his stomach, creep on his hands and legs, and eventually walk. He recovered his eyesight, regained his memory, and relearned an extensive vocabulary. With patience and devotion from his parents and hundreds of volunteers, David's tragedy had a remarkable conclusion: a brain-injured boy who was not relegated to an institution to be treated as insane. It was a miracle.

After seeing the film, we were finally persuaded. Dr. Wesloh sensed how quickly we identified with the dramatic account of David's progress. "You both must realize what will be required of you if Chris is going to get well. Don't expect sympathy from us when you tell us how hard the program is. We won't waste your time with bedside manners or sweet talk. We are in the business of making children well. Our goal is not to make your child a little better or help him hold his head up straighter. We define wellness as a *normal* child. Anything less is considered failure.

"This is an awful regimen. It takes energy, dedication, time and effort. It upsets your life completely! There are no shortcuts, no days off. You can't do just ninety percent of it. You have to do all of it to make your child well. There is only one thing worse than this program — a child with a problem for which there is no answer."

Spurred by Dr. Wesloh's persuasive presentation, we tried to imagine what it would be like to create a miracle for our son.

7
WALKING ON WATER

The possibility that Chris could go from a functional age of two months to a level of walking and talking was nearly unthinkable. But learning of the compelling progress of eight-year-old David made it more believable.

Dr. Wesloh was convinced that if we could bombard Chris' central nervous system in the same way as they had done with David, by communicating a *normal* pattern of movement to the brain many times a day, the undamaged part of Chris' brain could be trained to take over the activity of the damaged cells.

This process was known as *patterning*. It involved a technique in which his arms and legs would be mechanically moved through the basic crawling pattern as if he were actually crawling on his stomach. Each patterning session would require three people and would be done nine times a day. It would mean twenty-seven people a day, or one hundred eighty-nine people a week!

As new residents living outside the base, I wondered how we could recruit twenty-seven volunteers a day and maintain that schedule seven days a week.

The questions lingered until one morning I awoke early, sluggish after a frightening dream. Something was chasing me with such force I couldn't escape, leaving me with a feeling that I had to do what was being asked. When I shared my strange, but foreboding, dream with Phil, he looked puzzled, but later agreed it must have been the omen we needed to end our ambivalence about launching the program.

Three days later, determined to recruit as many volunteers as possible, I stood at the door of a neighbor whom I had never met. I nervously rang the doorbell and prayed for a friendly face. When she opened the door, I hurriedly introduced myself. "Hi! I'm Connie Wright. We've never met but I live just a few doors down."

She didn't invite me in and I didn't have time to chat, so I boldly continued, "We have a son who doesn't walk or talk. We're looking for volunteers to participate in a home therapy program. Would you be willing to help us for a couple of hours a week?"

"Actually, we just moved here," she replied. "I've been busy trying to get some flowers planted. As you can see, we're in the process of landscaping the yard. My two sons are returning next week from vacation...."

I bit my lip and closed my eyes, attempting to deny the brush-off. My heart pierced, I wanted to scream at her, *My son can't walk or talk. Yours are healthy and active. Please, this is our only hope for a normal child.*

Instead I managed a polite goodbye and slowly headed home. Momentarily, I allowed myself to indulge in a feeling of defeat, wondering if this rejection was a sign that I should abandon my impossible dream. When this neighbor turned me down, it was as if God had forsaken me.

After a good night's sleep, I decided to venture outside the neighborhood—a less threatening scene. I began making phone calls to local civic clubs, church groups, and even the Air Force Wives Club. I was surprised and pleased at the response. Many asked me to come and talk to their club. After only a few phone calls, and weeks of speaking engagements, we had a substantial list of recruits. Other community groups began to express interest in hearing about the program.

Even though the response quickly surpassed our wildest expectations, one hundred eighty-nine people a week was still an awesome number. To recruit more volunteers, Dr. Wesloh agreed to show the film *Whatever Happened To Eight?* After a group of thirty people came to our home to see how David had made progress, they enthusiastically signed on and agreed to find other volunteers.

Meanwhile, we designed a schedule that would reduce the number of volunteers. We calculated that if three volunteers in the morning could stay for two hours and conduct three patternings (one every thirty minutes), then the early afternoon group could stay for two hours and conduct three more patternings. The late afternoon group could complete the final three patternings. This way, we could confine the number to sixty-three people a week.

After a few weeks, we had one hundred twenty-six ready and willing recruits! It was unbelievable, twice the number we needed. They were comprised of Air Force personnel, some civilian families, and twelve teenagers. Now, instead of requiring people to come once a week, we could schedule each person to come every other week.

The program, however, called for more than organizing and training the volunteers. It required specific kinds of equipment. Most important, we needed a long padded table on which the patternings could be done. We also needed a wooden ladder six feet in length that Chris would hang on while volunteers stretched his spastic muscles. Another critical item was a wooden box, designed to encourage crawling. It had to be eight feet long and four feet wide, and we had to be able to elevate it three feet at one end. With specific plans and directions provided by the Institute, Phil carefully constructed everything we needed.

Finally, the table and crawling box were ready to be placed in the family room, transforming our living space into a physical therapy room. We propped the wooden ladder outside on the patio, which began to look like a children's playground.

The night before we were scheduled to start our patterning program, I was awake for hours wondering how I would get myself and our two babies fed and dressed, and the house organized by eight o'clock the next morning. Of more concern was Dr. Wesloh's ultimatum a few weeks earlier: *"The success of this program depends on YOUR careful and accurate training of the volunteers and YOUR willingness to carry out the daily patterning without missing a single day."*

Chris and **Connie** greet volunteers at the onset of the patterning program.
San Antonio, Texas - 1964

When morning finally came, the first three volunteers arrived at our front door. I greeted them and led them into the family room. In preparation for their training, they lifted Chris onto the foam-padded, vinyl-covered table. I showed them how they would move his arms, legs, and head, just as if he were crawling. One person wearing a pair of soft cotton gloves turned Chris' head from left to right, another person moved his left arm and left leg forward, and a third person moved his right arm and right leg back. This way, both sides moved together, but in opposite directions. While moving Chris' body they also had to brush the palms of each hand flat against the table to stimulate the nerve endings. Once the volunteers had grasped the concept and practiced a few strokes, I set the timer for five minutes. The person at the head of the table began counting, "One…two…one…two…"

When the timer went off to signal the end of the first five-minute patterning session, everyone stopped. Chris immediately lifted his head, raised up on his hands and smiled at his friends. One woman gave him a hug and held him upright on the table. Then I showed them how to place a plastic oxygen mask over his nose and mouth to encourage deep breathing and increase the amount of oxygen to his brain.

Next, the volunteers focused a small flashlight between Chris' eyes for three minutes. This was to encourage both eyes to converge on a single object and correct a condition called *strabismus*, where the eyes converge to the center at the same time.

After Chris was patterned on the table and his muscles stretched on the ladder, he was placed at the elevated end of the crawling box. Lying on his stomach with a toy placed in front of him, he was encouraged to slide forward and reach for the toy, giving him the idea of movement.

After training the first three volunteers and conducting three patterings, the boys and I had lunch. Then I put them down for their naps. At one o'clock, the next group of volunteers came. I did the same training with them, and during the next two hours, they performed three patterings. At four o'clock, the third group was given instructions, and then completed three more patternings.

Just as Dr. Wesloh had stated, the program would not bend to our schedules. Our lives would have to revolve around the program. With nine people a day, which was sixty-three people a week, it was clear there would be no short cuts or any time off. In fact, after the first week, each person was instructed to simply ring the doorbell, open the door, and go directly to the family room to a position around the patterning table.

It soon became apparent that with my schedule of supervising the patterning program, doing household chores, and caring for Chris and Thane, I had no time to answer the phone and find replacements for people who could not keep their appointments. We quickly created a substitute list so each volunteer could responsibly find his or her own replacement.

My anxiety about the mechanics subsided as, week after week, the program progressed in an orderly manner. The volunteers faithfully showed up on schedule and Chris cooperated beautifully, except for those days when he rebelled with a stiff body. This made it nearly impossible to perform the patterning. As for Thane, other children often came with their parents, and he always had a welcome lap to sit on. Phil was generally out of town three to four days a week, an escape I often envied.

With patterning nine times a day, I began to crave time alone, and needed a chance to go to the supermarket, clean my house, change the linens, and vacuum the floors. After numerous calls to an agency, we found a housekeeper named Laura who was able to come every Thursday. I had no idea what was expected of me, or what she would do when she arrived, but I didn't need to worry. After brief introductions, she expediently put the dishes in a sink of soapy water, went to the master bedroom to strip the beds, and started on the boys' rooms.

On my *day off*, which consisted of running errands and going to the market, Laura not only cared for my babies, cleaned the kitchen, handled the laundry, and maintained the tile floors, but she even filled in for the patterning when necessary. What Laura accomplished in one day at my house, before going home to six children of her own, was unbelievable.

One day when Dr. Wesloh came to our house to visit, he noticed that Thane was walking at ten months of age. "Connie, you need to get Thane down on the floor and keep him crawling. You know how important the crawling movement is to the development of a child's mid-brain, where most of the learning takes place. Every child goes through specific stages of neurological development during the first couple of years of his life. At this stage of mid-brain development, the more a child can be encouraged to crawl, the more enhanced the neurological development, and ultimately, a more advanced cortex stage."

"But Dr. Wesloh, now that Thane knows how to walk he doesn't want to crawl on his hands and knees."

"Connie, you can purchase one of those cloth tunnels to use in the hallway. He will have to crawl through it to get to his bedroom. You can use it in the back yard when other children come to play. As an added incentive you may need to crawl on the floor with him several times a week, playing hide-and-seek as you go."

As an education major, I knew the value of giving my children the utmost stimulation at a young age. And so, giving myself credit for being willing to do whatever it took to enhance my children's development, I strapped on the knee pads and crawled with Thane up and down the hallway and across the wooden floors of the family room.

In the midst of the daily activity, I kept my spirits up by cooking and occasionally, entertaining a few friends and neighbors for dinner. We enjoyed frequent get-togethers with my Aunt Joyce and Uncle Marvin, who lived in San Antonio. We were always entertained by Marvin's silly stories, and we delighted in the beautiful birthday cakes and candlelight dinners that Joyce created. I hoped that somehow they knew how much their love helped to dissolve the tension and soften our invisible scars.

Chris loves his birthday—especially the musical cake stand.
August 15, 1964

Second son, **Thane Richard**, celebrates his first birthday.
September 18, 1964

When Phil was home, we sometimes joined the colorful nightlife on the River Walk, where retail shops bustled with activity and Mexican restaurants came alive with mariachi music. At a riverfront cafe overlooking the San Antonio River, I had my first taste of Bouillabaisse, with chunks of fresh seafood in a sumptuous broth of saffron, fennel, garlic and wine. This particular evening I was reminded of how, with family responsibilities and a military lifestyle, we had forgotten how to have normal conversations with regular people. I often wondered what civilian folk talked about and what kind of marriages other people had. Even though our evenings at the River Walk were always too brief, they did offer a softer, more mellow view of the outside world.

Generally speaking, social life for Air Force wives was minimal. The base had formal dinner functions several times a year. With an upcoming event—a tribute to Phil's commanding officer circled on the calendar and the usual question of what to wear—I realized a compelling need to look good. But it seemed I needed more than the usual affirmation to satisfy a long-standing fear of rejection and deepening sense of unworthiness, even among people I hardly knew.

What I really wanted and rarely got from my husband was a hug and a simple compliment, such as "I love you" or "You look great." I wanted to believe that my need for love, affection, and approval, especially from my husband, was a normal desire rather than a narcissistic need. I thought perhaps my husband unconsciously withheld affection because of the rigid military rules that prohibited men in uniform from showing affection or carrying babies in public. It was possible the emotional setbacks in his early life influenced his capacity to show affection. Whatever the circumstances, they seemed to interfere with his ability to contribute to our relationship and to provide the inner security for which I yearned.

It was likely that neither of us realized how we had suppressed our true feelings because we had been in denial for such a long time. We couldn't admit to our fears of being unlovable and unworthy because those feelings were unacceptable. And while I was often aware of the subtle, but disheartening feelings of abandonment in my personal life, I depended on the success of the patterning program to fill the emotional void.

After just four months, Chris was consistently moving down the elevated box faster than ever before. He did this by reaching for a toy in front of him, which caused him to repeatedly slide forward, as if he were crawling. One night while Chris played by himself in the family room, he began to make his way across the hardwood floor, crawling on his stomach. I was stunned to see each arm and each leg working together in a cross-pattern crawling movement, just like the Institute had predicted.

"Phil, hurry! Come look at Chris!"

He came running from the living room and looked on while Thane, now sixteen months, cheered and clapped for his brother. No one was more pleased than Chris himself. His effervescent smile indicated how proud he was of moving across the floor on his own, an image that will be etched in my mind forever.

The news managed to reach the volunteers before their next patterning session. While their enthusiasm soared, my energy and strength of purpose were greater than ever.

Eight months into the program, it was time for another evaluation with Dr. Wesloh. While progress seemed to have slowed, he confirmed that Chris had advanced from a developmental age of two months to a developmental age of nine months. Committed to making progress, we continued our successful action of sixty-three people showing up at our house every week, daring to create a miracle. While Sunday services at the base chapel provided us with emotional support, a weekly Bible study group gave us an opportunity to join with others for companionship and comfort.

Over time, I became friends with the base chaplain who

agreed to come to our home to pray for Chris. Chaplain Wolf emphasized that the greatest suffering occurs in our mind and is acted out through our behavior. Unless we can understand and accept an imperfect world of disharmony and imbalance, we as human beings will always experience an element of pain. He said that sooner or later, all of us must face the reality of our own internal suffering, which actually has nothing to do with our circumstances.

As I struggled to find joy in the midst of the uncertainty of our circumstances, the hardest part was convincing myself there were others on the same journey, that I was not completely alone in my predicament.

Even though my tears might have indicated a lack of appreciation for Chaplain Wolf's visits, his strong presence and reassuring words gave me comfort.

One Sunday after Phil and I had attended early services at the Air Force Base, we had lunch before he and Thane left for the country as they often did. I had just put Chris in his crib for a nap before the next group of volunteers arrived. The house was quiet and peaceful when I received an unexpected telephone call.

"Hello?"

"Are you the mother of Chris?" a woman on the other end asked.

"Yes."

"I have heard about your son and the number of people who are working with him. Are you aware God can perform miracles for children like your son?"

"Yes, I pray every day that a miracle is possible."

"I would like to come to your home to see Chris."

She spoke with such confidence and authority, and her words were so thought provoking, that she stirred images in my mind of a normal child.

Without further deliberation, I gave her my address.

In fifteen minutes she arrived at our home. As I heard the doorbell and rushed to open the front door, I had the same gut-wrenching feeling as on my first date.

"I would like to spend five minutes alone with your son," she said.

"Okay," I answered, hesitantly.

I led her down the hallway to the first room on the right where Chris was resting in his crib. I quietly closed the door and left the two of them alone.

As I waited outside in the hallway, my fantasies went wild. What would Chris look like sitting up in his crib? Standing up? Reaching his arms toward me? I quickly got caught up in the possibility of normalcy. A surge of hope that I might be freed from the unrelenting responsibility of caring for a disabled child ran through me, momentarily numbing my thoughts.

Then suddenly, I was hit with a sense of shame for having trusted a complete stranger who might actually harm my child. After realizing I hadn't heard a sound from Chris' room, my shame, and now guilt, turned into a dreadful humiliation, and then an indescribable fear. When the door unexpectedly opened, I glanced beyond the woman to see my son still lying in his crib.

When Chris didn't pull himself up on the side of the crib or stretch his arms toward me, my short-lived fantasy was replaced with a sense of relief that he was unharmed and he was smiling.

The woman stranger quietly walked toward me and turned down the hallway in the direction of the front door. Before she opened it to leave, she turned to say, "God bless you."

When the door closed, I wept. I would always wonder who the woman was and what she had hoped to accomplish with my son.

8

THE ANSWER IS NO

In the course of a year, the love and compassion of one hundred twenty-six people confirmed our feelings that we were, in fact, living as the architects and designers of our lives. But now, particular happenings dictated a change—and more uncertainty. Many of Phil's peers were being relocated to military bases overseas. A transfer would not guarantee the medical services we needed, nor would it be feasible to continue the patterning program.

Fortunately, there were other options to consider. With Phil's background, he would likely qualify for a career with commercial airlines, so given the poor odds of our remaining in the States, he submitted his resignation to the Air Force. While waiting for confirmation of a release, he used his accumulated vacation time to attend aeronautical engineering school in California, a requirement he had to fulfill even to be considered for a position as a commercial pilot.

As Phil left for Los Angeles, I placed a sign in our front yard: *FOR SALE BY OWNER*. Though our lives were upset by another move, we approached it with courage and confidence.

In the next four weeks Phil completed his flight engineering training in Los Angeles. He returned to San Antonio just in time to receive official notice of a discharge from the Air Force. Two days later, he received confirmation of his acceptance by Continental Airlines. By the end of that same week, our house sold for full price.

There was, however, one hitch in our plan. Phil's acceptance by the airlines required six more months of training in Los Angeles. Until we were assigned to a permanent location we would be without an income, and would be forced to terminate the patterning.

It wasn't long before Phil's parents invited Chris and me to continue the patterning at their home in Lyons, Kansas. My mother offered to fly to San Antonio to bring Thane home to their ranch. After accepting their generous offers, Phil flew to Los Angeles for flight training; Thane went with his grandmother to western Kansas; Chris and I drove across several states to Lyons in southeastern Kansas.

Two days after our arrival, I stood in front of a group of nearly thirty people—neighbors, relatives, and friends of Phil's parents, who had crowded into a large family room where Phil's dad had already constructed and positioned the patterning table. Once again, I tearfully explained to an attentive audience how the fulfillment of our dreams depended on the exact application of the Doman-Delacatto technique. *"Chris' chances of learning to walk and talk depend on daily patterning, which means imposing the crawling movements on the brain nine times a day. It's critical that the program continue without interruption while our family makes a change from military life to civilian life."*

When I finished pouring my heart out, every man and woman in the room committed to a weekly position of patterning. A few days later, the *Lyons Daily News* featured a photograph of Chris being patterned by volunteers. The article proudly boasted of a community celebration when, as a result of their successful mission, Chris would be able to crawl across the floor on his hands and knees—for the first time!

Word quickly spread throughout the state that we needed more volunteers. We soon had eighty people. More calls came in daily. Understandably, most of the volunteers were committed to Chris' progress because of having known Phil or his family. Even though their lives seemed rich with friends and simple pleasures, many of them had dealt with their own pain and suffering. These beautiful people inspired me to get up every morning with renewed strength to pursue my dream.

It wasn't long before another article appeared in the

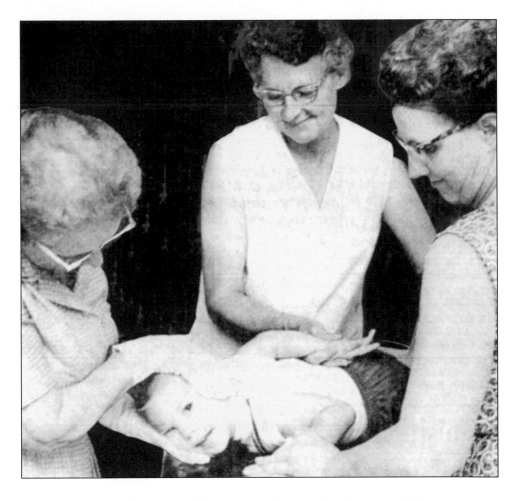

Chris's Therapy Becomes A Community Project - 1965
His grandmother, **Lillie Wright** (center),
and friends from Lyons, Kansas.

Lyons Daily News where editor Paul Jones wrote, *"If the volunteers are doing something for Chris, he is indeed returning something to them. Just observing the little fellow is a pleasure. Despite his limitations, he is remarkable in stamina, good humor, and alertness. Chris' spirit and pleasant personality are a joy to behold. Working in the program is, no doubt, the most worthwhile project in the week of any volunteer. Very few people can't afford two hours a week to help build a boy."*

The daily routine of caring for Chris would have been much easier if he were able to cooperate with me during the routine of bathing, feeding, and dressing. He was nearly three years old, but because of the ACTH hormones, he was heavier than most three-year-olds, and because of the daily patterning exercises, he was incredibly strong. When he got angry he defiantly grabbed my hair and, with fierce determination, held on. He often asserted his temper with a swift kick to my shins. But in spite of his strength and determination, he was unable to guide a spoon into his mouth or an arm into a shirt sleeve.

Since the beginning of the patterning program, a pain in my right side had persisted. I consulted numerous doctors, but they found nothing significant, only the aggravation of daily lifting. An orthopedist prescribed exercises to strengthen my lower back muscles, but the pain persisted.

Even though Chris was now more difficult to lift, I hadn't thought of using a wheelchair. The Doman-Delacatto staff repeatedly stressed that the injury was in the brain and that crutches, braces, and walkers simply treated the symptoms, not the injury. They didn't advocate artificial aids.

One day, as I thumbed through the newspaper, I discovered an ad that read: *Used Child-Size Wheelchair — $55.* But what would the volunteers say if I resorted to the use of a wheelchair? Would they think I had lost faith in the program? Would Phil be sympathetic to the relief it could give me?

I tried to put these questions aside while driving the

thirty-five miles to Hutchinson, Kansas. Inside the dusty antique shop, an elderly gentleman intuitively knew me from my telephone call. He directed me to the center of the store. I stood gazing at the smallness of the child-size wheelchair. My hand slowly moved across the brown leather seat, which was embossed with tiny western symbols. I carefully examined the tiny footrest and the hand brakes. It was perfect for a young boy. At the same time, it was nearly impossible to imagine my own son using a wheelchair.

My eyes brimmed with tears while I negotiated a price of $25. As the kindly gentleman helped me load the wheelchair into the back seat of the car I couldn't help recalling the dream of buying my son his first bicycle.

I polished the chrome to make the chair look new before anyone saw it. Much to my surprise, the volunteers reacted with relief and approval. It was only a matter of time before Chris and his friends readily adjusted to his new position, convincing me I had made the right decision.

The patterning program was progressing well, but I was increasingly aware of my own emotional deprivation. I appreciated the close relationship I had with my in-laws, but I missed Thane, who was still living with my parents in western Kansas. A ride across the state on the Union Pacific once a month to visit him was not often enough. Besides, I worried about how he and his grandparents would manage with toilet training and other developmental behaviors.

I also missed my husband. After three months of living in different worlds, the feelings of closeness and intimacy in our marriage had suffered. I hoped that when we were together again, I would feel the strength and reassurance of his love.

The details of our reunion in Los Angeles remain vague, except that when I arrived at Phil's apartment, I felt strangely alienated and helpless to bridge our emotional gap. In the awkward silence that followed, I felt like a specimen under glass, trapped by my own expectations of being able to seduce and romance my husband. In reality, I had very little knowledge of how to do that.

For most of our married life, I had focused on the practicalities of taking care of a home and family, just like millions of other women who were inherently more interested in the security afforded by marriage than the details of intimacy. In spite of knowing that Phil was just as naïve and uninformed on the subject, I was concerned about the theories that men are more promiscuous and more sexually aggressive than women. Also seeded in my imagination was the fact that my husband, because of the distance and time away from home, was more susceptible to opportunity.

I trusted that these strains would lessen when Phil was finally awarded a permanent assignment with Continental at their Los Angeles pilot base. Though we dreamed of relocating to Denver to be closer to our families who lived in Kansas, our priority, at least for now, was to bring our own family together.

Phil became interested in the fast-growing community of Thousand Oaks, forty-five miles west of Los Angeles. One Sunday morning, he decided to attend services at the Hillside Methodist Church. As he was leaving the church, he met another Continental pilot.

Jim and his wife Kay invited him to their home in a nearby suburban neighborhood. They talked enthusiastically about the activities of a community geared to young families.

Phil had to interrupt them. "Jim, I must tell you that we have different needs than most families. Connie and I have a three-year-old son who is seriously handicapped. At this stage of his development, he is unable to walk or talk. For more than a year now, we have been involved with a therapy program in which volunteers come to our home. Recruiting large numbers of people in an unfamiliar community is quite a challenge."

Jim was quick to reassure Phil of the kind of spirit that existed in Thousand Oaks. "I'm sure if you contact Reverend Andrews at the church, he will agree to place an announcement in the church bulletin. I feel certain that within a couple of weeks you will have many volunteers."

Phil turned to Kay. "Would you be willing to collect the names and phone numbers of those who respond?"

Kay was naturally apprehensive, but when Phil told her of our previous success, she agreed to head the project.

Phil then began to search for the perfect environment for us to live. It had to be one that was maintenance-free, affordable, and accessible to large numbers of people. He soon discovered a large apartment complex in Thousand Oaks, which was beautifully landscaped with lush vegetation and quiet courtyards. A *shared* environment could perhaps give us the illusion of support in a world that seemed chaotic and beyond our control.

Back in Kansas, as Chris and I prepared to say goodbye to family and friends, he made the headlines in the *Lyons Daily News* — one more time.

CHRIS MOVES AWAY

The best-known three-year-old in the community is, in one more week, going to move to California. With brain damage that occurred at birth, Chris is not just another little boy. At three years of age, he has not yet learned how to walk or talk. The story, however, is not only about Chris. It is about a labor of love from dedicated volunteers who would not accept hopelessness for him, people who after five months of a grueling daily therapy program, have definitely seen results. There is no doubt that Chris' remarkable stamina and humor will be missed. As the community of Lyons says goodbye, we hope the residents on the West Coast will feel the same kind of affection for Chris.

When I arrived at Los Angeles International Airport on a Monday morning with our two sons, Phil greeted us with news that the patterning program would begin at four o'clock that afternoon in our living room. It was hard to believe we could resume the patterning without missing a single day. Phil and Kay, with the help of the church, had structured a new program with well-defined teams of volunteers who were just as committed to participating in a miracle as our Kansas and Texas friends.

As the initial group of thirty volunteers grew to eighty and the momentum continued, we realized it was time for another evaluation. This time, the evaluation would take place at the Institute for the Development of Human Achievement in Chicago.

As the plane touched down at O'Hare International, I prayed that the collective efforts of so many people would result in *new* marks on the evaluation chart. After a brief, but thorough, evaluation by the doctor, we were encouraged to hear that he wanted to enlarge the scope of Chris' program. This *seemed* to indicate progress and required changes in the patterning.

When we returned home, the volunteers accepted the news of being *retrained* as evidence of their success. Based on Chris' strength and increase in size, the new program now included five people for each patterning session: one person for each arm, one person for each leg, and another person to move his head. That was a total of fifteen people a day, or one hundred five people a week. Excitement about the changes made it easier to recruit more volunteers, but training and supervising them was a laborious and ongoing task, which always became my responsibility.

A speech program was designed to encourage language through repetition and recognition of objects. We were told that even though the speech center in his brain had been damaged, Chris could learn to distinguish between an apple, a block, a ball, and a spoon, and that if he could learn to recognize objects, he could eventually identify words. When the volunteers showed Chris the various objects and he *just happened* to match the object with the name, we applauded his success.

One night when Phil was gone, I became crucially aware of the value of speech, especially in a critical situation. I had filled the tub for Chris' bath and put him into the water in his usual sitting position. I was aware the water was higher on his chest than usual, but it would only take me a few seconds to get two diapers. Running into his bedroom to grab them, I remembered the words that every mother has heard: *Never leave a child alone in the bathtub.*

I heard water splashing; Chris had never made that much noise in the tub! Racing back into the bathroom, I saw water all over the floor. Then I saw Chris in the tub, struggling beneath the water. Suddenly, my bare feet hit the slick, wet floor and flew out from under me. I fell with a startling impact onto the side of the tub. As I slumped to the floor, a sharp pain pierced my left side.

Gripped with fear and panic, I only had one thought: *I have to get Chris out of the tub.* With every ounce of strength I could muster, I managed to pull him over the edge of the tub onto the floor beside me. Gasping for breath, he looked terrified. In spite of the pain, I was able to get him dressed and into his bed.

It seemed like days before Phil returned from his flight, but it was only the next afternoon. When he took me to the doctor's office, the X-ray showed I had a cracked rib. I was given strict orders—No lifting! Thankfully, my wonderful mother-in-law flew out to help with the boys and the patterning.

During my much-needed period of rest and recuperation, the reality of the patterning program hit hard. Lying in bed, I tried to convince myself that I could cope with being confined to a small apartment with fifteen people a day for an indeterminate period of time. I also tried to tell myself I could endure the incumbent loneliness, which seemed to be getting worse. I prayed that tomorrow would be a *new* day.

The ultimate goal was to get Chris crawling on his hands and knees. An increase in physical stimulation was critical because we didn't know when his brain might begin to process the crawling movements. In addition to the nine patterning sessions a day, (five people each hour and a half, three times a day), our new schedule required an *assisted crawl* for two hours each day. This meant that in between the patterning sessions, volunteers would take turns bending his knees and pushing him forward, as if he were crawling.

The incentive for Chris to *crawl* was that magic moment when he could put his hand on the *moving* screen of the television that sat on the floor at the other end of the room. Equally motivating was a stack of red brick cardboard boxes, also at the other end of the room. After crawling across the floor to knock them down, he laughed with delight at his achievement, then turned to give his audience a big smile.

Naturally, some days his attention lessened and it was nearly impossible to push him. Yet, with months of dedicated effort, he finally mastered crawling on his stomach. Excited about the next phase of development, the volunteers learned how to place Chris on a triangular frame supported by three rollers, then took turns pushing his feet, which forced his hands to move as if he were crawling.

In spite of our progress, Christmas was bleak that year. Chris could crawl on his stomach from room to room and could grasp simple finger foods, but we felt the progress was not enough to compensate for our efforts. We struggled financially with doctor bills and trips to Chicago for the evaluations. Then, our portable television stopped working. Without the incentive of that magical picture, it was nearly impossible to get Chris to crawl.

The volunteers used this lapse as an opportunity to raise money for a new television, one that was larger and with beautiful color. Once again, as if there had been no interruption at all, Chris began crawling across the room to touch the animated screen.

I could only imagine that to Thane, who was only eight months old when hundreds of people a week suddenly invaded our home, the world must have looked very confusing. During the last two years, the stream of volunteers had graciously acknowledged him saying, *"Hi, Thane, how are you?"* But they quickly directed their attention toward his brother. *"Hi, Chris, don't you look cute in your short pants and matching knee socks. Let's see what you can do today."*

Aware of the imbalance of attention, I regularly took Thane aside to work on puzzles and vocabulary cards. We spent time doing art activities with clay, crayons, and water-colors. I loved reading him stories from his favorite books. His curiosity was keen and his comprehension level was high. I tried to demonstrate, as best I could, how much I enjoyed being with him.

Nevertheless, as a guilt-ridden mother, I enrolled him in a nearby preschool three mornings a week, with the intention of satisfying some of his needs through the association with other children. Even though I used our early morning walks as an opportunity to observe worm-like bodies of snails inching along on the wet sidewalk, and a chance to talk about the colorful succulent plants and budding flowers, Thane's tears and tantrums became a frequent part of the morning.

A month later, the rage of a confused little boy bubbled over with such intensity it frightened me. One day I entered Thane's bedroom and stood aghast at the results of a seemingly belligerent and defiant act. He had spontaneously heaped all of his books, records, building blocks, puzzles, toy cars and trucks from the bookshelves into the middle of the room.

When I tearfully confided my distress to the volunteers during the next few days, they tried to console me by saying, "Connie, Thane gets far more attention than most children. Look how you take him aside each day to work with him. My kids don't get nearly that much attention."

It was true. Thane was given far more individual time and creative instruction than most children. But considering that our home was *not* a normal environment, and that he was too young to understand the impact of his traumatic birth and the subsequent violation of his childhood, he was apparently acting out his repressed feelings.

Without understanding the meaning of his pain, it was impossible for me to know how to handle his aggressive behavior. Even with my educational background and my attempt to show him love and compassion, I knew his perceptions were as real to him as mine were to me.

Our neighbors, Geri and David, were teachers in the middle school and had two young daughters, Vicki and Debra. David was a coach and loved taking Thane to the park to play football. Geri was a wonderful mother who involved Thane in cooking, sewing, weaving, and other creative projects.

Grieving for the loss of a normal family, I searched for ways to mitigate the effect that our lifestyle appeared to be having on Thane. I tried to sort out the truth and the logic, but my mind seemed completely void of reason.

My friend, Jhonna, lived close by in the same apartment complex and was also married to a Continental pilot. She had two small children, so she understood my concern for Thane. She suggested a behavior-modification specialist who could help us evaluate Thane's behaviors and the effects of our lifestyle.

It was only a few days later when Phil and I, along with Thane, drove across town to Judy Algor's office. Inside the first-floor suite an attractive young woman greeted us. She jotted notes on our family history, and then gently persuaded Thane to accompany her into another room for a personal interview.

During the meeting that followed, we learned that our two-and-a-half-year-old son was grappling with more dark feelings and troubling fantasies than he could express, except through his rage. For a child with a disabled sibling in a highly restrictive atmosphere, it was natural for him to want to gain control by dominating every situation. His reactionary behavior was a way to compensate for his diminishing ability to trust his own feelings and judgments about being loved and included in the family. A home environment with a continuous flow of *guests* gave Thane the perfect opportunity to employ a power struggle against authority figures. In this situation it was even more difficult for me to maintain consistent standards of discipline.

For immediate handling of the situation, Judy advised us in two very important areas. First, she proposed some new parenting skills we could use with Thane. Then she guided us through a candid evaluation of the short-term and long-term consequences of the lifestyle that was required in order to conduct the home-therapy program for Chris. Her insight was crucial and pivotal; it caused us to make an honest self-appraisal and think about making a change in our home environment.

At home, I telephoned every Special Services agency in the area. I requested whatever kind of help they could give me, just one day a week. I repeatedly got the same response. *"Your situation isn't critical enough to qualify for assistance."*

Sensing that my life was in shambles because of the strongly suspected criminal conduct of a military doctor and his undocumented carelessness at the time of delivery, and now, the rejection of my pleas for help, I was close to a near breaking point.

Finally, one of the weekly volunteers offered her home for the patterning one day a week. The idea of being free from the mental responsibility and fatigue of the daily routine was nearly inconceivable, but a day of freedom would ease the emotional strain. On that first Thursday, Thane and I spent the entire day together visiting the children's section of the library, eating lunch in the park, and later, relaxing in the sun by the pool.

After three short weeks, the Thursday group reported that Chris was irritable and uncooperative, so I capitulated and regretfully, gave up my one day off.

Back to the routine as usual, I had no time to focus on the intangible aspects of my life — like what was happening to me internally, or what was occurring in my marriage.

It would have been easy to blame our disabled child for

the inhibited communication and the angry upsets between us. The truth is, neither Phil nor I really knew the person we had married. And now, we lacked the courage to acknowledge the *glittering images* we had fallen in love with. We also lacked the skills with which to bridge the gap between our fantasies and the real person.

Looking at the facts of our relationship, it seemed clear that neither of us had sufficiently invested ourselves in the marriage. In order to stop living in the past and create our future, we had to mutually decide to create something of value for *ourselves* and not the children. I wanted to feel that I was my husband's best friend. Sadly, I wasn't. Neither did I know how to create the kind of intimacy I desired or the kind of communication that I needed. Undoubtedly, his late-night flights, combined with jet lag, hurried meals, and sleepless nights in unfamiliar surroundings, took a toll on his mental state and his physical energy. I could only imagine getting on and off airplanes in different time zones and flying through tough weather patterns.

But from my perspective, his time and distance from home, and even his association with flight attendants and other pilots, gave him an escape from family conflicts. When he did come home, I hungered for his recognition of my strength in coping with the emotional overload and the *prison* in which I lived. I longed for someone who took my emotions seriously, and outwardly admired and respected me. This kind of validation from my husband was critical.

When I brought this up, he tried to acknowledge me by saying, "Geri and David next door think you are a saint. They can't imagine how you cope with people in and out of your house every day. They simply don't know how you do it!"

"I don't care what Geri and David think," I retaliated. "I only care what YOU think! I need to know that YOU think I'm doing a good job."

Painful emotions that seemed dormant from a million years ago suddenly gushed from a deep, dark and mysterious place, from a void that seemed impossible to fill. Phil's attempt to placate me with compliments from someone else, rather than accommodate my deep-seated desire to be directly acknowledged by him, fueled my anger.

I didn't understand that my husband might have suffered from the same lack of self-worth and was never validated for who he really was. Perhaps the prestige of college honors and military status filled a long-standing emotional void, but still left him susceptible to habits of rigid discipline and the effects of religious ideologies.

Assuming that my emotional needs were unimportant to him, I suffered from his silence and, therefore, put my feelings on ice. When a woman's sense of personal value slips away, it's easy to grow silent.

I further withdrew, not understanding why someone who supposedly loved me didn't want to share his thoughts and his apprehensions with me. While our mutual needs for comfort evolved into dreadful accusations toward each other, the thing I feared the most was happening—the loss of a relationship with my husband.

Years later, I learned that instead of coming directly home after a flight, Phil drove to a nearby shopping center where he chose to sit alone in his car rather than confront the situation at home. It was likely a way to cope with his fear of losing a responsible job, a fear that was undoubtedly intensified by the ongoing expenses of a disabled child. Perhaps it was also a way to avoid dealing with the intense therapy schedule.

While other people had time to enjoy their children, take trips together, or share picnics in the park, we lived with no shortcuts and no days off. I couldn't help remembering Dr. Wesloh's warnings to us at the outset of this program: *"The only thing worse than the grueling routine would be a child with a problem for whom there are no answers."*

After completing nearly two years of the Doman-Delacatto therapy program, we had doubts about Chris' progress and questions about the credibility of the program, but we still had hope. That is, until we flew to Chicago for another evaluation.

The professionals at the Institute persisted in their search for signs of progress that were not previously documented. To date, Chris had learned to crawl on his stomach from room to room, and he was able to grasp objects. His constant exposure to adults had fostered a loving, playful personality, but what about walking and talking? When would he learn to feed himself? When would he learn to sit up?

Doctors at the Chicago Institute seemed unwilling to state the obvious. There were no new developments. Chris was not progressing. When were they going to admit that he was at the same development level as a year ago? I felt wedged into a hard sticky place, my hopes contaminated with distrust.

Exasperated and fatigued, we returned home to Thousand Oaks. I could hardly drag myself out of bed to greet the next group of volunteers. I was depressed and even nauseated by an acute sense of self-sacrifice. My fantasies drowned in anger and flooded me with the truth of my own hopeless condition. I knew we had no choice but to stop the home-therapy program and Phil agreed.

Without hesitation and uncertainty, we had to face each of the volunteers with our decision. In spite of their support and optimism, we had to tell them they were no longer needed. How could I do that when my own identity was so closely connected to the possibility of a miracle?

In two years, approximately 6,600 volunteer visits in Texas, Kansas, and California had taken place in our household. The price of taking this risk was a future without guarantees. And now, in order to relinquish the hope ignited by the professionals at Philadelphia's Institute for the Achievement of Human Potential, we needed a different kind of courage. We needed the strength to realize that the *miracle* we had hoped for was *not* a child who walked and talked. The *miracle* was the thousands of people who had participated and were unwilling to succumb to failure.

Phil agreed to take care of Chris and give the news to the volunteers while Thane and I flew to Kansas to stay with my parents for a much-needed rest. As each group came to our apartment to perform the patterning for the last time, Phil gave them a typewritten note with news of our termination:

To our dear friends,
There is no way to thank each of you for your commitment to Chris. Over the last two years, he has benefited from hundreds of helping hands. There has been definite improvement. However, there has been very little progress during the last six months. I know you will understand it is not feasible for our family to continue with the investment required by this program. Thank you for every single day.

With much appreciation,
Connie and Phil

Word spread quickly until many of the volunteers knew that their next session with Chris would be their last. It would also be the end of a dream to see a young boy stand, walk, and run free.

9
TURNING THE TIDE
OF HUMAN SUFFERING

A brief respite at the ranch was the kind of solitude I needed, but I didn't know that disconnecting from the inflexible pace of the last two years would be so difficult. That first morning at home, after we finished breakfast, I stood up to clear the dishes and hurriedly began to clean up the kitchen. Mother yelled, "Connie, sit down! Those dishes can wait." I complied, but the effects of the unyielding routine of the past two years caused me to wonder what other compulsions I had developed, what personal needs and feelings I had put aside or buried while I concentrated on the needs of others.

After forcing myself to linger at the breakfast table a while longer, I walked outside and strolled down the dirt road and over to the barn. I continued onto a trail that led across the creek and up the hill to the south pasture. As I ambled along, my thoughts wandered to those times when I got up early to go with Dad in the truck to the wheat field just beyond the south pasture. I always felt important when he let me drive as he scattered *bait* from the back of the truck to prevent the grasshoppers from gorging on the wheat. On other mornings, I helped him place wool-covered traps in the ground to deter coyotes that attacked our sheep.

Life at that time seemed to center around survival and, subliminally, an ongoing attempt to feel my dad's approval. As a result of watching his impassioned, and sometimes inflexible drive, I decided that I wanted to *wear a tie* when I grew up. Even though I wanted to become fiercely indepen-

The road to the barn — and lifelong memories.

Connie's parents, **Larry** and **Isabel Morgan**

dent and successful like him, I also observed the religious tradition that dictated the rules for women. I intuitively sensed the rage of many women trapped in unhappy marriages and heard some of them regretfully state they had no other place to go. In those days, the virtuous stayed married and were supportive of their men at all costs.

During this visit back to Kansas, I realized I still wasn't strong enough to break away from the *adapted* person I had become. Even now, I was one of those women who lacked her own sense of identity. But when I went outside to observe the vast explosion of color in the sunsets, or gazed into a luminous galaxy on a clear night, I was comforted by a strong identity associated with something more powerful than myself. It was a kind of intangible knowingness that had always been part of my strength.

Two years ago, I had been convinced that if I had enough faith in God and the Doman-Delacatto therapy program, we could create a happy, purposeful life that aligned with society's expectations. But now, suffering from a loss of promised results, and even skeptical about a higher power—despite those moments when I felt a strong connection—I wondered what I was supposed to learn from this experience. In those dark and sorrowful moments, the only reward seemed to lie in constructing a new formula for happiness.

After nearly a week in Kansas, Thane and I returned to Thousand Oaks to join Phil and Chris. That first evening back, standing alone in the living room of our apartment, I looked out through the sliding-glass door to see only a barren slab of concrete surrounded by an eight-foot fence and a small patch of blue sky. I was unable to see rich colors stretching across the horizon as the sun faded into dusk. The high windows in the bedrooms also restricted a view of the outdoors. The fact that our living environment exactly reflected the lifestyle we had imposed on ourselves was hardly a *coincidence*.

With the lack of a predetermined routine for Chris, and a schedule where every hour seemed worth the effort, my life felt empty and meaningless. I got up in the morning on the ragged edge of a breakdown. Throughout the day, I merely occupied space while going through the motions. Rather than suffer from feelings of guilt or failure, I felt embarrassed and angry at having been involved with the program.

When my mind seemed completely void of creative solutions, I knew I could count on my friend Jhonna. At a time when I needed her most, she came knocking at my door. She had come to show me a newspaper article from the *Los Angeles Times*. Excitedly, she read me information about the Kennedy Center, a newly established medical center where every type of disabled child could be evaluated and parents could be given a realistic prognosis.

My hopes soared. I trusted that Phil, too, would be receptive to the idea of checking it out.

When he returned home from his flight, I was quietly ecstatic when he agreed to contact the clinic in Santa Monica. While I waited and speculated, he made the call. When he hung up, he smiled and said, "We have a date next Friday!"

The week passed quickly. On Friday morning we loaded the wheelchair into the trunk of the car, buckled Chris into the back seat, and joined the snake line of commuters headed for all parts of the city.

At the Kennedy Center the receptionist told us we wouldn't have to wait long. We barely had time to settle into our seats before a gentleman in a white coat walked toward us. He first shook hands with Phil and introduced himself as Dr. Hartke, the consultant who would be in charge of Chris' case. After saying hello to Chris and to me, he led us down the hall and ushered us into a handsomely designed conference room where we sat around an oval table. He explained that the evaluation would include comprehensive examinations from an opthamologist, audiologist, orthopedist, neurologist, and physical therapist. The team would then be asked to give a conclusive diagnosis as well as a prognosis. Participation in the program would inevitably require several months of doctors' appointments. When he initially discussed the cost of the program, it seemed beyond our means. But when he showed us how the respective charges were based on a sliding scale and would compensate for our lack of income, the cost of the program looked feasible. With only one car in the family, it would be necessary to coordinate the appointments with Phil's schedule.

During the following weeks, we endured many anxious moments as all the specialists respectively conducted their examinations with precise procedures. They listened to Chris' heartbeat, studied his grasp reflexes, examined his muscle reflexes, and checked his eye-hand coordination. With heartbreaking effort, he attempted to grasp objects with his thumb and forefinger. Determined to measure up to every request, Chris sometimes appeared to exceed his previous neurological age. When this occurred, the staff gave him additional chances to demonstrate his level of capability. We held our breath and prayed for good news, but when he was unable to perform even the simplest motor functions, our hopes were dashed. While we remained proud of his sense of humor and ability to laugh at his own failures, we were forced to accept the truth of his delayed development.

At last the fateful day came when we were to get the diagnosis—and prognosis. Having spent months agonizing over the results of every appointment, we nervously waited in the conference room for the pronouncement of our son's future. The Kennedy Center hadn't promised a quick fix, yet it seemed only natural to try to focus on a new beginning. As much as I wanted the world to stop and give me a hug, it would go on, and I would continue to love my son no matter what.

Staring out the window to an enclosed courtyard, I was appreciative of the input from so many competent specialists, and grateful for their many kindnesses toward Chris. But as I waited, the longing inside of me grew physically painful. I couldn't help knowing that happiness, for us, would include repairing a couple of broken hearts and restoring a child.

Finally, the door opened and Dr. Hartke, with his wonderfully compassionate smile, seated himself across the table from us. During those brief moments of silence, I tensed. I wanted to trust in the thoroughness of the examinations and believe in a positive outcome. I wanted to put aside all expectations and thoughts that could seriously mislead me. But I knew all too well that doctors could have lovely words for indisputable facts.

Dr. Hartke began. "Well, Mr. and Mrs. Wright, your son is certainly a personable little guy. He has won the hearts of us all. I see from the intake information you have spent two years doing the Doman-Delacatto program. Do you feel that you benefited?"

Phil said, "After having read more about the Institutes nationwide, I'm afraid we fall into the category of many disillusioned parents."

I added, "It's hard to say whether the progress that occurred came directly from the consistency of patterning techniques, the simple maturation of the brain, or the amount of time and training devoted to his care."

"Yes, I would agree," replied Dr. Hartke. "Here at the Kennedy Center, the conclusion of the team of evaluators is that *Chris is a cerebral palsy quadriplegic,* a condition resulting in abnormal movement of both arms and legs. It's important you understand that the cerebral palsy condition can occur from defects that originate before the time of birth, or from injury during birth, as well as disease or injury to the nervous tissues of the brain after birth.

"There are often misunderstandings about cerebral palsy. It is not hereditary. It is not contagious. Once it has happened to a child, its effects are not reversible. Brain damage can affect a child's motor abilities and mental capacity, as well as his speech, depending on how extensive the brain damage. Every child is affected differently.

"For many years, it was believed nothing could be done for these victims of cerebral palsy. Children were hidden away or left in inadequate institutions. We have since found that with the right training, children can show marked improvement. Naturally, the degree of disability depends on the extent of brain damage with any given child. Chris' comprehension is surprisingly higher than his performance of physical skills. His potential, however, remains in serious question."

Dr. Hartke's words came as cruel hard facts, marking another milestone in our devastated hopes that new scientific advances could further our dream for a normal child.

He continued with practical suggestions. "At this time, we recommend a good preschool where being with children his age and of similar abilities may help stimulate his development. With special therapy in a school situation, he may learn to sit up, feed himself, crawl, or walk."

We left the Kennedy Center and drove home, knowing the prognosis was bleak. The only consoling factor was the possibility of an educational program within the public school system.

At home, Phil and I began to make phone calls to schools throughout the San Fernando Valley. Some public schools had special classes if we lived in their area. Most, however, were not staffed to accommodate a child who could not feed himself or manage toilet training.

When we called the Kennedy Center for further suggestions, we were given the name of a school that might possibly offer a half-day program. When I visited the school and learned that I would have to make a ninety-mile trip each day just to give Chris an hour-and-a-half program, I was devastated.

I turned to Phil for solutions that orthodox medicine and public education didn't have. "What are we going to do if there isn't a school whose program can accommodate Chris?"

"Connie, I don't have any answers."

Feeling rejected and abandoned, desperate for emotional support, I lashed out with pent-up emotions that reflected the truth of my despair. "Phil, I can't live like this any longer. I feel like a prisoner in this apartment. I think I'm going to go stark-raving mad in this place."

He seemed stunned at my outburst. As in countless times before, he failed to acknowledge feelings that were real to me and simply left the room. Realistically, there was no way he could comprehend the limitations of a small apartment with only fragments of creativity and human relationships. I felt it was impossible for *anyone else* to understand the emptiness that existed inside of me, a barren soul shackled by agonizing and conflicting emotions. I knew the internal conflict was unhealthy. But the overwhelming responsibilities of the therapy program, the limitations of mundane household chores, and the constant accountability for my children had consumed me. Without the kind of affection and intimacy that made me feel loved, I felt I had nothing left to give.

Our relationship became increasingly tense, not because we didn't have anything to say, but because we didn't know how to share our loss of a dream and the loss of ourselves. In spite of a common belief in God, we were like many others who had depended on religion to help create a secure identity and further our connection with a *higher power*. We had always associated ourselves with the authoritative beliefs of the church and trusted that our faith and determination would sustain us. But at this juncture of our lives, we were unable to find the answers we needed.

When Phil left on a flight, the morning after my explosive outburst, I picked up the phone to call my friend Jhonna. "Hi! This is Connie. Phil's on a flight and Thane is at preschool until noon. Can you stop by?"

When she arrived at our apartment, knowing my concerns, she instinctively sensed my tension and gave me a hug. After we sat down at the table over a cup of coffee she asked, "Well, Connie, what are you going to do now?"

"I wish there were a place for Chris to go to school like other children."

"Connie, I have a friend who has a child who requires special schooling. Some time ago, in her search for an appropriate facility, Children's Hospital told her of the best facility in all of Los Angeles County. I'll call her and get the name of the school."

The morning flew by and soon it was time for me to meet Thane at his school. He seemed more content these days, but I still worried about him. I tried to appease my fears by knowing that I had always been there for him when he was hungry and when he cried. I had applauded his first steps, read him bedtime stories, and listened to his questions. I had comforted him when he was frightened by thunderstorms, and shared in the excitement of new rainbows. I had encouraged him to watch for delicate raindrops on the buds of flowers, and to create wild imaginings through paint and clay. Yet, somehow, I felt that wasn't enough to satisfy his emotional needs, and I suffered enormous guilt.

I could only imagine that a problem for many mothers was diminishing hope for their own future, feeling anxious, yet unable to communicate about that. At times, I would have given anything to come home to children who were happy and excited to see ME. I would have been thrilled to know that someone else had persevered with daily care and management of MY home. I knew that would never happen. Generally speaking, however, I felt that being at home with my children at an early age was an important opportunity. At the same time, it was necessary for me to emerge from the cocoon, and to provide a balance for myself as well as for my family. The question was, "How can this be done?"

A few days later the telephone rang. "Connie, this is Jhonna. The school that was recommended to my friend is located in southwest Los Angeles. The name of the facility is the *Spastic Children's Foundation*. They even provide bus service for children within a certain geographical distance from the school."

"Jhonna, I don't see how that could work for us because we live forty miles outside of Los Angeles, but if you can get some more information about the school, I'll talk with Phil when he comes home tomorrow."

I was apprehensive about Phil's response to another program, yet I also knew he wanted to give his son every opportunity. If the *Spastic Children's Foundation* could offer us a new beginning, it would be worth investigating.

After Phil had a few moments to himself, I approached him with the idea. "Honey, I have some news about a school that might work for Chris. Jhonna says there is a place in southwest Los Angeles that comes highly recommended by Children's Hospital. She told me they accept children with all kinds of disabilities."

I waited for his response, allowing him enough time to grasp the bigger picture before his mind flooded with doubt and resistance. Thankfully, Phil was receptive and made the call. While I endured the many pauses in the conversation, I prayed for a new beginning.

When he hung up the phone, his face radiated optimism. "It sounds as if there is nothing that could prevent Chris from being accepted into their program. We have an appointment for the three of us to meet with the executive director next Tuesday morning."

My feelings of despair disappeared like chaff in the wind and were replaced with a sense of renewal.

Phil and I excitedly made the seventy-five mile drive from Thousand Oaks on the Ventura Freeway to an area called Watts, located in southwest Los Angeles. The predominantly black neighborhood was comprised mainly of tiny, unkempt stucco houses crowded together. The area was disheveled and filled with people hanging out on the corners with bottles of liquor in their hands. We pulled up in front of a small frame house with a wooden sign that stood in the yard and read *SPASTIC CHILDREN'S FOUNDATION*.

Before Phil got out of the car, he said, "Connie, do you realize that if Chris is accepted into the school we'll have to move into the city? That would be a big change for us."

"Yes, it would, but if Children's Hospital recommended the school, it must be a good program. A move into Los Angeles would be closer to the airport, a shorter drive for you."

Phil got Chris' wheelchair out of the trunk of the car and came around to lift Chris out of the back seat. At four years of age Chris weighed about sixty-five pounds, so I was grateful Phil was there to help with the lifting.

Inside, as we anxiously waited to see the director, the secretary instructed us to look across the street at a large two-story contemporary building. It had replaced another small frame house to become the first classroom of the *Spastic Children's Foundation*.

The secretary then told us about a woman named Eileen Allen who claimed it was her pride that refused to accept the diagnosis of *hopeless* for her premature spastic child. Doctors told her he was not intelligent enough to recognize her, but Eileen believed he did. She figured if the doctors were wrong about *that*, they could be wrong about her son's entire future.

With ingenuity and bold determination, she battled the standards of the time. She bombarded newspapers with letters. She campaigned with clinics and orthopedists and fiercely resisted anyone who saw only her son's handicap. She enlisted the loyalty and help of other mothers of children with a handicap. Together they created the *Spastic Children's Foundation*. Mrs. Allen's son was unable to walk or talk until the age of eight, but later he became the manager of the Hollywood High School football team. He graduated with honors from Claremont Men's College in three years. He earned a master's degree from UCLA, he married, and became a partner in an attorney's service business. Needless to say, our hopes were aroused by a victory like that.

While we waited, the secretary told us of another woman who dared to think beyond the constraints of her time. We learned that she first offered her services as a volunteer. And before long, her attention turned to the enormous need to make a better world for these children. With a firm and resolute vision of their needs, Anne Wendt became their spokesperson, the executive director of the *Spastic Children's Foundation*.

A few minutes later, a statuesque woman came into the room. She was wearing high-heeled pumps and a tailored shirt in cobalt blue that richly contrasted with a white wool skirt. Her blonde hair was worn in a twist on top of her head.

She greeted us warmly, "Hello, I'm Anne Wendt." After shaking hands with both of us, she bent down to shake hands with Chris, indicating her regard for him as a human being. She then ushered us into her small office.

After Phil and I were seated with Chris between us, Mrs. Wendt began to relay the history of the Foundation. "During the early years, when I became part of the building blocks of faith and hard work, I observed a tendency for people to react with repugnance to the physical problems of the child. It was my conviction that the total child must be treated. You can't treat just the acceptable part of a child and turn your back in rejection when he's sick or dirty.

"Secondly, and by no means less important, the Foundation has a passionate concern for families who are not geared to being twenty-four-hour parents. Our goal is to help the entire family. There is no place in this world where you can put your child and forget him. He is always yours and his problem is no greater than your ability to meet it. We never deny entrance to a child because he would be too much of a problem, nor do we ever turn families away because of their inability to pay. On the contrary, since we have a waiting list, we take children from families who have the greatest need."

Pausing to gaze out the window at the rapidly growing complex of buildings across the street where other small houses were being torn down, she thoughtfully stated, "The *Spastic Children's Foundation* brings the dawn of brighter days for children. These are not handicapped children. They are children with a handicap. There is no reason for a whole family to be handicapped because of one child. Parents must think about the future."

Mrs. Wendt then escorted us across the street for a tour of the classrooms and the dormitory. Inside the building, we observed teachers working with children in pint-sized wheelchairs, technicians guiding them across the room in walkers, and therapists dedicated to transforming the children's twisted bodies. One child inched along the floor on his stomach with both legs in braces. He didn't ask for help and he didn't receive it. But success was written on his face.

Suddenly a young boy about Chris' age stumbled toward me. He reached out and grabbed my clothes. Fearful that he might tear my dress, I backed away. He persisted by grabbing my hand and trying to talk to me. Saliva drooled from his mouth as he tried to get me to hug him. I started feeling ill; I wanted to vomit.

My thoughts darted back to the time when my special education class from Kansas State University went on a field trip to Nebraska. We had toured the residential facility and interacted with children like this. I had to leave the building because I felt sick.

Now, standing in the hallway looking at these kids, I felt guilty because I felt sick. I had to accept them as they were— recognizing that they had a need to be loved just as I did when I was a child. When I thought of their sense of emotional abandonment, I felt a deep shame. When I looked at them with their suffering I wondered, *How could a God of love allow this? But even if I didn't believe in a God of love, suffering would still exist.*

Returning back across the street to the small house and her executive office, Mrs. Wendt concluded, "Mr. and Mrs. Wright, here at the Foundation Chris will have every op-portunity to develop to his fullest capacity. It appears from his medical and developmental history, as well as your family circumstances, that we can accept Chris into our program. It is the only residential and day treatment center west of the Rocky Mountains. Our focus is on the education and training of children with a cerebral dysfunction known as cerebral palsy. Through the total commitment of custodians, cooks, teachers and therapists, we are turning the tide of human suffering. Our children are symbols of health and happiness and represent a brighter future. For these children we dare to dream large dreams and endure great hope. We don't play God, but we do give our kids a chance."

The last thing Phil and I wanted was sympathy. Instead, we needed day-to-day collaboration with professionals who could give care to our son and help us face the reality of a re-tarded child. The commitment and reassurance of this unique program gave us hope for the future.

At the age of four, Chris enrolled as a day student at the *Spastic Children's Foundation*, located at 1307 West 105th Street in Los Angeles. It was later renamed and is hereafter referred to as the *United Cerebral Palsy Foundation*.

10
PEBBLES IN THE POND

With our discovery of the *United Cerebral Palsy Foundation* in 1966, it was easy to imagine that hardship was behind us. However, in order for Chris to receive bus service to the school, we had to live in a particular Los Angeles neighborhood. Homes for rent in Westchester were scarce but finally, from an ad in the *Los Angeles Times*, I located a ranch-style home near a park and a playground, only a mile from the beach. The house was badly run down, but with fresh paint, new carpeting, and window coverings, it would soon feel more comfortable.

As I took pictures off the walls and dishes out of the cupboards in our apartment, the enticement of big-city living and the anticipation of new friends added to my momentum. Having lived in nine cities in five years, with little time to develop relationships, I was accustomed to moving without having to say goodbye.

Now I looked forward to being plugged into a normal life in a *real* family neighborhood. Soon after we settled into our home on Ninety-First Street, I surprised new neighbors with an invitation to a party at *my* home. With candles and music, my favorite chocolate cake and rum coffee, and friends mingling in my living room as if we had known each other for a long time, I felt myself detaching from the loneliness of the prior two-year commitment. Even though few of us have the capacity to prevent the past from haunting the present, I looked forward to the best of everything—a new life and an opportunity to unleash my repressed creativity.

Months before, while we were still living in Thousand Oaks and doing Chris' home therapy, my gynecologist had spoken to me about having another child.

"Another child! Dr. Westcott, you don't understand. I have a disabled son and sixty-three people a week coming to my home to do therapy. I have a hyperactive two-year-old and a husband who is gone more than he's home, and you're telling me I should have another baby?"

Dr. Westcott answered, "You should think about Thane growing up as an only child, and how old he might be if you decide to have another child."

I didn't know what to say. I had only scheduled the appointment to refill my birth control prescription.

Sensing my hesitation, he said, "It's just something to think about."

My gynecologist seemed to understand the deep commitment a family has toward a retarded child, but he was also aware of a second child living in the shadow of a sibling's disability.

After recovering from the shock of his suggestion to have another child, Phil and I decided to forego birth control, and conceived shortly thereafter.

It wasn't long before I told my neighbors that I was expecting our third child. Perhaps for the first time, I was able to give myself credit for being more capable than I had ever believed. I awakened each morning in a joyous frame of mind, anticipating the new addition to our family.

It was impossible to forget those early months of fatigue, the staggering responsibility of a newborn, the repetitive routines of feeding, dressing, bathing, and laundry. But I saw pregnancy as an opportunity to reinvent myself. It was a matter of reconciling the realities of motherhood with my fantasies of being the ideal parent. Now that the therapy program was over, I dreamed of picnics in the park, bike rides, outings at the beach, and time to really watch my children's curious, exuberant faces.

I hoped my husband would let me know when the maternal glow had kicked in and a more sensuous nature was evident. It would be great if I could talk to him about my fears, the funky things my body would be doing, and the euphoria of becoming a Mom again. If only I could encourage him to express what he was feeling. Unfortunately, we rarely indulged in a relaxed two-way communication that would have made each of us feel important. Rather we talked *at* each other.

Aside from my other concerns, I wanted the morning of Chris' first day at school to go as smoothly as possible. The new schedule would include organizing his clothes the evening before, setting the breakfast table with placemats and dishes, and carefully laying out my own clothes. When the alarm sounded at six o'clock the next morning, I would have no time to linger.

Chris was generally good-natured while I dressed him and put on his diapers. He would never argue, "I don't wanna wear that shirt." When I put on his leg braces and laced up his high-top shoes he would never ask, "Who's gonna help me tie my shoes?" When he was cooperative and playful, and I didn't feel so rushed, our time together was really special. But since the bus would be pulling into our driveway promptly at seven o'clock every morning, the timing was critical. The routine of dressing him, giving him his breakfast, and getting him ready for the bus depended on his cheerful cooperation. Most important, I had to keep him from seeing his jacket and diaper bag, which were usually placed by the front door. Once he saw them, he began to moan with angry rebellious sounds, and then lapsed into a sorrowful wailing, which merely reflected the painful uncertainty of a young boy leaving home. When the bus driver sounded the horn in our driveway, Chris' crying got louder and even more painful to endure.

Once outside, the driver helped me lift Chris into a car seat that had been secured to the bus seat so he could sit up high and look out the window. While boarding the bus, Chris stopped crying, but when the bus driver pulled out of the driveway, he again wailed with heartbreaking tears. Eventually, after about twenty minutes, this tearful episode stopped as abruptly as it had started. After several months, he gave up the tears for good. Thankfully, he arrived home each day in a happier mood.

Naturally, I couldn't help wondering what my neighbors would think when they observed the large black letters CEREBRAL PALSY FOUNDATION on the side of the yellow bus. But even without the glaring indicator, they would soon learn that Chris was an exceptional child, and that this bus wasn't the usual school bus.

The inevitable day came when children and their parents became curious enough to ask questions. One afternoon, while Chris sat in his wheelchair on the sidewalk, a group of

Chris arrives home after a day at school—age four.

kids began asking questions. "Why does he have to sit in a wheelchair all the time? Why doesn't he talk to us?"

My teaching instinct brightened. I began educating the neighborhood kids. "All of us have a mechanism inside our body that tells our body what to do. Do you know what that is?"

One young boy spoke up, "It's a brain."

"Do you know where your brain is?"

"It's in my head."

"That's right. And the brain in your head works like a computer. It gives a message to your body that tells your arms and legs what to do. It can tell your body to sit, stand, or walk. But if your brain is injured, it can't tell your body what to do. Chris was born with an injured brain and because his brain cannot tell his legs how to walk, he has to use a wheelchair. Chris is not able to use words to talk to you, but he understands most of what you say to him. He would like for you to talk to him just like you do with your other friends. Would you be willing to do that?"

The children nodded in agreement.

In the sixties most people had never encountered a child with a disability. It would be a long time before an increase in exposure to the problems of mental retardation would result in greater understanding, eliminating the looks of pity that could make parents feel inferior. Ultimately, I would be comforted when our neighbors on Ninety-First Street fell in love with Chris' gregarious personality, and would have no problem relating to his special kind of energy.

Wherever we lived, Chris soon became part of the community. Not long after we moved into the area of Westchester, the local Elks Club adopted him as their *Child of the Year* and featured his picture in one of the local newspapers.

Freed from the relentless routine of patterning, I awoke each morning with renewed energy and approached life with a sense of gaiety and aliveness. I eagerly planned my daily household routine and even cooked my famous beef stew for a neighbor, Irene LeBlanc, who had five children and had just given birth to twins. It wasn't long before a new neighbor, Carol Gilger, along with her husband and two sons, moved across the street. She was surprised that with my busy schedule I would bring them a tuna casserole. I soon met Ann Murdock, Hazel Peeler, Winnie Hobbs, and Barbara Dickson—other young mothers who lived down the block. The Plotnick family, who lived a few houses away, had seven children and a well-organized household that was the envy of the neighborhood. Jean and Bob next door had two children, Larry and Kathleen, who were nearly the same age as Thane. Charlie and his wife, an older couple who lived on the other side of us, enjoyed a quieter existence.

A fascination with the culture of Los Angeles and the opportunities it provided to artists led me to enroll in an Architectural Studies course at UCLA. From our many short-term residences, I had gained much experience in turning a house into a home *overnight*. After five years of frequent moves and a military lifestyle, I was acutely aware of the internal effects of one's environment, and was inspired to create a warm and wonderful place that nurtured my soul. My idea of *home* was a refuge from doctors and hospitals, a place where I could look at life with assurance and optimism. Now I was motivated to learn more about the mechanics of creating that special kind of environment.

After learning the basics of interior design, my final project was to design three major rooms with a master color scheme, selection and placement of furniture items, and appropriate accessories. I was fortunate to become close friends with Barbara and Max Ward and their four daughters, who had recently moved into the neighborhood and lived across the street. They gave enthusiastic support and helped with the more technical aspects of my final project. When I completed the course, I received high marks for my work, and was confident I could apply the principles of good design to any home in which we lived.

This new life would not have been possible without the *United Cerebral Palsy Foundation*, which by now had become the primary instrument in turning our earlier frustrations and disappointments into positive and satisfying actions. For the first time since thousands of volunteers in three states had crossed over our threshold to try to produce a miracle, we found new support through the wisdom of the Executive Director Anne Wendt and social worker Nancy Harris.

One day, while sitting in Nancy's office, Phil and I observed her provocative but practical demeanor. She had an unassuming way of getting directly to the issues at hand. With her short reddish-brown hair sweeping down over one side of her forehead, she leaned forward with both elbows resting on the desk and began talking to us about the reality of a disabled child.

"As parents, we all think about our child becoming something special, even though most of us disguise the truth of our expectations by saying, *'We only hope he is a healthy baby.'* All parents of disabled children have to accept the fact that the child of their dreams never was and never will be. Your challenge is to get beyond the image of the expected child and to realize it's normal to grieve when your dreams are not fulfilled.

"There are no ideal family systems. All families have their particular strengths and weaknesses and are forced to deal with their circumstances in the most creative way. The Foundation doesn't ignore family problems, but our concern is primarily with the child. We try to minimize the problems at home by building the child's ego, by giving him individuality and status that will help him become as self-sufficient as possible.

"Chris has a right to a normal day with other children. His classroom activities will be geared to his specific needs and development. In a program called *Daily Living Activities*, he will work toward achieving independence in the areas of feeding and dressing himself. His educational program will focus on increasing his attention span and teaching him to distinguish colors and numbers. He will work on manual dexterity and eye-hand coordination.

"While the Foundation addresses the emotional and practical needs of the child, we understand how parents are affected by long-term responsibilities. Therefore, I encourage you to become acquainted with other parents. You will be able to gain support from them that is not available in the outside world."

Not long after that, I was invited to attend a Mothers' Auxiliary meeting. While driving to the school, or the Foundation as it was called, it was hard to believe that in four years I had not met a single other mother with a disabled child. And even though one might assume there would be comfort in meeting other parents, I was now painfully reluctant to expose myself to the group.

Thankfully, at that first meeting, another young woman named Norma DeHaan sat next to me. She had a son the same age as Chris who was also newly enrolled at the Foundation. Norma's infectious energy and positive attitude reaffirmed the devoted spark of the human spirit. For the first time, I felt I had a friend who knew my anguish, but even more important, I felt there was someone who understood the unconditional love I felt for my son.

At a later Auxiliary meeting, a staff member emphasized a crucial element in the adjustment process. *"In the case of giving birth to a child with a disability, there is NO TIME to grieve and work through the loss of the 'expected' child – the child you had lovingly anticipated. Instead, you are forced to accept and invest in your 'new' child – your disabled child.*

"As soon as time allows, you must try to find fulfillment beyond the care of your child. It's extremely easy to get so involved with the needs of your family that you lose yourself in the process. Studies have shown that parents who are able to achieve mutual satisfaction from their own personal goals, fare better in life than parents whose parenting roles prevent the accomplishment of other goals."

When Phil and I came together in marriage, we attempted to create an emotionally integrated life. But when children (and especially a child with disability), became part of that system, we failed to take the necessary time to work on our marriage or accomplish meaningful goals outside the family.

When I attended another Mothers' Auxiliary meeting, a staff member named John Siepp introduced what he called the *Reactionary Stages*, or family coping mechanisms. For the first time since Chris' birth, I felt relief in knowing that certain emotions, even volatile ones, are a normal part of the grief process.

First, there was *Shock*, which was nature's way of providing a cushion against the reality of the doctor's words, *"Mr. and Mrs. Wright, I'm very sorry to inform you that the EEG has shown conclusively that Chris..."*

I had responded, *"Yes, Dr. Thomas..."* but my intellectual powers were disorganized by the enormity of loss and grief. The intense shock lasted for days, then gradually faded. For some people, this stage could last for weeks or months.

John Siepp explained the next phase, *Denial*. During this stage many parents begin a costly and futile search for a better diagnosis or a miraculous cure. They want to believe the results are not conclusive, and that eventually the findings will be reversed.

Even when my denial eased and I was able to say the words *disability* and *cerebral palsy*, I still wanted to deny the fact of brain damage. John had described how the denial phase helps assuage anxiety and depression, but also requires the support of family and friends. Without this support it's easy to feel overwhelmed by the reality of a child's development, or even the intensity of one's own emotions.

As the denial stage softened into *Guilt*, I had feelings about having caused the retardation. Sometimes I felt I was being punished. At other times I wondered if I was a carrier of questionable genes. Perhaps my prenatal exercises, or the ghastly pink liquid I took for heartburn, were the cause. My guilt feelings led to a nearly exclusive dedication to the welfare of my son. In the first three stages of shock, denial, and guilt, I used my energy to try to alter reality rather than deal with it.

The next stage, *Resentment,* was easy to recognize. The anger, turned inward during the guilt stage, was then directed outward. I was angry with people who stared at my child in the supermarket. I was enraged at insensitive doctors. When Thane spilled his milk, my upset was proportionately greater than the incident. Sometimes I resented my neighbors when I saw them with their normal children, enjoying traditional family outings or valuable time as a couple.

When Phil and I couldn't experience enough satisfaction with each other to replace our loss, it was easy to direct our anger toward each other. Naturally, each of us had separate reasons for punishing behavior, not realizing how our defense mechanisms failed to relieve the stress and sabotaged our relationship. Additionally, neither of us recognized how our child could become the scapegoat for tensions that developed between us.

Then came *Intellectualization.* During this stage, I began educating myself. Within the broad scope of mental retardation, I soon became an *expert* on certain aspects. My energies were focused on child development patterns. I enthusiastically promoted the Doman-Delacatto theories to other parents who could potentially enhance the development of their *normal* children. Without my being aware of it, this preoccupation often hindered my emotional availability for personal and family needs. Unable to see my situation objectively and create other responses, I vacillated between stages of terrible and bearable.

Normally, one moves into the sixth stage known as *Involvement.* The activities of the Mothers' Auxiliary were ideal for this phase of adjustment. They included white elephant sales, spaghetti dinners, pancake breakfasts and luncheon-fashion shows. We launched massive fund-raising campaigns for the construction of new buildings and important educational programs. We appealed to other donor groups throughout the city, hoping they would be willing to raise money exclusively for our children and the *United Cerebral Palsy Foundation*. Thrift shops were organized and managed by volunteer services. Golf tournaments and tennis events were hosted by celebrities and contributed hundreds of thousands of dollars to the annual budget. As important, parents appealed to political groups for *human rights*.

As a result of being involved, it was hoped that parents could begin to feel a *Resolution*. This meant we would no longer feel the need to over-invest *or* under-invest in our retarded child. We would be able to appropriately allocate our emotional and physical energies to meet other needs. However, due to the lack of time needed to grieve the loss of the desired child while investing in the disabled child, a progression through all these stages could take more than a decade, with some stages lasting longer than others.

We learned that a sense of resolution is hindered by the fact that retardation is an ongoing process. The child is not gone. Parents who are not enlightened and disciplined enough to create a life apart from their children generally have difficulty transcending the problems posed by a child who requires so much attention. Each family has to decide how much they owe their child with disability, and must evaluate the potential results of the efforts invested in his care and training. *For most parents…resolution never comes!*

A few months after I heard John Siepp's lecture on the stages of coping, Phil and I attended the annual Mothers' Auxiliary dinner dance. It was reportedly the most exciting event of the year. On a balmy, near-perfect evening, and looking elegant in our evening attire, we walked across a quaint wooden bridge surrounded by a small lake that rippled with reflections of a full moon.

As we entered the ballroom, we joined nearly two-hundred other parents from diverse social, racial, and economic backgrounds. For most of us, being told that we had a child with a disability was perhaps the most severe shock we would ever experience. Our internal suffering was possibly as painful and devastating as any physical injury.

Somehow I had imagined that *these* parents would be more inhibited, even depressed, but instead they were having a shamelessly good time. I was shocked, however, to learn that one of the mothers at our table had given birth to three children with birth defects; two of whom had died. I later learned that my friend Norma also had a second child at home with cerebral palsy.

No one knew I was having another child in six months. Some might have considered it a foolish risk. Many in my situation might have felt guilty because of the amount of time another child would take from their existing responsibilities. Others, deciding to forgo another pregnancy, might have unconsciously blamed their retarded child for their decision not to have another child.

On this evening, as each person dropped a pebble of friendship into a great reservoir of humanity, I watched an ever-widening bond of fellowship and love. As I observed a deep compassion for one another, I felt the indestructible power of the human spirit.

In the final analysis, our child's disability may have appeared to be a deterrent to our potential success and happiness. But it wasn't our circumstances that would elevate us to a higher condition—or sink us to a lower one. It would be our *response* to the circumstances.

11
ANOTHER ROSEBUD

Only a razor's edge existed between my blissful expectations of a normal child and my fear of an abnormal birth. But right now, feeling an abundance of love, I relied on my inner resources and trusted that things would go right.

With only a week or so to go in my pregnancy, I announced during dinner one evening that I didn't feel well. Nothing specific—just a stifling discomfort. It was the only night of the month Phil was scheduled for a flight. Before he left, he tried to reassure me. "Connie, I'm just going out on a short flight. I'll be home by midnight."

I crawled into bed and was finally able to sleep. Three hours later, I awakened to what seemed like a popping sensation inside. Without warning, my muscles tightened and waves of panic heaved through my body—the reality of labor. The possibility that Phil might not be here to share in this birth in a civilian hospital was disconcerting, but when I realized labor pains had started and were three minutes apart, I frantically called my doctor. When his answering service paged him, he ordered me to the hospital—immediately!!

First, I notified the personnel office of Continental, asking them to leave an emergency message for Captain Wright. Then I called a babysitter across the street to come stay with Chris and Thane while they were sleeping. I alerted Jean and Bob next door, and they rushed over to drive me to the hospital. When I insisted on waiting for my husband, they flatly refused. "Connie, you can't wait for Phil! We have to leave NOW!"

Even as they loaded me into their car, I was determined to have my husband present for this delivery. As we backed down the driveway, I saw headlights racing up the street. Thank God, Phil had gotten my message! Just as soon as he reached our drive, I was moved into the front seat of his car, and he took over from there.

While he swerved through freeway traffic toward Santa Monica Hospital, I endured what seemed like one interminable labor pain. Panic quickly set in when it looked as if I might give birth on the freeway with the assistance of a policeman or passing motorist.

"Phil, how much farther?"

"We're almost there, just a little bit farther," he replied, trying to disguise his own panic.

When we saw the sign at the west side of Santa Monica Hospital, I trusted I could hold on until I got inside. As we came to a screeching stop near the emergency entrance I was relieved to see two attendants waiting outside with a wheelchair. Acute labor pains made it impossible for me to sit upright in the chair. They managed to get me to the elevator and upstairs to the examining room. While Phil dashed down to the front desk to check us in, a nurse quickly examined me, and then screamed at her assistant, "Give this lady a shot. Qu- i- i -ick!"

Hospital staff scattered out of our way as a nurse wheeled me down the hall and into the delivery room. By now, my intentions to share this experience with my husband had been cast aside. All I wanted was to get this baby born.

When Phil got back to the maternity ward, a nurse burst forth with the good news.

"Congratulations, Mr. Wright. You have a new son."

"It's not my son. We just got here."

"Yes, I know, but your wife delivered a beautiful baby boy three minutes ago!"

I don't remember much of anything about the delivery except that I survived without incisions, and my husband missed the delivery-room drama that dads brag about. At eleven o'clock that night, May 5, 1967, the nurse came into my room holding our seven-pound, six-ounce miracle. She carefully handed me the tiny bundle, a beautiful dark-haired, brown-eyed baby. When I looked at my son for the first time, a kind of rebirth took place. Looking at this spiritual being who had come from my womb to be part of my life, all pain, disappointment, and anger were replaced by love and tenderness. Perhaps only when the dream to have a child comes true, does one truly grasp the greatness of the gift.

Phil carefully and lovingly took his son into his arms. He gingerly unwrapped the blanket and counted ten perfectly formed toes and fingers. Then gazing down at his face and his delicately shaped features, he said, "Welcome to the world, Mark Sterling."

I had vowed this delivery would be different from my other two, and that it was. In addition to my harrowing ride to the hospital, my roommate Judy had unexpectedly delivered twin girls. With the arrival of her double flower arrangements, which was customary for twins, and extra tables brought in for my flowers, our hospital room looked like a florist shop.

After leaving Santa Monica Hospital and arriving home, I faced the task of managing the daily schedule. Phil was frequently on overseas flights that lasted a week to ten days. Mark would be waking up for his six o'clock feeding about the same time Chris needed to be dressed and given breakfast, ready for the bus by seven o'clock sharp. That's when I relied on Thane. At the tender age of four, he positioned himself on the sofa and waited until I handed over his baby brother. Then he securely held him in his arms while giving him his early morning bottle. It was a sweet scene, one that even Frau Schmidt would surely have approved.

After Chris was on the bus and Mark awakened for his second feeding, it would be time to drive Thane to his morning preschool.

Domestic help wasn't financially feasible, although one agency that listed our family as an *emergency* continued to search for a Spanish-speaking woman who could take care of Chris and would be more affordable.

It wasn't long before we welcomed a young woman

Third son, **Mark Sterling**, adds joy to the family.
May 1967

named Elya into our family. Her primary responsibility was to manage Chris: dress him in the morning, take him for walks in his wheelchair after school, help with his dinner and bath, and dress him for bed.

Even though she was the equivalent of divine intervention, it was only a matter of time before the differing philosophies of two women sharing in meal preparation, child care, and household duties in a small home would be at cross purposes. Whether Elya discarded my flowers without my permission or handed Thane a glass of orange juice and complained when he promptly poured it onto the newly waxed floor, the conflict of authority was ever present. But in spite of her *intrusion*, my survival depended on her.

During this time, I concentrated on regaining my independence. Even though my doctor had suggested a full month of recovery before driving, I couldn't wait to introduce my new son to the world. For his first outing I dressed him in a light blue outfit, bundled him in a matching blanket, and drove to a trendy cafe in Westwood Village close to UCLA. At one month of age, he was a blissful being that filled my life with the softness of new love. Nothing more was expected of him than to be a peaceful companion.

At home he was easy to care for. He cried very little and slept a lot. Whenever possible, we snuggled back into my bed for the mid-morning feeding, then took a nap together.

The early morning routine continued to be daunting, especially when Phil was away on a trip and Elya had the day off. But as soon as the routine of those early months became more manageable, I dismissed Elya and felt relieved to be on my own again. As I began to anticipate Mark's progress, I was reminded of how the experience of disability can easily create doubt and uncertainty. Often parents are aware at birth that their child is brain-deficient or brain-injured. Others begin to suspect problems when their child is the *best* baby anyone has known, quiet and sleeping most of the time. More frequently, parents must depend on a later diagnosis when damage to a child's mental and physical processes is more evident. Yet, even then, symptoms of brain injury can be subtle, such as poor hearing, lack of motor coordination, or mild seizures. Needless to say, Phil and I were watching Mark closely for any signs of abnormal development.

When Phil returned home from trips, he was always eager to know about his son's development. "Is Mark rolling over yet?" Months later he asked, "Is Mark sitting up yet?"

Through letters and phone calls the grandparents too, eagerly inquired about his progress. Even Thane's questions indicated concern. "Mom, is Mark going to be able to play with me when he gets older? Will he talk to me?"

Thane, Age 4 - **Chris**, Age 5 - **Mark**, 8 months
At home on Ninety-First Street—Westchester, California.
January 1967

During those early months, I repeatedly referred to the child development chart, which had become a point of reference during Chris' therapy program. I had learned that the most important consideration is allowing a child to progress through *all* the stages, and so far, Mark was doing that.

As he got older, bath time became a wonderfully playful scene where all three boys could participate equally, making clown faces with soap bubbles, and laughing hysterically at each other. Afterward, when they were wrapped like mummies in their bath towels, their animated faces were worth a thousand words. During these times, the two younger boys could easily see that Chris' body was much like their own, except for a few differences. His body was not as fully developed, his knees didn't straighten out, his feet remained in a stiff downward position, and he couldn't sit alone.

After I dressed Chris in his pajamas for bedtime, Thane and Mark delighted in showing him how to fold his hands, then put his head down so they could say their prayer: *Now I lay me down to sleep, I pray the Lord my soul to keep.* When they finished, Chris' broad smile reflected his joy in being able to participate with his brothers.

Playing outside after school, Chris' greatest thrill was having me *pilot* him in his wheelchair, racing down the sidewalk over the bumps, the wheelchair tipped at half-mast. He exploded with excitement as other neighborhood kids gathered to run with us. At times like this, nothing else mattered except to show the rest of the world how to have fun.

At home in our living room with his brothers or neighborhood kids, Chris loved having his hands moved through the motions of *patty-cake* or *two little blackbirds.* Always bursting with enthusiasm, he anticipated simple activities such as dropping bean bags in a basket, tearing up the daily newspaper, or crawling over to the organ pedals to create deep mysterious sounds. Thane and Mark took turns stacking the red cardboard blocks at one end of the living room, then waited for Chris to crawl on his stomach to deliver the fateful blow. Once he succeeded, their joyful noise of cheering and clapping, along with their brother's infectious laughter, filled the room. These were times I would always remember.

Phil made a wooden box with corresponding shapes of a circle, a triangle and a square. Each of the wooden pieces had a large knob on top so Chris could easily pick them up. Sometimes by accident he dropped one of the shapes into the matching hole. When we applauded his achievement, Chris reacted with his typical heart-warming joyfulness, never failing to be his own cheerleader.

One day I happened into the living room where Chris was playing. I stopped dead in my tracks! He was sitting upright in the middle of the floor, smiling with his remarkable sweetness and goodness. "Chris, look at you. When did you learn to sit up?"

He grinned as if to say, *"I just wanted to surprise you, Mom."*

When I questioned the teachers at school, they told me that several months ago they started putting him in a sitting position on the floor with his legs crossed and his hands at his sides to help him balance. When he seemed confident with this new position, they placed him in the same position on a small round skateboard. On this movable platform, he was forced to work harder to maintain his balance.

Another red-letter day occurred when he received a new wheelchair. Doctors had drawn up specifications for a light-weight, chromium-plated wheelchair with a vinyl seat and back. The two larger wheels with hand rims, and two smaller wheels that swiveled easily, provided stability. After a brief period of watching other students, Chris learned how to simultaneously grasp the rims on the large wheels and push himself forward. By moving only one rim he could turn to the left or to the right. His wheelchair became a measure of security as well as a source of freedom and pleasurable activity.

During the two years of our home-therapy program, Chris had learned to grasp simple foods such as a grilled cheese or peanut butter sandwich, but was never able to hold a spoon. At school a special spoon was designed with a

Chris learns to sit up on the balance board.
United Cerebral Palsy Foundation
1307 105th Street — Los Angeles, California

curved handle that perfectly fit his grasp. He was also given a plastic bowl with an edge on one side so he could scoop the food against it, and a tray that fastened onto the wheelchair for mealtimes. By being allowed to feed himself, Chris became more self-sufficient, even though the task of cleaning up was a messy ordeal.

As grateful as we were for the remarkable gain in his ability and confidence, his more assertive behavior often led to potentially dangerous situations. One day while I was driving on the freeway, Chris was buckled in the front seat and unexpectedly reached across and grabbed the steering wheel. While attempting to hold the car steady, I endeavored to release his grip. When I finally succeeded and scolded him, he responded with a tantrum followed by his infamous heart-breaking tears.

At home, while parked in his wheelchair in our narrow hallway, he delighted in getting a fistful of Mark's hair as he tried to squeeze past. As Chris held on, Mark screamed bloody murder. On other days, when Chris wheeled himself from room to room, I was reminded of how we would be painting our walls sooner than most homeowners. Ever so many times, I heard the sound of books falling off the bookshelf in the living room, or I caught a glimpse of Chris reaching for the stereo and portable television set. During these times I cringed, but was forced to realize he had his own needs for purposeful activity.

Beneath the rewarding times lie the grim tightness of constant vigilance and, of course, the ongoing financial needs. We made too much money to qualify for welfare. Even though we were a middle-class family with generous contributions from our families, our income didn't handle the medical needs outside our insurance. Those needs included tuition for school, medication for seizures, and neurology appointments.

Twice in one year Chris underwent surgery. By lengthening the heel cord muscles, giving his feet a more normal posture, we hoped that we could strengthen his chances to stand and walk. The second surgery, designed to relax the muscles in his upper thighs and correct his tendency toward a

A Family Portrait—1968
Chris, **Connie**, **Mark**, **Phil**, and **Thane**

scissoring effect, required a full-length cast on both legs for six weeks. I depended on assistance from neighbors to change his position every four hours.

Increasing our income was a difficult leap, especially when Phil accepted a schedule of overseas flights, which dictated his being gone from home seven to fourteen days at a time. When Continental Airlines contracted with the military to fly troops and supplies into Saigon during the Vietnam War, Phil became one of those pilots.

Even though the troop-carrier planes landed at night to avoid the anti-aircraft fire, I wondered if someday my husband might not return. I championed myself for being hopeful and strong, but the unmitigated responsibility for a five-year-old in diapers, braces, and a wheelchair, a hyperactive four-year-old, and a one-year-old caused me to feel, on many days, that I couldn't hang on alone. Without the support of family living nearby, the mental fatigue of *solitary confinement* was a challenge.

I didn't have to wait long, however, before a new outlook came knocking on my door. One Sunday evening, a saleswoman came to our home for a short business presentation. When the business portion was over, Phil retired to the bedroom to begin packing for a flight the next day. The saleswoman, aware of my responsibility for three small children, began sharing her philosophy about how anyone can be happy by doing what they love to do and living each day to the fullest. Her theory not only sounded impractical but, in my situation, impossible!

The next morning, shortly after Phil left for a five-day trip, the woman's viewpoint continued to be uppermost in my mind. Deciding to test her theory, I put together some lunch, gathered up the gear, and proceeded to load the boys into our van for a trip to the museum. The van had been customized with a table, a refrigerator, a countertop stove, and enough open space for the wheelchair, a playpen, and a stroller. Instead of being used for family trips or overnight stays for Phil and myself, it had become our primary mode of transportation.

Arriving downtown at the Museum of Natural History, I was delayed by two double lanes of cars ahead of us waiting to enter the parking area. When I finally announced to the boys, "We're here," each of them responded with his own brand of excitement. Luckily I found a remote parking space at the outskirts of the parking lot, which made it easier to unload. Thane was assigned the job of pushing Mark in the stroller while I managed Chris in the wheelchair. As we neared the entrance to the museum, I wondered why I had dared to expose all of us to public scrutiny.

Inside the museum, I tried to anticipate Chris' unexpected outbursts, which sometimes sent shock waves through a crowd. Except for one brief episode, everything went well. Even though the boys were too young to benefit from the history of the exhibits, I wanted to give them the experience of vivid colors, textures, and sounds which I knew would later enhance their artistic expression.

Outside at lunchtime, we tossed breadcrumbs to the ducks

and devoured peanut butter sandwiches. At the end of the day, feeling exhausted, yet quietly exhilarated, I was proud of having done something so bold and unconventional.

Encouraged by another successful day, I planned an outing at the beach. Knowing we were only a short distance from home, this trip seemed easier. At least, until I tried to maneuver the wheelchair and stroller through the sand. It was tedious and unrealistic, but I was determined to show the boys the ocean. Luckily we discovered a concrete path partially covered with sand, which took us closer to the water. While gazing out over the ocean, I felt a salt water breeze. Life seemed promising and worthwhile.

The next morning, rested after a good night's sleep, I marveled at how I had been able to reinvent my life. Since it was only Wednesday, I decided to load everyone into the van and visit the children's art museum. Suddenly my thoughts reverted to the unfinished household chores and the piles of diapers that were heaped on the living room sofa waiting to be folded. I hadn't been to the supermarket. The house hadn't been cleaned. But, I reasoned I could handle those chores on Thursday before Phil returned home on Friday.

After loading the boys and the gear into the van, we joined the never-ceasing freeway traffic and headed toward the heart of the city, hoping to reach the museum before noon.

On the way into the city, Chris grabbed Mark's hair and he started screaming. Instead of loosening his grip, Chris held on even tighter and added his own screams of delight. My focused thoughts immediately scattered, and my excitement about our trip turned into panic.

Arriving at the museum parking lot, with a calmer scene in the back of the van, I found a place where I could safely unload. While Thane pushed Mark in the stroller, I maneuvered Chris in his wheelchair. Inside the museum, the boys were wide-eyed and mesmerized by the fast-moving mechanical displays. They were reluctant to interact with the live clowns that mingled among the crowd, entertaining all of us with their costumes and occasional juggling acts.

At the end of the day, I was gratified to know the boys had received a healthy dose of sensory stimulation. As for myself, I was just happy to be able to play with the rest of the world.

On Thursday morning I woke up energized and ready to tackle the household chores, grateful Phil wasn't coming home until Friday. About ten o'clock, still dressed in my bathrobe, the doorbell rang. I opened the door expecting to see one of the neighbors. But when I saw who it was, my body went numb. Had I lost a day?

There was my husband, standing on the front porch in his airline uniform. A sudden panic swept through my body. What about all the chores I had planned to get done before he came home?

When I opened the front door, Phil stepped inside, gave me a quick kiss, and put his flight bag on the floor. He hung his black double-breasted jacket in the coat closet and started toward the living room. "Something is different," he said, as he turned to look at me.

Immediately I jumped to my own defense. "Yes, the house is a wreck. The laundry isn't done. And I haven't been to the market."

"That's not what I'm talking about," he said. "You look happy."

I was stunned by his observation.

When I described my adventures of the last three days, he said, "I'm amazed at how you managed."

My reward was being able to indulge in creative activities I didn't think were possible. An added bonus was the idea that an immaculate home was not so much a part of my husband's expectations as it was *my* perception of a perfect wife and mother. Convinced there was some truth to the philosophy of the saleswoman who had come to our home only a few nights before, I was grateful for a new perspective.

As the weeks went by, I began to wonder how many women in my generation had imposed on themselves the burden of an impeccable household, especially without help from anyone else. But given the standards of the times, even if we had respected ourselves more and forfeited the idea of being the perfect wife and mother, we would undoubtedly have tried to live up to our husband's expectations, just to get his approval and his love. For many married women, those expectations included a clean, well-organized house-hold, dinner at six, well-behaved children, and *his* control of the money.

Even with my growing awareness of women's issues, it seemed impossible for me to let go of the little-girl dream of being the perfect, desirable wife, rather than simply being in charge of my life. As I watched Phil pack his tennis racket and swimsuit, it was hard not to feel envious of those times when he could *play* with fellow pilots and flight attendants during their layovers in Hawaii. The occasional gifts he brought back from exotic places were beautiful, but they didn't replace my need for adult conversation or cherished moments of intimacy. Besides, the gifts often seemed like a gesture of obligation rather than an expression of his deeply felt affection.

When I considered how I might compensate for my isolation, especially during the unalleviated hours of loneliness with only the children, I considered the unrealistic idea of a babysitter. The cost was not only prohibitive, but finding someone who could manage *my* three children was impossible, even if I were willing to pay $25 an hour.

One Saturday morning, determined to reshape my attitude, I planned a trip to the beach. With my car parked at the top of our sloping driveway, I proceeded to buckle Mark into his car seat in the back. I counted on Chris to wait patiently in his wheelchair next to the car, with the brakes on his wheelchair securely locked. While making the final adjustments with Mark, I noticed through the rear window of my car that a man and a woman had parked their car out front by the curb. Thinking that they were unsolicited salespeople, I immediately felt intruded upon.

Suddenly, I saw my neighbor Charlie sprinting across his front yard, a fast pace for a man his age. When I looked toward the street to see where he was headed, I gasped, "Oh my God!"

Chris was turned upside down in his wheelchair, still fastened by his seatbelt. He apparently had released the brakes, rolled down the steep driveway, and crossed over the jagged cracks in the sidewalk—all before turning upside down in the street. The salespeople had pulled over to avoid hitting Chris.

While Charlie struggled to get Chris upright, I left Mark in his car seat and ran down the driveway fearing the worst, a broken nose, missing teeth, serious bleeding. I held my breath until I saw there were no large cuts or bleeding, only a pockmarked face from the impact. Charlie said I should call a doctor right away. I went inside to call and the doctor told me there wasn't much to do. Even if his nose were broken, it would have to heal on its own.

I was embarrassed to send Chris back to school on Monday, but I put him on the bus anyway. I also feared the reaction from his dad when he returned home from his flight in ten days. Thankfully, there would be time for Chris' injuries to heal.

That incident caused me to realize that a mother's job frequently extends beyond heroic measures, even without the care of a disabled child. Fathers might not understand the day-to-day commitment and the emotional challenge of rearing children, but at the very least, I felt it was their responsibility to nurture the mother of their children. One way of doing this was to acknowledge what their wives did for the family. Far too often, a woman's contribution to her children and the family goes unacknowledged.

In spite of my efforts to maintain a smoothly run household and manage the daily care of everyone else, the needs of all the family members were not being met, particularly mine. Never in my wildest dreams, however, could I have envisioned something terrible happening to me, especially at home.

One unusually warm evening, when Phil was on an overseas flight for nearly a week, I was working at the table on the patio, making a dress to wear to Hawaii in preparation for the first vacation with my husband in five years. Mark had been crawling in and out through the open glass door that led to the patio. Later, after I tucked him into bed for the night, I went outside to finish sewing. As I closed the sliding glass door behind me I noticed how the lights inside caused the luminous panels of glass to look invisible. When I realized the dress was ready for a second fitting, I excitedly threw it over my arm and dashed toward what I thought was an *open door* to the living room.

With incredible impact, my head hit the thick plate glass, causing it to shatter onto the concrete. Instinctively I covered my face with my hands, and then I felt blood gushing from the left side of my face and oozing from my leg. When the sounds of broken glass finally stopped ringing in my head, I peered through my outstretched fingers to see large jagged shards of glass protruding from all sides of the patio door. Fortunately, my eyesight was still intact.

Suddenly I remembered Thane playing in the back yard. I turned to see him frozen with horror.

"Thane, I'm just fine, but go get Mrs. Brogan. Quick!" Though he was only five, he scaled our six-foot fence to get help from Jean and Bob next door. I managed to get to our back door, blood still dripping from my face and legs. Too terrified to go inside and see myself in the mirror, I waited. Within seconds, Jean came running to the back door and Bob came tearing through the living room.

Still dazed, my trip to the emergency room didn't seem significant until the glaring overhead lights brought me to my senses. Stretched out on a table waiting to see the physician on duty, I felt lucky. When he walked in and saw the gaping wound dangerously close to my left eye, he said, "Young lady, it's a miracle you survived. Only recently, a man severed an artery and died at the scene of the accident."

After summarizing the extent of my injury, he asked, "What kind of doctor would you prefer, a plastic surgeon or a regular doctor?"

"I don't know, whatever it takes to fix my face," I replied.

The doctor hesitated, then he explained, "Because the wound is deep and precariously close to the corner of your eye, I suggest we call a plastic surgeon, one who is capable of suturing the layers so it will heal without a scar."

"That sounds good," I said.

Lying there waiting, I never imagined that in an emergency I wouldn't be able to call my husband, even when he was on an overseas flight.

After returning home that evening, I took medication for the pain and for sleep. As I dozed off for the night, I was grateful Jean and Bob had been able to drive me to the hospital, and appreciative for neighbors who came to stay with Thane and Mark.

When I looked in the mirror and saw the sutures close to my ominous bloodshot eyes, and patches of black and purple bruises on my face, I could only speculate that it would be months before I would feel comfortable going out in public.

Days later, after a week of travel, Phil called from Los Angeles International. "Connie, I just arrived home. Can you pick me up at the flight personnel building?"

"Yes, but first, I have to find Thane. He's outside playing with his friends. I'll call Jean to watch Mark while he's taking his nap; I should be there in about fifteen minutes."

While Thane rode in the back seat, I reflected on what had happened during one week of Phil's absence. How could I tell him that his son was almost hit by a car? And, that this was my first day out of the house after walking through our plate glass window?

As I had done so many times in the past, I pulled alongside the curb outside the personnel building and waited. Thankfully, my large sunglasses covered most of the injured area around my eyes. While Thane and I watched planes taking off in the distance, time inched forward. Without warning, Phil opened the passenger door and slid in next to me.

"Hi! How are you?" he asked.

"I'm good," I replied. "How was your trip?"

"A lot of flying in seven days. How are the boys?"

"It's been quite a week, but they're okay."

As we pulled away from the building, I was thankful the drive home was short. Somehow I still had to break the news. Thane, sitting in the backseat, armed with nuggets of information, timed it perfectly. He proceeded to lean forward and eagerly blurted, "Dad, while you were gone, Mom broke the living room window out! Clearrr Out!"

"What did you say?" Phil asked, turning to look at Thane, then at me.

Slowing to a stop at the next corner, I lowered my sunglasses and turned to show him my face.

"You went through *our* plate glass window?" he inquired.

"Yes."

"How did *that* happen?"

I explained as briefly as I could without adding to the stress of his trip—that is, until Thane announced the rest of the odious news.

"And Dad, Chris rolled down the driveway in his wheelchair and almost got hit by a car."

After a dreadful silence, Phil asked, "Is that *all* that happened while I was gone?"

"Yes," I calmly replied.

After we arrived back at the house, Phil carefully inspected the boarded-up window and sighed with relief when I told him the neighbors had already scheduled new glass to be installed.

Later that afternoon, Chris' school bus pulled into our driveway. Phil rushed outside. As Chris was lifted off the bus and placed in his wheelchair, my stomach knotted. I could sense Phil's apprehension as he carefully examined his son's face. Fortunately, it had healed well, almost as if nothing had happened.

It would take longer for my bruises to disappear and for the layers of scar tissue to heal. In the meantime, I searched for a way to feel better about my severely bruised face, so I scheduled an appointment with the plastic surgeon to have my ears pierced.

While I was in his office, I noticed other women who seemed to be recovering from face lifts and breast implants. When I inquired about the procedures, I wondered if these women had the surgeries to feel more beautiful inside, or if they merely wanted to slow the aging process.

At home, I showed Phil my newly pierced ears and told him that because of my curiosity, the surgeon had explained breast implants to me.

"How much would they cost?" he inquired.

"I don't know. I didn't ask. I wasn't really serious."

Because I was still feeling fragile after my accident, his questions caused me to wonder if he desired a more sensuous figure, like the bikini-clad woman in the close-up photographs he had taken during his recent trip to Hawaii. While he claimed he wanted me to see the unusual conch shell she was holding close to her voluptuous breasts, I couldn't help wondering if there was something more he wanted me to know.

Perhaps the photographs were his way of expressing his resentment over the fact that my desire for sex had all but diminished. Perhaps he blamed himself for no longer being desirable. Nevertheless, due to the anxiety caused by my suspicions, as well as a need for retaliation, I sometimes started a fight just to get out of *doing it.* Or I would go to bed later, hoping he would be asleep by the time I crawled in next to him. The next day I endured self-imposed guilt from his punishing remarks. "Connie, you're cold. You're frigid."

I considered a healthy sex life a beautiful thing, but continued to wonder why I couldn't enjoy a sexual relationship with my husband. Perhaps there was a physical problem. Perhaps my hormones were out-of-whack, or there was a problem with my adrenals, thyroid, or pituitary gland. Or maybe I just needed a compliment—reassurance that my husband loved me.

While Phil was away on another trip, I picked up the latest *Reader's Digest* and immediately noticed on the front cover, an article about women's sexual issues. As I sat down in the living room to read, I couldn't help reflecting on the shame I had endured for so many years, envious of others who I assumed enjoyed a healthy sex life.

Quickly turning to the article, I saw it was written by the famous Dr. Kegel, known for his *Kegel exercises.* My interest peaked when I read how every woman could benefit from developing a strong pubococcygeous or PC muscle, the major muscle of contraction during orgasm. To engage the PC muscle, one had to contract the band of muscle that circles the vagina. The article stated that women who have strong pelvic muscles also tend to have more fulfilling sexual experiences.

Though I had no phone number or address, I was determined to find Dr. Kegel who, according to the article, was located somewhere in Los Angeles. One night I drove across town to a small hospital in an indigent neighborhood where it was rumored he worked part time. I parked near the entrance and slipped in through the front door. The barren hallways didn't offer much hope of finding him. Finally, a nurse appeared.

"Is there a Dr. Kegel on staff here?" I asked.

"Yes, he occasionally sees patients at this location. In fact, he was just here tonight, but left about an hour ago."

Sensing my despair, she located a phone number where he could be reached during the day.

Weeks later, having persevered long enough to get an appointment with this well-known specialist, I arrived at his office located in a remote part of downtown Los Angeles.

Seated in a plain and sparsely furnished reception area plastered with certifications, I wondered what I might say. *My marriage has more than suffered. It has collapsed. My sense of myself as a woman has disappeared. I'm on the verge of a nervous breakdown, but I don't know what's wrong.*

When my name was called, I was ushered into another modest office where I came face-to-face with a handsome, professional-looking gentleman dressed in a crisp white coat. As he warmly shook my hand and motioned for me to have a seat, I admired his strong cheekbones, his tanned and weathered skin, and graying black hair.

After taking down a brief history, Dr. Kegel instructed the nurse to prepare for a pelvic exam. When the exam was over, Dr. Kegel said, "Connie, it appears that when Chris was born, the major muscle that runs along the vaginal opening was severed during the episiotomy and, like a rubber band, it snapped. Without that muscle, there is nothing to give you comfort or a feeling of sensation during intercourse. If the doctor at the time of delivery had known he cut that muscle, he could have sutured it back into place. Or he could have avoided the procedure altogether.

"An episiotomy is usually not necessary. Women who undergo an episiotomy are fifty times *more* likely to suffer from severe lacerations than those who don't have it. The cuts from an episiotomy frequently extend farther into the vaginal tissues during the delivery and later cause painful scarring and unnecessary postpartum pain. Doctors typically do it because they are trained to do it, even when there are no long-term benefits.

"In your case, the muscle that affects a woman's sexual sensations is missing. It's no wonder you have physical pain and painful emotions during intercourse. There is really nothing I can do except recommend the *Kegel exercises*, which would only strengthen the band of muscle that circles the vagina."

My anguished thoughts flashed back to August 15, 1962, when I was assured that the birth of my first child had gone well. My baby was perfect, I'd been told. There were no complications. I remembered, however, that during the following two weeks, I questioned why I had difficulty in walking, sitting, and putting my shoes on. I had called my doctor and he confirmed that in spite of some thirty sutures, the procedure was normal.

Two weeks later, the same doctor had done a pelvic exam and told me I could resume making love with my husband. Naturally, I looked forward to the return of the erotic energy I had experienced during our first year of marriage before I gave birth. My sexual energy, however, had never returned, and I agonized for years.

Now in Dr. Kegel's office, it all made sense. The apparent negligence of a military doctor had destroyed the sexual pleasure that adds to the esteem and enjoyment two people rightfully expect to enjoy throughout their marriage.

The truth of my damaged body, and the emotional abandonment from my husband, was a wound nearly as punishing as the news of brain damage, seizures, and mental retardation. Enraged by another disheartening consequence of a military doctor's incompetence, I was close to a complete emotional breakdown.

Dr. Kegel, empathetic with my pain, placed a tissue in my hand and said, "Connie, I want to schedule an appointment with you and your husband."

"Okay," I responded, my voice barely audible.

Days later, Phil arrived home where, by now, upsetting news almost seemed commonplace. I told him about the article in the *Reader's Digest* that talked about women's sexual issues. Then I described how I had found Dr. Kegel and went to see him.

When I said he wanted to meet with the two of us, Phil looked surprised and asked, "When is the appointment?"

"It's next Wednesday," I replied.

Phil left the room to check his schedule. When he returned he said, "Yes, that should work."

On a chilly March day, Phil and I fought our way through freeway traffic that was slower than usual. The air was moist with drizzle. Arriving at the older brick structure in downtown Los Angeles, Phil eased into a crowded parking lot and finally found an unreserved spot.

We entered the lobby on the first floor of the building, and then walked the stairs that led to the doctor's second-floor office. Suddenly, my head throbbed. I felt helpless to deal with another *irreversible* condition. I began to sob uncontrollably. Too embarrassed to sit in the reception area with the other patients, I waited outside in the hallway while Phil checked us in. He then joined me as I silently tried to absorb the truth behind all those years of unfulfilled sexual pleasure.

Hours seemed to drag by before Dr. Kegel was able to see us. But once we were seated inside his office, he wasted no time getting to the point.

"Mr. Wright, I want you to know there is nothing wrong with your wife! This is what happened. During the birth of your first child the attending physician made a lot of incisions. During the episiotomy, he unknowingly cut one of the main muscles along the vaginal opening. Out of unthinkable, criminal neglect, he failed to suture it back into position. And without the cushion provided by that muscle, there is extreme pain during intercourse. However, there is really nothing I can do."

When the facts were finally presented, I expected that Phil would respond in outrage. Instead, he said nothing. I questioned whether his lack of response to the diagnosis was a matter of indifference or shocking disbelief. Perhaps it was guilt.

Back home, I longed for his support and ached to feel his arms around me, just holding me. Mostly, I needed someone who understood that female sexuality is a sensory experience which involves the whole body, and that love-making includes attentiveness and tenderness, not just orgasm.

But Phil and I were never able to talk about the truth that had changed our lives forever. Those weeks and months after seeing Dr. Kegel were a tumultuous and sad time for me. It was only natural to want to experience the kind of sexual energy that is actually part of *all* creativity, and adds joy to life. The impact of this recent diagnosis, on top of all the other traumas, felt like a force leading to death. Without knowing why, I persuaded Phil to schedule a meeting with our social worker at the Foundation…just to talk about Chris.

As we sat in front of the familiar walnut desk in Nancy's office, we told her of the recent news. Sensing the emotional overload, she stated, "It's perfectly normal for you to want to give Chris as full a life as possible, but you must understand the traumatic impact that retardation can have on the family unit, and how easily it can reduce one's personal esteem."

Aside from a discussion of family issues, Nancy focused on the need for a more expanded program for Chris. We all agreed that his removal from an over-protective home environment, and his enrollment in a more controlled school program, had created a positive shift in his development. As he experienced more freedom to participate in social activities with his peers, he seemed happier. His level of anxiety and frustration had diminished. An improved attention span made it easier for him to comprehend instructions.

However, to accelerate his total development, the staff recommended a five-day residential program, which meant he would live away from home during the week and join his family during the weekends.

Intellectually, I could see the advantages of supervised training in a more structured environment, but emotionally, I wasn't ready to accept the separation. I had never considered the option of my six-year-old son living away from his home and family.

As the three of us momentarily sat in silence, fatigue settled into my body. I had prayed for so many things. I had prayed for a miraculous breakthrough in the ACTH treatments, and for strength to conduct two years of patterning, but I had never prayed for strength to accept Chris' going away. He was part of my deepest love and delight, a child who had the capacity to evoke all of my laughter, or all of my tears.

I was relieved when Nancy announced there were no openings for a residential program and that most likely, it would be a year or more before an opening would occur. Feeling the depths of a mother's love, I agreed to have Chris' name put on the waiting list.

12

COURAGE TO SURRENDER

In the midst of uncertainty, Phil and I planned our first vacation alone. Hawaii, with its raw natural beauty, seemed a perfect place where romance with my husband could surely be rekindled. Photographs of this tropical paradise looked romantic, with beautiful people basking on sandy beaches against a background of waterfalls and volcanoes, seductive island music, open-air restaurants, and exotic seafood.

Phil's sister, Jane, saddened by the recent death of her husband, had proposed to stay with Thane and Mark in Los Angeles. One of the teachers from the Foundation generously offered to take Chris to her home during our absence.

Friday morning, four days before we were to leave, the telephone rang.

"May I please speak with Phil?" a woman's voice asked.

I handed him the phone as he sat at the kitchen table. His tones were hushed, as if what was being said would be difficult to accept. I had put Chris on the bus earlier that morning. Was there a problem?

After a brief conversation, Phil turned to me and calmly announced, "He's in."

"What are you talking about?"

"The Foundation has a bed for Chris. He can live there five days a week. He can start on Monday."

My heart and my mind just stopped. Was I the last person to know about the opening for my son? When we agreed to put Chris' name on the waiting list we were told that a bed would most likely not be available for at least a year.

"Why didn't you tell me?" I asked.

"Connie, they didn't want you to know until the opening occurred."

Tangled thoughts darted through my mind. Emotions of blame, anger, and deceit blurred together. But one thought was clear. I couldn't possibly go to Hawaii without taking Thane and Mark. Perhaps in years to come, I would see that forfeiting a vacation with my husband was a poor choice. But right now, the idea of Chris leaving home darkened my world in such a way that a family vacation seemed like the only way to survive the devastating news.

We began to organize Chris' clothing and finalize the arrangements for him to begin his weekly residency. One of the teachers agreed to take him to her home for the weekend. Three days later, all of us, including Aunt Jane, boarded the plane for a flight to Oahu.

Upon arrival at our beachfront hotel, I opened the sliding door to our third-floor balcony. Stepping outside, I inhaled a deep breath of thick tropical air. The sandy beaches of Waikiki stretched as far as I could see. Diamond Head loomed in the distance. Directly below me, palm trees swayed in the breeze. The alluring scene was enough to momentarily distract me from my thoughts of Chris, until the mesmerizing mood was interrupted by a terrifying fear that Thane or Mark could fall off the enclosed balcony. I quickly stepped back inside and locked the door.

Later that night after the boys were asleep, I lay awake in the living room of our suite. A blanket of warm humid air swept in through the open doors and wrapped me with temporary comfort, replacing the need to be with my husband.

Lying there in complete solitude, I could hear the relentless crash of the waves in the distance. I could imagine their delicate peaks forming with perfect rhythm, then unfolding at their own pace before surrendering their power to the arms of the shore, where the white, frothy foam would be absorbed by the porous sands of the beach. There was a kind of un-explainable power in the repetitive cycle of the waves. Perhaps I, too, could achieve that kind of power by learning how to manage the vicissitudes of life—the uncertainties, the unpredictable, the shifting sands beneath my feet.

The next morning the sun followed me as I fell into a rhythmic pattern of jogging on the beach. With each step, my feet pressed into the sand and a lifetime of dreams unfolded in front of me, dreams that would lead me to search for a new purpose in life. Along the way I watched the waves splashing against the rocks, envious of their resilience. I prayed there would come a time when my spirit would be less vulnerable to the perceived obstacles and tormenting restraints.

When I came back to the place on the beach where Phil and the boys were camped, Thane was building sand castles. Mark joyfully watched from his stroller.

"Mom," Thane commanded. "Watch what I'm making."

"Okay," I murmured.

Seconds later, "Mom, you're not watching!"

How could I tell him I was watching and was absorbed in his creativity even though I appeared not to be watching? Someday he would understand how much I admired his spontaneous and artful play.

I was grateful when the daylight hours turned to evening shadows and I could bask in the security of solitude. As I was walking along the beach, back to our hotel, darkness glided across the ocean. My mind filled with thoughts of our son who couldn't be with us. *Chris, where are you? I thought I heard you crying last night. Can you feel my touch? Can you see my footprints in the sand? The tide will soon wash away these footprints, but tomorrow there will be new ones. Chris, my darling, we have a long way to go. A thousand nights will pass. Listen to the seagull. He's searching too.*

While the waves continued their steady, unwavering pace, I wondered how long it would take for me to surrender to a life without my son, a child who was too young to be living away from home.

A few days later, five suntanned passengers boarded a Continental 747 for the return flight to Los Angeles. While flying 35,000 feet above the Pacific Ocean, passengers and flight attendants cheered for Mark, who was barely a year old when he boldly took his first steps down the aisle of the jumbo jet. I was grateful for that exhilarating moment.

Back home, it wasn't surprising that Phil and I had trouble accepting Chris' five-day residence. In reality, we had spent the last four years in an endless quest for a normal child, convinced that if we tried hard enough, we could redesign our life for the better. Now, two years after the termination of the Doman-Delacatto program, it was nearly impossible to think that our son living away from home could be a solution. No matter how much we had wanted to feel safe in a world we could relate to, very few people in a highly competitive, materialistic society, with cultural stereotypes of the *ideal child*, would understand the constant adjustments we had been forced to make.

The staff at the Foundation had told us that Chris would eventually feel secure in the classroom setting. In spite of their reassurance, I frequently went to the Foundation to observe him through a small window in the door to the classroom. When Chris saw me, his clenched fist went to his mouth. His piercing screams, which turned into one of his usual tantrums, disrupted the classroom. When I realized the pain of separation was mutual, it was tough for me to walk away.

Chris' explosive reactions were possibly a reflection of his anger as well as his fear, but they also indicated a brain injury that involved the intellectual spheres, as well as the personality. These factors made it difficult for him to cope with new situations.

On Friday afternoons, Thane and Mark joined me as we eagerly waited in the lobby to pick up Chris for the weekend. When he first saw us, he squealed in his loudest voice and kicked the metal heels of his braces against the footrest of his wheelchair. In the midst of his delirious excitement and spastic movements, it was difficult for Thane and Mark to hug him as they wanted to, but somehow they managed. Mark helped me carry Chris' diaper bag while Thane pushed the wheelchair.

After we were all buckled into the car for rush-hour traffic on the freeway, Chris' happy mood soon turned to pandemonium. In angry defiance, he sometimes grabbed Mark's hair or Thane's shirt and held on with an unyielding grip. At other times, he reached for the steering wheel. When I scolded him, he cried piteously. After only a few weekends, it was apparent that the transition between a structured five-day residence and a weekend at home was going to be difficult.

At home, Chris reacted sharply to the new routine. Deeply attached to his dad, he cried hysterically every time Phil left the house to go outside and work in the garage. The uncertainty about when or if his dad would return was clearly painful. When neighborhood kids came to play, Chris was often left behind. Even when I wheeled him outside to watch the others, his mournful sounds, combined with his fist in his mouth, indicated the agony of rejection.

More often than not, Phil's flights took him away from home during the weekend. And once again, without adult interaction, or a diversion from the pressures of the daily routine, I often felt trapped in an endless cycle. The only thing that could ease the feeling of going over the edge was to seek companionship with other members at the Westchester Methodist church.

After breakfast one Sunday morning, I diapered and dressed Chris, laced his high-top shoes, attached his leg braces, wheeled him into the living room, and parked him in his wheelchair near the front door. After dressing Mark and helping Thane, I returned to the bedroom to finish getting ready.

During those moments, Thane decided to help by getting Chris outside. He had watched many times while I tilted the wheelchair back, then pushed it forward with the weight distributed on the two larger wheels. In the same manner, he had undoubtedly attempted to wheel Chris across the threshold of the front door. When the weight was too much to manage, Chris went headlong onto the concrete porch.

From the bedroom, I heard screaming. I raced to the front door to see what had happened. As I wrestled to get Chris and the wheelchair upright, Thane said, "Mom, I was just trying to help."

"Honey, I know. It's all right."

I would have to talk with him later to soothe his failed purpose. But right now, I had to handle myself. With each successive crisis, I felt internally ripped apart and emotionally out of control.

In spite of the circumstances, going to church still seemed like a good idea, but we all needed a dose of reassurance. As we set out, I trusted that we could find a way to improve our morale and feel a sense of contribution.

On the way to church we happened by a field of wildflowers, and I immediately pulled over and stopped. While Chris stayed in the van, Thane and Mark and I hurriedly picked handfuls of flowers to take to the boys' Sunday school teachers. I felt that this example of spontaneity was the most precious thing I could pass on to my children, and whenever I created something of beauty, my own spirit soared.

Inside the sanctuary, sitting with hundreds of other people, I could easily acknowledge a divine power as the source of my strength and intuition. Of course, I still had questions of immortality, and I wondered about God's purpose for my life. But I knew that when I was ready to wrench away from the trap of self-pity, I needed only to listen for the next step.

Unfortunately, the sermon wasn't enough to conquer my self-doubt or cause me to stop comparing my life to others. My condition was probably no different than millions of others, but that hardly spelled freedom from my suffering.

The two-day weekend flashed by before I realized. Sunday was cut short, and by three o'clock in the afternoon, I was already preparing for the return trip to the Foundation. I had to organize Chris' clothes for the week, prepare dinner, then bathe and dress the boys in their pajamas. Sadly, by then, Chris had just begun to make a transition to *our* routine. Even though his adjustment came late, it was an achievement in a weekend that, otherwise, could have been considered a complete failure.

As I loaded the gear into the van, anchored Chris and the wheelchair, and buckled the other two boys into their seats, I could feel anxiety stirring just beneath the surface.

Arriving at the Foundation just before bedtime, I barely had enough time to take Chris to his room and put his weekly wardrobe in the chest next to his bed. The least I could do was to make certain he was handsomely dressed in his color-coordinated shirts, short pants, and matching knee socks. After tucking him into bed, I parked his wheelchair at the foot of his bed. Thane and Mark hugged their brother and said, "Goodnight, Chris."

As they walked toward the bedroom door, they didn't notice Chris turning to look at all of us, his big brown eyes filling with tears.

The weekend, with all the aspects of homecoming and a sorrowful separation, broke the shell that enclosed my lifelong understanding of how a perfect life would be. It also provided harsh evidence that I could not meet my child's needs at home. Still, I wasn't convinced he was happier at the Foundation.

As I pulled away from the school I grappled with relief and guilt. Joining the freeway traffic for the drive back home, tears flowed.

"Mom, why are you crying?" Thane asked.

"Honey, I just don't like leaving Chris at school."

"Well Mom, that's the way it goes," he responded.

His innocence was so pure, his objectivity brilliant. Mark, in his tender and beautiful first years of life, was equally unaware of life's struggles. On the faces of my two sons, I saw rosebuds unfolding. I prayed that Thane and Mark would someday understand that out of a situation that was both tragic and good, their brother was a child born of love, a spiritual being who would eventually cause all of us to look beyond our human needs and develop our deeper nature.

13

A CHILD OF LOVE

Many people go through life attempting to influence others with their best behavior, or apologizing for who they are, as if asking permission for their existence. I didn't believe in a heavy dose of politeness, and I didn't believe in hiding from the truth. I could only trust that with good intentions, my undesirable habits could be broken and negative attitudes replaced.

One Tuesday morning, standing in the kitchen with my husband, I was desperate to talk to him about my concerns regarding Thane's behavior, which was again becoming a problem. I thought the earlier attitudes and the acting-out that had occurred during the patterning program were resolved, but now he seemed to be regressing to those earlier behaviors. I knew there was a chance I could be ignored by my husband or misunderstood, but I had to confront it.

"Phil, I'm worried about Thane's aggressive actions. He seems to be angry and irritable much of the time."

"Connie, Thane is the way he is because he's around you all the time," he angrily retorted before leaving the room.

I blinked hard. Was I the crazy one, without any reason to be concerned? Or was this, again, Phil's way of needing to be in control? As if in slow motion, I gathered the dishes from the table and turned toward the kitchen sink. While attempting to bury my pain in the warm soapy water, his words created internal wounds that would likely never heal.

After Phil left for a week-long flight, I came across an article that listed signs of an abusive relationship. Never dreaming they might apply to my situation, I was surprised when some of the characteristics fit. He needs to be in charge; he blames everyone else; he insults you with degrading and discrediting remarks or implied threats. The article told how women tend to rationalize these behaviors, thinking that if they avoid the things that upset him and behave the way he wants, their husband's attitude will change. However, after years of being subjected to this kind of damaging behavior, a woman begins to lose faith in herself, and feels more and more isolated within the relationship.

On the verge of thinking I was a horrible mother and an unreasonable wife, I suddenly recognized an unhealthy pattern of restricted communication and verbal attacks. Worst of all, this behavior not only seemed to be something I had to endure, but caused me to feel that I was unlovable, even deserving of being abandoned in one form or another. Realistically, the only way I could be abandoned by someone was to remain in denial myself. I began to question how I could protect myself from my husband's hurtful accusations, and wondered with whom I could share my most intimate concerns.

Determined to at least find some peace regarding my son, I called the principal at the private school where Thane attended first grade. I had to know whether I was imagining things or dealing with a child in need of specialized help. Surprisingly, the staff at his school validated my concerns and agreed to schedule a battery of tests. Confident I had taken the right steps, I hung up the phone with a sigh of relief.

In the weeks that followed, I was haunted by simple, but relevant, questions. When does a little boy stop being difficult to manage and become emotionally disturbed? What degree of responsibility do parents realistically have for the adult life of their children?

After all, my children were my achievements. I worked countless hours caring for them; I hurt for their troubles and their sicknesses; I racked my brain for solutions to their problems. When they were beautiful and happy, I took credit. And if they were unhappy, I assumed blame and suffered guilt. On the other hand, my children were not MY children.

Each one of them had come into this world as a unique and amazing expression of intelligence and creativity; each was a prodigy in his own right, a jewel without a price.

Whether unfounded or not, our culture seems to support the opinion that children are what their mother has made them. Regardless of possible influences from our own upbringing, or the theories of Sigmund Freud, the famous Dr. Spock, or *Family Circle* magazine, the idea was imbedded in our thinking by the time we are adults: "It's the mother's fault when children don't turn out as society expects."

I had counted on setting up a time to review the test results at the school. Instead, the counselor dropped the news over the phone that my son was nearing an emotional breakdown. Without understanding exactly what she meant, I automatically blamed myself.

Phil was on a flight to Saigon; there was no way to reach him. I was uncertain whether or not my parents would really understand my concern, but I had to talk to someone. I called them.

Their response was as I expected. "Connie, we're certain it's not true." Needing emotional support and trying to hide my disappointment, I told them I would keep them informed. As I eased the phone back into place, tears moved freely down my cheeks and into my mouth.

For nearly a week, I saw no one but my children. During my seclusion, I wondered if I had to endure depression and a sense of inner emptiness just to survive — just to maintain some degree of sanity.

On Sunday, when my motivation was at its lowest ebb, I knew I had to do something to force myself out of this condition, so I loaded the boys into the van and drove to church, hoping to receive counsel from a higher power.

Sitting alone, I realized that my entire life had been devoted to satisfying the needs of others, all while suppressing my own desires and unwanted emotions. I had been fearful of not being loved when I was angry or upset, and concerned that others wouldn't understand if I insisted on setting boundaries for myself. It was no wonder that my strength of purpose felt so diminished, and that my courage and determination had suddenly waned. Right now, I was barely hanging on.

That afternoon, when I thought I had received all the bad news possible, Thane's Sunday school teacher called. "Mrs. Wright, I don't want to alarm you, but my observations of Thane's behavior concern me a great deal. Based on my firsthand knowledge of emotional problems with my own son, I believe that your son needs professional intervention."

Her straightforward, yet empathetic, approach confirmed there was a problem. Our son needed help!

When Phil came home I took the risk of telling him everything.

"After you left on your trip, I made a phone call to Thane's school. I needed someone who could help me determine whether his behaviors and attitudes were reason enough to be concerned. They agreed they were. After that, his Sunday school teacher called to tell me she was equally concerned. In fact, Thane's school recommended a child psychologist whose office is in Beverly Hills."

"Connie, I don't want to see another doctor, especially some fancy shrink in Beverly Hills, but if it will make you feel better, I'll go."

In our first interview, Dr. Shusterman broke the ice by stating that a mother who is emotionally available during the first three years and responds with a sensitive, caring attitude has a profound effect on her child's happiness. He emphasized that other experiences in a child's early life, including the prenatal period, can likewise affect his behavior. However, with testing and proper intervention, these patterns formed during infancy and early childhood can be altered.

We readily gave our approval for a series of tests.

The results of Thane's testing revealed he was a gifted child with outstanding perceptual abilities, extraordinary reasoning, and a good vocabulary. He demonstrated capabilities of achievement two years beyond his peer group. The fact that he required a special reading teacher at school indicated a gap between his exceptional capabilities and his present performance. This fact alone was evidence of moderate emotional disturbance.

Dr. Shusterman suggested tutoring to help close the academic gap. He recommended a specially trained therapist and a technique known as play therapy, which could help Thane deal with his anger, whether toward his parents or his brother. Through play therapy he could likely shift his negative perceptions to a more positive view of the world, and alleviate feelings of vulnerability.

Faced with the harsh reality of more therapy, I resigned myself to driving Thane across town for appointments twice a week. As he sat next to me in the front seat, my heart went out to him. I felt such empathy for his pain and confusion that lay hidden beneath his behavior.

As we got closer to the therapist's office, I was thankful to be addressing the problem. After all, this was my son's life at stake, a childhood interrupted by responsibility that was perhaps too heavy a burden for the shoulders of a child. It was a life that had been greatly influenced in the womb by emotional trauma, a painful birth, the sudden invasion of patterning and volunteers, and a five-month separation from both of his parents—all before the age of two.

Inside the reception area, Thane was hyper and unsettled. I was relieved when a compassionate-looking woman, probably in her mid-thirties, walked in and warmly said, "Hello," then persuaded Thane to join her in another room. Fortunately, he didn't resist.

Because I was unable to focus on any reading material, the minutes ticked slowly. Struggling to get comfortable on the over-sized sofa while waiting for time to pass, I prayed Thane's first session was going well. I happily recalled how we made our own play-dough at home, and how I had en-couraged Thane and his friends to paint on sheets of paper clipped to the backyard fence. Watching them as young artists dressed in large white T-shirts, I knew the value of creative play. Even at birthday parties, I instructed the neighborhood kids to gather around a long low table to make their own placemats, and then decorate their cupcakes with frosting and sprinkles. From my study of Montessori principles, I structured my children's activities to help expand their organizational skills and heighten their imagination. Using my knowledge to encourage and enrich the thinking of my children was the best part of being a mother.

In the months that followed, the play-therapy sessions slowly produced a change in Thane's behavior. He seemed less irritable, and more capable of integrating his aggressive impulses, possibly reassured that the world existed for him. Once it appeared that he had acquired a more manageable perspective, we terminated the therapy.

Most of the time, I felt confident in the way I had coped with the difficulties and frustrations of full-time parenting, the insistent needs of a disabled child, and the low status of housework and child care that inevitably pose a threat to a mother's self-esteem. When I was able to meet most of my children's needs, as well as my own, I felt good about myself and experienced growth beyond my wildest imagination. In my attempt to remain impervious to the scrutiny of public opinion and the harshness of self-evaluation, it was amazing how much of my individuality had survived.

But in light of stubbornly complex marital issues, and other fixed patterns and conditions which seemed futile to change, it often seemed that suppressed pain from my past interfered with the present, and left room for depression to take hold. Perhaps it was just the daily grind and the ongoing needs of young children that hindered my happiness and created unwanted emotions. Or was it something else?

One particular weekend when Phil was away on another five-day trip, the demands of being home alone only *seemed* like the worst kind of isolation. I wanted to enjoy the laughter of my children and their never-ending noises, but I also longed to go shopping, have lunch with a friend, or simply chat about things that might never come to pass.

Without warning, my emotions began to unravel, causing me to feel I could no longer single-handedly cope with the responsibility of three dependent children. As if I had simply run out of staying-power, I was consumed by a feeling of wanting to end it all. After Chris returned to school on Monday, I knew the situation would appear different, somehow more manageable. But fearful that I could sink into that vulnerable place again in the future, I sat at the kitchen table and hastily scribbled a note to my husband.

Dear Phil,
I cannot endure another weekend like this one. The cumu-
lative pressures of responsibility and my emotional reaction
to them greatly concern me. I am concerned not only for
myself, but for Thane and Mark. I can no longer live like
this. We have to find full-time residence for Chris.

Connie

When Phil returned from a weeklong trip, he found my tear-stained note on his bedroom dresser. I trusted he would view the note as a plea for help, rather than use it as evidence of my weaknesses. Feeling neither wise nor valiant, I was grateful for the moral strength it took to reveal the truth of my barren soul.

I don't recall a conversation between the two of us, except that Phil quickly made a call to the Foundation and scheduled an appointment for us to meet with Nancy Harris, our social worker.

Looking back over the years, it seems unbelievable that he and I had never discussed how, week after week, in his absence, I could continue to tend Chris and manage the emotional stress. We had no guidelines from other parents, or even the luxury of family living close by. My interaction with mothers during our Auxiliary meetings was a source of emotional support, but due to the logistics of travel across the city, I wasn't able to interact with them on a regular basis.

Instead, I just got up every morning and tackled the daily routine by myself. When Phil did return from a flight, after ten to fourteen days of absence, the extended separation hindered meaningful communication. When we were together, we perhaps avoided conversations about Chris because it was simply too painful, just one more reality we couldn't face in a life that had been irrevocably changed by a child's disability.

And now, we sat in front of the familiar walnut desk in Nancy Harris' office. My eyes, swollen from a night of turmoil, brimmed with tears. My heart broke into tiny pieces as Phil began to speak with his usual authoritative and controlled voice. "Nancy, we have decided we must have full-time residence for Chris. We can no longer stand by and watch what's happening at home without feeling completely responsible."

His request sounded as if we had made a unified decision. But when he stated, *"Connie can no longer cope,"* it became clear that I was the reason we were there. I was the one who was responsible for having to place our son in residence for the rest of his life.

My cheeks were on fire. Flashes of emotion ran up the back of my neck. I clenched my fists, fighting to restrain myself. Finally, I could no longer hold back the tears! The idea of giving Chris a more complete school program, with fair and equal competition and identity with his peers, was suddenly impossible to justify. Certainly, at this moment, it didn't seem like an act of love.

Nancy interrupted my punishing thoughts. "Connie and Phil, there are no openings in any of the residential schools in southern California. Even if there was one available, how are you going to pay for it?"

In desperation, Phil urged, "Nancy, our family simply cannot go on like this. We will visit every school in California until we find an opening. If we have to borrow the money we will. As a last resort, we'll consider a state institution."

"There's been a change in policy with the state institutions,"

Nancy replied. "They only accept children who require full-time medical attention. Chris doesn't need full-time medical attention, therefore he's not eligible for placement."

After we left Nancy's office, three months passed with no further discussion of residence.

One day when Phil returned home from a flight, he said, "Connie, Continental Airlines is reducing the number of crew members based in Los Angeles. That will force a move to Denver."

"What about residential schools for Chris?" I asked.

He shrugged his shoulders. "I don't know."

We began extensive correspondence with directors of residential facilities in Denver, only to discover that schools offering therapy and educational programs were not available to children who did not walk, were not toilet-trained, and were not educable.

Until we were able to make permanent arrangements for Chris, the only option was for Phil to schedule his flights out of Denver and commute from Los Angeles to Denver.

A few months later, I got a call from Nancy. "Connie, there may be an opening soon in one of the residential facilities southeast of Los Angeles. A vacancy could occur if another young boy is moved to a different school. I can't be certain of anything right now, but it might happen within a few weeks. I'll call you just as soon as I know anything."

When Nancy called again, sooner than I had expected, her news of an opening for full-time residence was heart-rending. No words or actions could relieve the pain of my son leaving home.

Just days before Chris was scheduled to leave for his new residence, Anne Wendt, the director of *United Cerebral Palsy Foundation*, called me at home with words that would help soothe my aching heart.

"Connie, you've worked hard to meet Chris' needs at home. But in ninety-nine percent of families, the disabled child does not need or want all that parents are inclined to give. There is no reason for an entire family to be handicapped by a focus on one child. Chris has a right to his fullest development along with the rest of us. He will never be able to live safely or independently in the community. A full-time residential program will give him the greatest opportunity to grow and learn. It may surprise you to know Chris has been ready for residence for a long time. *Placement is never rejection."*

From all outward appearances, August 5, 1969, was just another day. The roar of jetliners taking off from nearby Los Angeles International confirmed the normalcy of the rest of the world. When I awakened to *Handel's Water Music* on my clock radio, I knew it was a day that would change my life forever. In a surprisingly relaxed manner, considering the circumstances, I dressed in a pair of camel gabardine slacks and a cotton sweater, took time to put on my makeup, and set the table for breakfast.

As I walked down the hall to Chris' room, I felt an enormous lump forming in my throat. I didn't turn on the light as I had done so many mornings before. Looking at him asleep in his bed, his tousled head on the pillow, I was reminded of all the times I had tried to visualize him as a young man. Now, lying there wearing his cowboy pajamas, with his small brown teddy bear at his side, he looked even more childlike.

I didn't hear Phil's footsteps behind me, but when he put his arm around my shoulder and pulled me close, I knew he must feel the agony inside me. We stood together for a moment as tears streamed down my face.

He turned on the light and said, "It's for the best. Let's get ready to go."

He quickly headed back down the hall. Before he closed the bathroom door, he shouted, "It's almost six o'clock."

The glare of the overhead light broke the spell. Brushing away my tears, I slowly moved to the side of Chris' bed and kissed him gently on the cheek as I had done many mornings before. Today would be the last time.

The *Intercommunity Exceptional Children's Home* was a stucco structure with Spanish-style arches and a courtyard designed to enhance the front entrance. Inside, the reception area was warm and inviting with a fireplace, game tables, colorful sofas, and matching draperies. The supervisor introduced us to a therapist and a few teachers who would be working with Chris. Then, with compassion in his voice, he reminded us, "A child with a disability can easily absorb you. He can be a burden on your family all your life. Here, he will be loved and cared for in the best manner we know."

Without notice, a technician came forward and began pushing Chris in his wheelchair across the room. Realizing what was happening, we followed. Moments later, they disappeared behind a closed door. Through the small window of the door, I saw Chris being wheeled down a stark corridor. Twisting in his wheelchair to see us, his lips quivered. His big brown eyes filled with tears. He knew we weren't coming. With great difficulty, I turned to walk away, knowing that if I stayed I could never leave. My body was bleeding inside with the deepest pain a mother can feel.

Outside the air hung heavy with a mixture of anxiety, relief, and guilt. I felt tired and bruised. The emotions of shock, resentment, and hostility came flooding back. It was hard to know Phil's thoughts as he relinquished a cherished dream for his son. His anguish undoubtedly penetrated the depths of his soul, just as mine did. This step was a final acknowledgment that our son's life would never unfold in accordance with the usual American dream, the expectations of a perfect child.

As we made the seventy-five-mile drive back into Los Angeles, a million thoughts churned in my mind. Only one thing was certain: I felt a bond with my son that death itself could not break.

Arriving home to a mailbox chock-full of the usual unimportant stuff, I discovered a letter from my dad. Tearfully I opened the envelope and began reading.

Chris leaves home at the age of 8.
August 1970

Dear Connie,

I have said a lot of prayers for Chris, but I must admit that after the patterning program, my hope for a miracle diminished. I know you and Phil continue to hold the faith. And God loves you even more because of your steadfast belief in him. Perhaps you are already doing what he wants you to do. He may have answered your prayers in giving you Thane and Mark.

But, you need to know that more will come. As long as I live, I will say a daily prayer for Chris. Your courage has been a blessing to your mother and to me. We love you all.

With love always,
Your Dad

Receiving a letter from home, and especially from my dad, was the kind of validation I needed. His comforting words would be read a thousand times.

14
THE LOST NOEL

There were no rules, no handbook for regulating my sorrow. Worst of all, no one was grieving with me. Aside from being able to confide in a few close friends, I didn't expect others to comprehend my loss. In fact, even our minister, who had recently visited our home, didn't understand the finality of our decision. He said, "You mean Chris is never coming back?"

With the harsh reality of Chris' going away, and the impending move to Denver, I needed to know I could make it through this terrible period of grief. The feeling of loneliness was excruciating and overwhelming. The policy at Chris' new residence didn't allow visitors until after a three-month period of adjustment. By then our family would be living in Denver.

Once again, during my grief-stricken state, I received an unexpected phone call from Anne Wendt. "Connie, I want you to promise me that you will go to Denver to live, love, and enjoy life. Chris will do just fine without you. In fact, he will not even know you've gone."

Even though the experience of disability had challenged the fabric of my existence, and in many ways, had made me stronger, it seemed impossible to believe that we had diligently pursued success, only to have our happiness so acutely affected by our failure. Right now, I had to simply trust that our decision to restructure our family was evidence of our strength in overcoming unexpected and painful hardships. Having dealt with them in the most creative way possible, we were satisfied we had made a difference in the life of our child.

As if the universe were reaching out to support me, I was strengthened by the love and encouragement from wonderful neighbors on Ninety-First Street. Carol Gilger gave a surprise brunch with French crepe's and champagne, and Jean Brogan gave a neighborhood coffee. With thoughtful remembrances and gifts, I said goodbye to Carol and Jean, Barbara Dickson, Agnes Mocsny, Barbara Haddad, Helen Hinkle, Eve Hoble, Norma Volk, Karin Leiberman, Irene LeBlanc, Ann Murdock, Barbara and Max Ward, and all the other wonderful neighbors.

With our move to Colorado, the exhilaration of unknown adventures would eventually transcend the mere pleasures of hiking, biking, and skiing. The opportunities for outdoor recreation, however, were second only to finding the perfect house in a family oriented neighborhood with good schools and athletic programs. It was comforting to have my sister Brenda, her husband Jerry, and their children Heather and Brian also living in Denver. My parents still lived on the ranch in western Kansas, only two hundred miles away.

Earlier, I had flown to Denver to meet with a realtor. We spent nearly a week eliminating houses because of ugly wallpaper, unworkable floor plans, or outdated carpet. But when he showed me a two-story brick and frame house on Easter Circle, it seemed to speak to my soul. The house was barely two years old, and even though the existing décor of gold sculptured carpet and matching window treatments were hardly my taste, they could be replaced. I immediately fell in love with the black slate foyer and the rust-colored brick wall in the family room. The large kitchen and eating space overlooked an open backyard where we could easily interact with other neighbors and their kids. Even though a home with a formal living and dining room, three bedrooms, two-and-a-half baths, and a guest room (to be used as an office) seemed perfect for a new life, I had to remember that the journey into ourselves would be the most important part of our new life.

Three inches of freshly fallen snow provided the perfect opportunity for Thane and Mark to join with their new play-mates and pack together a six-foot snowman detailed with a tattered straw hat, a wool scarf, and a broomstick tucked securely under his arm. As I stood watching, tears welled. I was thankful for their creative spirits and encouraged by their rapid adjustment to a new environment.

One morning, shortly after our move to Denver, a woman rang the doorbell and introduced herself. "Hi, I'm Betty. I live next door. Welcome to the neighborhood. It looks like your boys have already made lots of friends. How many children do you have?"

"We have two boys, ages three and seven."

Thane was standing nearby. "Mom, you have three boys," he shouted.

I was embarrassed and confused. I hadn't thought that it was necessary to include Chris in conversations with my new neighbors. I finally said to Betty, "We also have an eight-year-old son who has special needs and requires a residential program. He lives in one of the best facilities in the country, which is located in southern California."

It seemed we barely had time to settle into our new residence before more snow fell, just in time for Thanksgiving. Determined not to have my energy diminished by the move, I tried to enter into the spirit of the season. I prepared dinner for eight people, wrote a Thanksgiving script, and made cos-tumes for the children. After dinner, everyone took turns swinging at the homemade turkey pinata. My energy was fueled by a need for artistic expression, which helped me cope, at least for the moment.

It wasn't long before I began to look closely at our new suburban neighborhood of traditional two-story brick and frame homes with beautifully manicured yards. I noticed that other people lived with appearances, just like I did. We all had faces and personalities that represented images, but we had no real idea of who we were. Perhaps out of an unconscious fear of being isolated, and even forgotten, we felt an urge to create an identity for ourselves. We decorated our homes, we filled our closets, and we depended on our men to be there to support us. None of this was wrong; it was simply our means of survival.

Perhaps we felt a need to avoid choices we didn't think we had a right to make, and feelings we would rather not have. For myself, I was learning to live with my own frailties, which was even more difficult than acknowledging the limitations of my disabled child and the dark days of his absence.

In an attempt to satisfy my need to create something beautiful, I convinced my husband we could advertise and sell the out-dated carpet and draperies through the Denver paper. This would allow us to purchase new wool carpet on sale, and to select different window coverings. On a budget and using my intuition, I was determined to design some respectability into our family room and kitchen-dining area. Just as I had planned, the carpet and draperies sold and the reshaping began.

My artistic boldness in decorating our home created a sense of self-worth, but those creative energies didn't always align with my husband's more conservative views. While he was gone on another trip, I finished decorating the downstairs powder room. I painted the cabinets, moldings, and baseboards, and was proud to be able to match the pattern in the paper we had chosen, especially since I had never hung wallpaper.

I looked forward to Phil's approval, but when he saw it he lashed out, telling me how he still liked the old wallpaper that was now outside in the trash.

Months later, I anticipated his enthusiasm over the custom-designed wallpaper which he had approved for the foyer. It was a more sophisticated pattern in pewter and shades of off-white and gold, which beautifully coordinated with the charcoal slate floor and rust-colored carpet on the stairs.

When Phil returned from a flight late one evening and opened the front door, he shouted, "I hate this wallpaper. It looks like bulls' horns."

I wanted to believe his reaction was simply due to the tension from a difficult flight, or exhaustion from a change in time zones. But no amount of rationalizing could counter the fact that my joy was suddenly quashed, and my anticipated excitement about our new home quickly smothered. The worst part was that instead of realizing I couldn't always manage the unmanageable, I felt responsible for his actions and his words. I readily assumed feelings of inadequacy and guilt.

The next day, when I was able to think more rationally, it seemed my husband's angry outbursts stemmed from something other than the wallpaper. What was it I didn't know?

Winter inched forward with grim determination. The frozen landscape and the long, dark nights pressed into my empty soul. Nevertheless, I trusted that behind the heavy clouds and the coming Christmas season was a personal and caring God. As part of a commitment to a new beginning we joined the Methodist church. Phil, surprisingly, joined the choir.

Sitting in church one morning, Thane and Mark snuggled next to me as they watched the choir members walking down the aisle in their black robes. They whispered, "There's Daddy." We all beamed as he passed our pew. Then came the sentimental moment when the congregation sang *Silent Night*. My voice wavered as I thought of Chris.

In the adult education class Phil and I attended on Sunday morning, I learned that another class member, whom I had known only briefly, had recently lost her three-week-old baby. Her mother had also been diagnosed with terminal cancer. I overheard someone comment, "It's been nearly three months since Freda's baby died. She's still grieving. Don't you think she's had enough time?"

How could anyone put a limit on someone else's grief? I wondered what yardstick they would use to measure mine.

In preparation for Christmas, we gathered fresh greens and pinecones to decorate the fireplace mantel, and to use with candles on the kitchen table. The house was filled with the aroma of freshly baked cookies and a faint scent of wood smoke from the fireplace. Christmas letters with our family photograph had already been mailed. Packages wrapped in holiday paper waited beneath the tree. In spite of the beauty of the season and our intentions to create a new beginning, a dark emotional undercurrent stubbornly prevailed.

Just a week ago, I had asked Phil, "What are we going to get Mark for Christmas?" He said, "I don't know what you're getting him, but I'm going to buy him a bicycle."

My heart sank. When I recognized we were no longer a team, my sense of loss deepened. Perhaps it was the dispiriting symbol of shared failure that was represented by a child's disability, or the emotional strains imposed on our marriage by separation, that caused a feeling of alienation. But, in my mind, there was no reasonable excuse or explanation for Phil's thoughtless and inconsiderate words and actions.

Along with my attempt to move forward, the usual complaints about a commercialized Christmas permeated the season. The real meaning of the holiday, with its sense of joy and peace, seemed to disappear in the scurry of material madness, only because it was what our culture had chosen. When I heard the Salvation Army bells ringing with a message to remember the friendless and the poor, I dropped a few coins into the kettle. I felt better, but it wasn't enough. Perhaps I could find a battered women's shelter, call the Denver Rescue Mission, or visit a family on welfare.

At bedtime one night, Thane and Mark voiced their own sentiments. Mark, at the tender age of three, remembered Chris in his prayers: *Dear God, I like Mom and Dad and my brother Thane. And I hope you can make Chris well. Amen.*

Thane looked at me and quietly asked, "Mom, will you die before I do and leave me all alone?"

"Honey, I will be here as long as you need me." I hugged him for a long time and kissed them goodnight.

It was late when I was ready to go to sleep. Indulging in

the luxury of solitude while my husband was away, I stood for a moment looking out the bedroom window. The neighborhood roof-tops had nearly disappeared behind blankets of white snow. Smoke curled delicately from a few chimneys. Blinking lights danced merrily around some of the windows, creating miniature rainbows on the snowy sills. Even with the wonder and glow of the season, I questioned how long it would take for me to fashion a new life, to move beyond the impact of a loss which was not as final as death, but, in some ways, infinitely more devastating.

A week before Christmas, the four of us flew to Los Angeles where we picked up a rental car and drove to the *Intercommunity Exceptional Children's Home* in San Bernardino. As we pulled into the familiar circle drive, my emotions were fragile. What would Chris look like? Would he recognize us?

When a technician wheeled Chris into the lobby, I noticed his hesitation, wondering who we were. After each of us quietly introduced ourselves, he started to bang his shoes against the footrest of his wheelchair. As his leg braces clattered noisily and shrieks of excitement filled the room, it was obvious his confusion had melted into recognition and happy surprise.

While Thane and Mark helped tear the wrappings off the Christmas packages, Chris' screams intermingled with bouts of laughter. The joyous festivities continued as we placed him on the floor and began demonstrating his toys. Then Thane, determined to see if he could do *wheelies* in Chris' wheelchair, gaily pushed himself around the room. Finally, Mark insisted on his turn, and hung on tight as Thane raced him up and down the hallways.

We all piled into the car to go to a nearby restaurant. Sitting in a booth surrounded by other people during the lunch hour, I realized that a year ago I would have been offended by their stares. Now, with a greater appreciation of Chris' sensitive and beautiful spirit, and more tolerant of my own insecurities, I was less concerned about their reactions to his noisy outbursts and messy eating style.

We drove a short distance to the amusement park,

thinking Chris would enjoy a boat ride. However, while Phil held Chris beside him in the boat, his moaning indicated he was restless. After the boat ride we strolled over to the picnic area where we saw other residents from Chris' school.

"Hi, Chris! You gonna go home with your parents? When ya comin' back? Did you tell your mom and dad about Santa? Well, did you, Chris?" Chris smiled his tenderhearted smile, then clasped his hands together like he always does when he understands and approves.

Another student told us how excited Chris was on their train ride to visit Santa at the shopping center. Her enthusiasm about other coming events, and especially the big party on Christmas morning, convinced me that we had given Chris a life that wasn't possible at home. Still, I felt a deep sadness in knowing that it was the end of a dream that our son would walk and talk and go to school like other children, the dream that never included his leaving home at such a young age, depending on another family for love and security.

On our way back to the residential facility, Chris nervously put his fist to his mouth and began crying. Did he not want to go back? Was he afraid of being left again? Or was he frightened that he might *not* be going back?

As we neared the circle drive that led to the entrance, Chris' agitated mood became more relaxed, more peaceful. It suddenly occurred to me that he wanted to be there. It was his home. It was where he belonged.

Inside the lobby, the mood was somber. Tears teetered on the edge. A staff member insisted on brief goodbyes. And before I knew it, a technician began pushing Chris in his wheelchair and soon disappeared behind closed doors.

This process of separation is one that parents of a disabled child must eventually endure. It is an experience that, for parents of normal children, is impossible to explain. For parents of a disabled child, no explanation is necessary.

At Los Angeles International Airport, we boarded the massive 747 for the return trip to Denver. I wearily dropped into my seat next to the window and fastened my seatbelt. As the plane ascended into the darkness above Los Angeles, the vibration and noise from the engines quickly distracted me, and I was once again alone with myself. I was traveling to a new place in time, wondering if it was possible to create a purposeful life that could replace the daunting challenge of the last eight years.

Back in Colorado, we celebrated Christmas Eve by attending a traditional candlelight service. Swags of pine boughs decorated the sanctuary. Candles flickered at the altar. Phil and I sat near the front of the church with Thane and Mark snuggled between us. We joined the rest of the congregation in singing *The First Noel* and *O Come All Ye Faithful*. Prophecies from the Bible sounded familiar, stories of people who professed to reveal the will of God through pain and struggle. One of the most repeated themes in scripture was the search for a meaningful life.

The minister followed the scripture readings with a message that sounded like it was written just for me: *"This is a time of great blessing, a time to love yourself unconditionally. It's a time to break away from destructive thought patterns and see purpose and good in all things. Sometimes we have to prepare for a new life, which can't happen without some discomfort and pain. It means uncertainty and inconvenience. It means giving up your expectations.*

"I urge you to get in touch with your feelings and develop your talents. Discard everything that inhibits the magnificent creature that lies within you. Your greatest purpose is to be a light unto others."

Then came the moment when candles were given out and lighted wick to wick. The organ began a medley of carols. A sea of lights rippled through the church. We carried our candles toward the door and into the night, keeping them alight as long as possible.

With each step, I surrendered to the power of my intuition, more willing not to know where the next step would lead me. The images would come, some quietly, some boldly, but they would come. I trusted that darkness would soon yield and the way would become clear.

15

An Unconscious
Cry for Help

When I began to look at my life, which was no solemn journey, and a soul that felt splintered and confused, it was clear I needed a new perspective. Perhaps I just needed to find more practical ways to contribute to others, or explore ways to develop my worldly interests. What I really needed was a confidence that no one would hurt me again. Perhaps all my life I had tried to find this assurance outside myself, never realizing that working through issues of trust was part of my journey.

I was beginning to realize that I needed more time just to be alone with myself. But when I considered what it might take to allow the rays of an invisible sun to penetrate my weary soul, I felt the agony of uncertainty. It was like the mental and physical struggle that apparently precedes death, a sudden, but all consuming, feeling of confusion.

Designing a few rooms in our home helped satisfy an artistic need and provided a way to channel my grief. Getting together with my sister and her family was great, even though I often felt envious of their seemingly normal family. I was happy that my brother had returned from Vietnam, having also received the *Bronze Star* for heroic combat action as a Marine Lieutenant. In some ways I felt that our experiences, and the possibility of post-traumatic stress syndrome were similar, but he likely wouldn't see it that way.

As time went on, I continued to feel alone and different. Subliminal thoughts of living a life with fewer restrains and expectations had been present for months, perhaps for years, intensifying when Chris left home. I felt bound by my thoughts, unable to control where they might lead me. As I grew more intolerant of others who seemed to be able to cover up their emotional conflicts, my despair deepened.

Sitting at the kitchen table with a cup of coffee that was barely warm, I gazed across the open back yards of our neighborhood. With a hint of wind, the leaves on willowy branches of our newly planted trees moved only slightly in a mesmerizing rhythm.

In those moments, it looked pointless to carry on, especially when I felt the life I was living wasn't my own. It was hard to remember anything other than trying to please my parents or a husband, or striving to do the right thing for my children. Even now, with Thane in second grade at the nearby elementary school and Mark at pre-school for half a day, my mind felt barren of resources.

I wondered how I could move beyond the compulsion to create perfection for the sake of feeling good about myself. How long could I live with the enduring loss of a child without causing myself accidents, illnesses, or an emotional breakdown? Even if I were willing to overcome a sense of failure and try to reason away my feelings of over sensitivity, it wasn't likely I would make much progress without help. The question was, *"Where to go to for counseling or therapy?"*

Suddenly I remembered a conversation that took place in Los Angeles nearly a year ago. At a party where I knew few people, I overheard a woman saying, *"Every major city has a Family Service Center that can assist people with any type of problem."*

As I glanced reluctantly at the telephone above the desk, I shuddered at the aspects of myself that might be underlying the image of poise and confidence which I had maintained for so many years. The process of penetrating that illusion would undoubtedly require a great deal of effort and introspection. It would require a willingness to look at my childhood, the changing role of wife and mother, my early illusions of a perfect life, and even the shortcomings in my marriage.

Looking outside, I hoped for some kind of distraction, but there was none. Perhaps with enough determination, I could simply adapt to my depression. But after realizing I had no other solutions, I dialed the Family Service Center.

A warm and compassionate voice answered, "Hello, Family Services. How may I assist you?"

"I don't know. I just can't stop crying."

"Is there anything you want to tell me?" she asked.

I told her something about having moved to Colorado without my eight-year-old son, and the difficult time I was having.

The friendly voice continued. "It sounds like you need to speak with a counselor."

"Yes."

"Would you prefer to meet with a man or a woman?"

A million thoughts passed through my mind before I finally decided that another woman would likely understand a mother's feelings.

The receptionist said, "Fine, I have you scheduled with Rebecca Wade next Tuesday morning at nine o'clock."

On Tuesday morning, I pulled into a parking lot next to a three-story, brick office building, arriving at least thirty minutes early. I sat in the car hoping no one would see me. Minutes before the appointment, I got out of the car, walked to the front entrance, then I took the elevator to the third floor. Halfway down the hall I came to a door with black letters etched into the opaque glass — *FAMILY SERVICE CENTER.*

Even though I had made the bold decision to get help for myself, I felt guilty for turning to a secular solution instead of taking refuge in my faith. In the waiting room, still wracked with conflict, I tried to bury my shame behind a magazine while I thought to myself, *Religious people don't have problems.* Seconds later, I reconsidered that position. *But even religious people have difficult times. It's perfectly okay to seek the guidance of a professional during difficult times.*

When my name was called, I was glad I hadn't succumbed to logical reasons for not keeping the appointment.

In Rebecca Wade's office, sitting face to face with someone

I hoped could at least be objective, my irrational thoughts seemed easier to confront.

As I unraveled the numbing mixture of anger, bitterness, sorrow, and denial, I again felt the silent knife-like terror that comes a hundred times a day when you want to be with someone you love, and want to say goodnight when they are not there.

After Rebecca listened to my pain and distress, she said, "Connie, it sounds like you're trying to kick nine years of your life under the rug and pretend they never happened. You can't replace those years with a new home in suburbia, activities for your sons, or even new friends. The loss of a child is not replaceable."

She encouraged me to grieve the loss of my expectations and to grieve without restraint or feelings of embarrassment. "Give yourself permission to cry as often as you need. There are no timetables to gauge the healing, and no judgments against experiencing the entire gamut of emotions."

I came away from our first meeting with a better understanding of the grief process and how my roller-coaster emotions were part of dealing with the loss of a child.

In my second session, I was able to pinpoint another aspect of my grief, a fear that because Thane and Mark were so young (seven and three) when Chris left home, they would not remember the thousands of people who had become a part of our family. They were too young to know the impact their brother had on all of us.

Suddenly I blurted, "Rebecca, some days I think I would like to write about our experiences with Chris. I feel it's important for Thane and Mark to know what we went through during those early years, and to understand the decisions we made."

"Connie, if you have any talent or desire whatsoever, I strongly advise you to do it! Writing would be good for you. When you spend time alone recounting the truth of your journey, you will begin to think less about your loss and more about what you've gained from the experience. The process of questioning your life can be painful and disorienting, but well worthwhile."

In the third session, I talked about my need to know that my eight-year-old son was still a part of our family. But Phil refused to have photographs of Chris around the house, or include him in conversations. While I struggled with how to cope with my loss, Phil coped by choosing to withdraw or by flinging hurtful accusations, which caused me to retaliate with my own abusive remarks.

I didn't understand how a *loving* spouse could inflict this kind of illogical pain. Neither did I understand that my husband's angry remarks could stem from his own unacknowledged guilt. I only knew that I ached for someone to hold me and tell me I was going to be okay.

In the remaining moments of that third session, Rebecca stressed the importance of being able to grieve in our own way, and urged me to remember that the expressions of hate and resentment *can* be a way of surviving.

Without knowing how to handle the uncertainties that come with grief, Phil and I became vulnerable to the damage inflicted by each other, as well as self-punishing behavior. And even though we were advised to seek counseling together, Phil saw no reason. For myself, it seemed I had gained enough insight with which to manage my own situation.

At home in a neighborhood of wonderful people, I continued to share interior design ideas and exchange recipes for carrot cake, pumpkin bread, and dishes like Chicken Marchand De Vin from the famous Brennans's restaurant in New Orleans. At Little League games, I swapped stories of our exciting wins and devastating losses. But in spite of warm and friendly interactions, while living the *good life*, nothing seemed important enough to exert the kind of energy required by the patterning program, the fund-raising activities in Los Angeles, and the exacting care of a disabled child. Even though I knew it would take time to focus on new goals and get back into the mainstream, I seemed unable to overcome the expectations of a quiet suburban lifestyle.

It was difficult to put a label on it, but as far as I could tell, it was a feeling of anxiety that stemmed from a fear that I was making a mountain out of a molehill by insisting that my needs were important, and that they were not being met.

As Phil left the next morning, he kissed me goodbye as he usually did. His kiss was an indicator of two people inextricably connected in a morass of obligation, with occasional shared pleasures. Indeed, we seemed to have nothing in common except the children's excitement over the first snowfall, or their delight in new friends.

On my thirty-third birthday, my family had wished me another happy year. Their good wishes somehow added to the dichotomy of being an unhappy, but well-cared for, suburban housewife. My friends also wished me another great year, saying, "You've got it made—a nice home in a great suburban neighborhood, a handsome husband with a prestigious job and two beautiful, intelligent children."

But for me, the good life wasn't enough to compensate for the loss of a son and, subsequently, the loss of my husband. I needed a new formula, one that gave meaning and excitement to my life.

Another weekend rolled around. Phil left early Saturday morning for a seven-day trip. I remember thinking: *Another shitty weekend alone. Other husbands are home for a family barbecue, a movie or dinner with their wife, and I'm home alone with two kids.* As hard as I tried to escape the trap of feeling lonely and deserted, it seemed that nothing could shake what seemed like mental fatigue.

To cope with *this* weekend, I drove the boys to a nearby mall to shop for items for their bathroom. Inside the department store, where merchants appealed to a woman's femininity in a profoundly material form, we passed a counter of fragrances where an exotic bottle of Chanel No. 5 spelled seduction, and gold serpentine jewelry created desire for the female psyche. I feared Phil would be critical of money spent on *unnecessary items* such as perfume and jewelry. He likely wouldn't understand the kind of superficial nurturing that women sometimes need.

On the opposite side of the store I saw a large table of sunglasses. Just a few weeks ago, I had purchased a pair for six dollars at this same store. Soon thereafter, the wire frames became loose and the glasses kept falling off. Instead of taking them back and requesting a refund or a new pair, I harbored resentment about inferior merchandise, without realizing what was really bothering me. It wasn't the cheap merchandise; it was my deep-seated feeling of impoverishment, my emotional bankruptcy.

Standing next to the display table, which was laden with hundreds of choices, I couldn't decide which style I liked best. As I continued to search the table, I noticed two other women who were casually sorting through the pile at the other side of the table. It seemed strange that I would even care what they were doing, but in spite of that flashing thought, I couldn't resist the temptation any longer.

I stuffed a pair of sunglasses into my purse and walked away. It was a risky move, but I escaped without notice, and the boys and I rode the escalator to the second floor.

What I failed to realize then, is that my contempt for the faulty merchandise had served as a defense against a tide of unwanted feelings. I stole those sunglasses as an act of revenge, without recognizing that revenge was a weapon of the weak.

In the linen department, we searched for towels and a shower curtain for the boys' bathroom. While I waited impatiently to pay nearly two hundred dollars for our selected items, I reached into my purse for the new pair of sunglasses. Unconcerned that someone might be watching me, I removed the sticky price tag, crumpled it between my fingers before dropping it on the floor, and then put the glasses on.

When I completed our purchase, the three of us took the escalator to the first floor. Walking toward the front entrance, nearly obscured by the large bulky package I was carrying, I felt strangely fatigued and eager to get home. Without warning, a stocky blonde-haired woman in a pink pantsuit crowded next to me. *What's going on? Why is this woman walking so close?*

Suddenly, she stepped directly in front of me and flashed a badge in an open leather folder, which was cradled in the palm of her hand.

"You had better come with me," she said quietly.

My heart stopped. Something inside of me just died. Perhaps it had died a long time ago. And now I was paying the price.

I motioned for the boys to follow as we took the escalator to the lower level, which conveniently opened to the toy department. I told them to wait there while I talked with this woman.

As she escorted me into a small room, I wondered if in the shadow of depression and another shitty weekend alone, shoplifting was an emotional outlet. Terrified by what had just happened, my mind was void of coherent thoughts, my body numb with fear.

During the interrogation, I was afraid Phil might be notified. What about my parents? What if neighbors found out? Would my name appear in the newspaper?

After the questioning was complete, I joined Thane and Mark in the toy department. I trusted they didn't know what was happening, even as a security person escorted us to a patrol car waiting outside.

While Thane and Mark sat on each side of me in the backseat, I barely noticed the rush-hour traffic. It wasn't long before we arrived at a light-colored brick structure near downtown. Large black letters on the building identified it as the DENVER POLICE DEPARTMENT.

After pulling into the circle drive, the officer stopped and opened the car door, then ushered us into the lobby and past a security desk. While the boys were directed to a room with sofas and a television, I was taken behind two wire doors for fingerprints and photographs, and then escorted to the second floor.

Wearing a bright orange, tunic-length pant outfit with a colorful sash and matching sandals, I endured the humiliating stares of the less fortunate behind bars, or sitting on benches. At the end of the hallway, I suddenly heard a door slam shut behind me. My mouth went dry. My hands were wet. As I stood facing the wall in the shadows of a semi-dark cell, I was too numb to feel remorse, too paralyzed to cry.

Two hours later, I was dismissed and told I would receive notification of a hearing to be held within the next ten days. The boys and I were escorted out of the building and into the backseat of the police car.

During the ride back to my car, the policeman glanced over his shoulder and loudly inquired, "So lady, how much did you get away with? Two-hundred-dollars worth?"

"No! I took a pair of six-dollar sunglasses."

"You're kidding," he retorted.

"No, that's all I needed."

Back at the shopping center, fatigue penetrated every bone of my body. The day's rush of excitement had moment-arily given me a strange sense of accomplishment. But now, I was ready to go home.

Later, learning that shoplifting was a crime committed almost exclusively by women, I questioned why anyone would risk an arrest for a lipstick, a piece of lingerie or a six-dollar pair of sunglasses. With fear and humiliation forever etched in my mind, I was relieved to know the court hearing would be over by the time Phil returned home.

On a Monday morning, after the boys went to school, I stood in front of the judge's bench at the Denver County Courthouse. Taking a deep breath, trying to look and feel confident, I waited for the judge to speak. "Unfortunately, the costly price tag of unresolved problems is one that can easily lead to shoplifting. I see it in my courtroom every day. Look-ing at your folder, it appears this is your first offense. There-fore, I'm going to grant a motion to temporarily dismiss the charges. It's what we call a *deferred prosecution*. But first, you must fulfill six months of probationary counseling. After that, your record will be reviewed. If no further incidents have occurred, your case will be dismissed."

I was given a file number and told that my case would be passed on to Probation Services. I was then scheduled for weekly counseling.

Driving home, I calmly accepted the consequences, but wondered what prompted this hideous and insane act. Was it simply frayed nerves? Was it revenge against unacceptable feelings? Or was it rage toward my husband? Whatever the reasons, it came with its own problems.

The most pressing issue was how to tell Phil that his wife had been arrested for shoplifting. The situation would likely be seen as confirmation of a wife with a flawed character and a dysfunctional family, for which I was solely responsible. I could count on being shamed and degraded for an act I already knew was a bizarre, immature, and self-defeating reaction to life's painful moments.

At last, the time came to tell Phil. The temperature on that particular Saturday evening was just plain hot. Sitting in lawn chairs on our front porch, Phil surprisingly refrained from his usual complaints. Even my sarcasm was in remission. And although the prolonged silence was uncomfortable, it allowed me time to organize an explanation of how this good and virtuous woman became a shoplifter.

As I began to unravel the incident, Phil appeared calm. When I finished speaking, he remained quiet. Then, ever so slowly, a devilish smile formed beneath his mustache, twisting his indifferent expression into a look of contempt.

"Well, Connie, if anyone knows you're in counseling, you had better tell them why. Otherwise, they will assume it's marriage counseling and will automatically think I'm having an affair with a flight attendant. So, Connie, if you don't tell them, I will tell them!"

My heart sank. Who did he think I was going to tell? I only wanted to know that I could trust the man to whom I was married. But now, it seemed that he valued *his* image more than our marriage.

"So, *are* you having an affair?" I asked.

He didn't answer.

Regardless of what else might be going on in his life or

mine, I felt that if he really loved me, he wouldn't throw my past in my face. He would look for a way to understand and to help. In reality, both of us had resorted to forms of escape.

While driving toward the Denver City and County Building to report to Probation Services, I wondered who my husband's lover was. The flight attendant he visited in the hospital with a gift he had asked me to purchase? Another flight attendant who sent me a pair of leather gloves from Spain, after telling me my husband was one of the nicest, most honorable men she knew? Or was she the bikini-clad woman in the photograph from Hawaii?

Finding a parking space downtown was nearly impossible, but one finally opened as I came around the block for the third time.

Frozen with fear, I headed downstairs inside the City and County Building, and followed the signs in the hallway that read *PROBATION SERVICES*. The basement of the building was barren except for wooden courtroom benches that lined the stark white walls.

First-time probationers were easily recognized as they nervously puffed on cigarettes. The more seasoned probationers slouched half-asleep on the benches.

While waiting, I smoked my first cigarette since final exams in college, and made several trips to the ladies' room.

Suddenly, from the end of the long hallway, a gruff-sounding voice called, "Connie Wright."

When I stood and walked toward the voice, I saw a man with a surly expression and a harsh demeanor that was softened only by a more professional-looking coat and tie. His graying curly hair and mustache contrasted with the dark skin of his African-American heritage.

"I'm Lester Thomas. Come with me."

My fear heightened as we walked into a small, disheveled office and he gestured for me to sit down in front of his desk.

"At the last minute your case number was unexpectedly given to me instead of another counselor. So here we are."

Quickly noting his credentials on the wall, a Ph.D. in

education and Director of the Probation Department, I felt honored to have been referred to him.

The first thing on the agenda was the Minnesota Multi-Phasic Personality Inventory, commonly called the MMPI. This evaluation tool was a way to explore the possibility of underlying personality disorders and neurotic tendencies. Consumed with anxiety, I tried to mentally prepare myself for the written test.

After being seated in a small room, I began to answer the questions, terrified of discovering some sort of aggression or defect that would mark me forever.

At home, I anxiously awaited the results and was even more terrified when Dr. Thomas called to tell me I needed to take the MMPI a second time. As I drove downtown to take the test again, my thoughts went wild. Was I suffering from some hidden psychosis, a mental disorder in which the personality is seriously disorganized and reality is impaired?

The following day, sitting in his office, I steeled myself for results from both tests. Dr. Thomas, with a cigar in one hand and papers in the other, was impossible to read.

Finally he said, "Connie, I'm relieved that you have no serious emotional disorders, only some narcissistic needs that typically evolve from the tragic loss of oneself. Your tests clearly indicate you were not looking for a father figure when you married your husband. You already have a strong father figure. And the loss of your son is not the issue. However, the way in which you respond to the world around you stems from a sense of wanting to be different. You don't necessarily *want* to be different, but you feel you *need* to be different in order to be accepted. In technical terms, it's called obsessive individuation. Fundamentally, it's a denial or invalidation of the person you really are.

"The test shows that much of the time you feel degraded, like you haven't played the game adequately. It appears you willingly assume responsibility for some areas of your life, but easily fall victim to situations in which you are not responsible.

"When one suffers from the loss of his own individuality

and uniqueness, it's easy to become blind to the strong and talented person he really is."

When he dismissed me and I started to walk toward the door, he said, "You have a beautiful smile." I glowed with the warmth of a compliment and no longer felt alone, burdened by my arrest.

As the weeks progressed, my fear of being discovered lessened, but I was still curious about the recent behavior. I would learn more about that in my next session with Dr. Thomas.

When that day arrived, he concluded that the shoplifting was an act of defiance against perceived constraints. "Clinically speaking," he said, "the behavior stems from two things. The first is an *unconscious aggravation* or a feeling that the world owes you more than you are getting in return. The second is *emotional deprivation* or a feeling of being deprived in the most intimate parts of your life, specifically in the areas of sexual and emotional intimacy."

As Dr. Thomas spoke, I reflected on times when I resented my husband's control. Like the time I purchased two different dresses and proudly displayed them on the bed, then was told I had to decide between them. I was provoked to think that I even needed his permission to buy my clothes. Another time, I was accused of putting more food on *my* plate than his. When the backyard awning was finished and installed, he instructed me to write a check, and then he berated me for overdrawing the bank account. The desk in the upstairs study was kept locked *for privacy*, but I never dared to question the reason.

Another time, when our family was getting ready for a particular trip to Los Angeles, Phil asked, "What are you and the boys wearing?" Surprised, I thought to myself, *Why is he so concerned about how we look? The airline dress code for employees and family members has always required that we dress appropriately, and we always have.*

I wondered who else was going to be on the same flight. Coincidentally, en route to Los Angeles, a female flight attendant stopped to talk to Phil, who was sitting next to the aisle.

After their flirtatious dialogue, he introduced me by saying, "This is Connie, my *first* wife."

I laughed, but in reality, it was just another one of those times when I tried to disguise my inner pain.

Returning to the issues in Dr. Thomas' office, he explained how intelligent women in middle and upper income groups act out repressed conflicts. Studies indicate that women who are angry and fearful, for whatever reason, are more vulnerable to becoming one of the millions of American women who engage in shoplifting, who momentarily benefit from the reward of having gotten away with it.

Nearing the end of the session, Dr. Thomas revealed how weeks ago, Phil had come into his office and angrily asked, "Are you the one? The one she's having an affair with?"

Dr. Thomas admitted that aside from being surprised, he was ready to go for the gun in his desk drawer. Instead, he asked Phil, "Why did you marry Connie?"

"I guess I loved her," Phil had replied.

After hearing this, I was even more certain that Phil and I had fallen in love with an image and thought that marriage would make us whole and complete, not realizing we had to be willing to take charge of our own healing and happiness.

Referring again to the shoplifting incident, I said, "I still can't believe it happened."

Dr. Thomas asked, "You can't believe you did it, or you can't believe you got caught?" I wasn't able to give him an immediate answer, but the question would linger for a long time.

Actually, I was glad it happened. It was an unconscious cry for help. It was true that when people don't feel acknowledged and appreciated, they look elsewhere for fulfillment.

Dr. Thomas startled me with his next question. "Why don't you leave your husband?"

I looked up and said, "It never occurred to me."

"Connie, please! We don't have time for games. You must be as frank as possible. You have continued to complain about your feelings of inadequacy, your feelings of loneliness and emptiness. But your perceptions of yourself appear to stem from your husband's comments, what he and others have caused you to believe about yourself."

Then he glanced at his watch. "Our time is up."

Leaving his office, I knew that until I recovered my self-respect, I had nothing to give to anyone.

During the final week of probation, I wondered if my marriage had been a mistake. Had I been in love with the promise of security, the promise of a perfect life rather than being in love with the man I married? Was the shoplifting incident a way of forcing me to give up my dream of living happily ever after?

Dr. Thomas summarized my challenge, "Connie, if what exists for you right now is more important than your future, your life is over. It's time you take responsibility for what has happened to you instead of complaining about it. If you are looking to others to solve your problems, you are only betraying yourself. Out of a devastating period, you *can* create a new life. You *can* recover your self-respect.

"Someday, we will all be called to testify to the crimes of others by the way in which we live our own life and learn from our own experiences. By finding creative solutions, we can potentially free ourselves and, ultimately, others."

16

A TIME TO WEEP

On my life's journey of adventure and challenges, my path had turned sharply in a surprising direction. Unaware of how an unconscious cry for help would influence the rest of my life, it was now clear that the extent to which I might fulfill my potential depended upon how I responded to these challenges. If I could muster enough courage to start writing about my experiences, as the counselor had encouraged, a new beginning seemed possible.

Initially, Phil encouraged the writing by bringing out a stack of Chris' medical records, which had been given to us by an Air Force doctor who was leaving his military career about the same time as Phil. The records included eight years of appointments with military doctors, the civilian pediatrician and neurologist, and correspondence with specialists across the country.

I was also surprised and thrilled to discover a large manila envelope stashed among my belongings. It contained references to scripture and philosophy, a record of a wide range of emotions, notes scribbled on church bulletins, airline tickets, cocktail napkins and other pieces of paper. The envelope also contained a spiral notebook with eight years of fragmented medical history and expressions of emotional chaos. It seemed uncanny that I had jotted down so much information without conscious thoughts of writing.

The task of sorting through the material seemed endless. The challenge of where and how to begin was daunting. After three months I had one typed page. Needing emotional and intellectual support, I called Joan, a friend and wife of another pilot living in the same area. I knew she would be an honest critic.

Seated in a brown leather chair next to the fireplace in our family room, Joan read the first page. When she finished, she looked up and smiled, then handed me the page, saying, "Well, you've started."

It was hardly the response I had hoped for.

After she left and I recovered from my disappointment, I decided if I forfeited a belief in myself and depended only on the approval of others, I might always resent their opinions, or even their efforts to help.

I didn't have any way of knowing what this project could look like. I only knew I had a compelling desire to organize the facts and put them on paper. I hoped that with long hours of scrawling on legal pads and sometimes falling asleep at the typewriter, my efforts would result in a worthwhile journal.

It wasn't long before I saw an ad for a *Beginning Writer's Class* offered through the adult education program at a nearby high school.

Weeks later, I sat in a classroom with a few women, a couple of men, and a short stocky instructor named Dr. Netrick. He introduced himself by saying he was proud to have earned a Ph.D. and proud to have grown up in the Bronx. In the beginning class he told us his philosophy was very simple. "You are never free unless you are following your passion. Learn to trust your inner voice and write as if the words are already inside of you, just waiting to come out. If you are willing to persevere with a sincere effort and hard work, anyone in this class can learn how to write first drafts, create characters, dialogue, and plot."

In his intermediate class, we were asked to write a story about a *triangle love affair*. My story began with a snowmobile accident in Colorado and concluded with a romance in the Swiss Alps, a story my instructor liked.

Months later, in the advanced class, I was thrilled to be given permission to work on my manuscript. Research on medical issues and details of personal struggles made my head spin, not to mention the necessity of learning the difference between a tearful catharsis and a piece of good writing. But if I could effectively document my experiences for my family, and help others, it would be worth it.

After the boys went to bed, our empty dining room provided the space and solitude I needed. With a Smith Corona typewriter on a small card table and my collection of haphazard notes, I began the task of organizing our first eight years with Chris.

To my surprise, when friends encouraged the idea of a book, Phil began to withdraw his support and ceased to have any conversations about the writing. He complained that my typewriter was keeping him awake in our second-floor bedroom.

The criticism and complaints didn't end there. At neighborhood parties, when I felt good about myself and was having a great time, he scolded me for holding my wine glass in a pretentious manner and talking way too much. Perhaps a wife who appeared to be coming out of her despair was somehow threatening. Perhaps even my writing was viewed as competition.

While I teetered on the brink of regaining confidence and achieving some individuality for myself, his ongoing attacks slowed my progress.

During the summer months, Thane and Mark went fishing with their dad, cooked over a campfire, and slept under the stars. Occasionally, I went along. We stayed overnight in our van, which was customized with a counter-top stove, a sink, a small refrigerator, and sleeping accommodations for two adults and children. When the boys returned to camp carrying fistfuls of wildflowers, I hugged them for their thoughtfulness and found a discarded can to put the flowers in for our picnic table.

With the onset of another winter, our family took to the slopes of Winter Park. It was a wild and crazy time when we taught the boys how to ski by taking turns coming down the mountain with each of them skiing between our legs. Later, after taking lessons with the Eskimo Ski Club, Thane and Mark became accomplished young skiers.

Phil and **Thane** with the "Catch of the Day"
at Taylor Lake, Colorado.

At home in our back yard, which happened to be the largest and flattest on Easter Circle, Phil frequently organized football games, baseball games, and soccer matches, and participated as one of the key players. It didn't matter what season it was, there always seemed to be activity outside our family room window. Nothing, however, compared to the adventure of bringing a baby lamb from my parents' ranch to a pen filled with straw that we had built behind our garage. One by one, the children on our circle discovered *Annie* and fell in love with her. It was a humorous dichotomy to see the neighborhood kids leading a lamb, with a twenty-foot rope, down our suburban block of beautifully manicured yards, then back home to feed her from the bottle and watch her graze in our back yard.

While I loved planning creative activities for my children, I craved something I could really sink my teeth into—a stimulus that went beyond my children. Phil, on the other hand, having achieved the status of a senior airline captain early in his career, and consumed by a second career of organizing games and outings with his sons, appeared to be enjoying an utterly fulfilling life.

I was, therefore, shocked when he suddenly asked, "Connie, what are we going to do now that Mark is in kindergarten?"

Swallowing in disbelief, I said, "I don't know what you're going to do, but I sure know what I'm going to do."

"We could always have another child," he said.

Managing to maintain a sense of composure, I calmly replied, "I think I've made a contribution with three sons."

Internally, I raged at his inconsideration of my needs. How could he even think about another child after all I'd been through?

It seems that the decision to have a baby is rarely a rational or logical one, but feeling as if I might never be free to pursue personal interests beyond my children, I wanted a more permanent form of birth control. Phil wasn't keen on the idea of a vasectomy, so we agreed to consult a gynecologist for other choices.

Mark, Connie, Thane, and **Phil**
with their pet lamb "Annie."

The following week, sitting in the doctor's office, Phil and I were questioned as if preparing for a court hearing.

"Phil, if something happened to Connie, would you like to have more children?"

"Yes."

"Connie, if something happened to Phil, would you have more children?"

"No."

"The best solution, then, is a laparoscopy for Connie. It's a relatively simple procedure that is done through the navel and cauterizes the Fallopian tubes."

Before I knew it, the day of the surgery had arrived. Feeling groggy from a sleepless night, I stepped into a pair of sweat pants and pulled a long-sleeved shirt over my head. En route to the hospital, I endured a sickening silence. Even while knowing that another child would tax my emotional resources in an unhealthy way, the biological pull was strong. There was no doubt that a woman's experience of pregnancy, labor, and delivery was empowering. It was also true that when a baby is brought into the world to fill the unmet needs of an adult, a child can feel the burden of parents' unspoken expectations.

Nearing the doctor's office, I wondered what Phil might be thinking, perhaps how he was going to adjust his life without the possibility of another child.

Hours after the surgery, I remember thinking my child-bearing days were over. While recuperating at home, I was satisfied in knowing that the life of each of my children had been a conscious creative act. Even in the womb, they were a source of inspiration and inner strength.

As a well-educated and capable woman of the seventies, I had intended to stay at home and be a full-time parent. However, when Chris left home and my heart was so broken I thought it would never heal, I determined never to depend exclusively on my children, or any one person, for happiness.

My decision, however, was contrary to the customs of the times. During that period, most women thought they had no choice except to rely on the image of the wonderful man they had married and depend on him for their happiness. I was beginning to see, however, that a woman who stood completely in the shadow of her man, might also lose sight of where she is going.

Thumbing through *The Denver Post* early one morning, I stumbled onto an intriguing ad. All I had to do was fill out the questionnaire connected with the ad, return the questionnaire, and receive one free hour of interior design consultation.

Having completed Architectural Studies at UCLA, and proud of the final project for which I received high marks, I jumped at the chance to get an objective evaluation from a professional.

A week later, a designer by the name of Sarah Porter arrived at the front door of my home. When she began scrutinizing three of the nearly finished rooms, I swallowed hard. My muscles tightened. While I waited for her evaluation, I realized how much I really wanted her approval.

She graciously proposed some minor changes and complimented my efforts, saying, "Connie, you have a very nice way of putting things together."

"Thank you," I proudly answered.

As I watched her drive away, I admired this woman who appeared to be self-sufficient without a desperate need for power. Most important, she had used the strength of her feminine intuition to accomplish what she wanted in life.

Sarah reflected qualities I desired in myself, if only I could break out of the prison of self-doubt. Perhaps I had convinced myself that I had no talent, or simply believed it was impossible to move beyond the conventions of domestic bliss.

As the days went by, I could only imagine what it would be like to be passionately submerged in a new activity.

Then one day, Sarah Porter's BMW edged to a stop in front of my house. On this unexpected visit, I was certain she had come to show me items I couldn't afford.

Barely inside the front door, she said, "Connie, you are very talented. I would love to have you work in my design studio."

"Sarah, I can't go to work. I have two children, one in kindergarten and another in third grade."

"Well, it would be great if you could work at the studio even a few hours a week. You can create your own schedule."

Her recognition and acknowledgment of my talent meant more to me than anyone could possibly understand. She not only admired what she saw, but was willing to capitalize on it.

Perhaps I just needed to take myself seriously, like my neighbor Mary Ellen. Even though I envied her going to graduate school and writing a thesis for a master's degree, I couldn't imagine that I was capable of doing anything like that.

Soon thereafter, I learned she had not only graduated with a Master of Arts degree, but she planned to divorce. Perhaps her ambition was fueled by something more than her intellect. Maybe it was a realization that she no longer needed to earn love from a husband who left her feeling empty-handed. Her separation was indicative of the changing times, and was recognition that a woman could be more than a wife and a mother.

A year later, another neighbor who appeared to have created a workable balance between managing a family of four and writing children's stories, also separated from her husband, and divorced after ten years of marriage.

Despite the changing times, I continued in the tradition of seeking validation through domestic accomplishments. It was easy to think that delicious smells emanating from my kitchen, my ability to create a farmer's breakfast, a hearty lunch, and a three-course dinner would translate into affection and appreciation. Part of the problem was thinking that I had to create a fabulous presentation instead of enjoying the pleasures of family interaction.

Later, I questioned my motives for the elaborate surprise birthday dinner I had painstakingly prepared for my husband and thirty guests, and the notes and cookies I often put in his suitcase. I wondered if these things were being done out of love and spontaneous affection, or did they represent duty and compensation for the emotional void?

The role of women was in the process of change long before women's liberation finally had a name. And even though I hadn't been taught to be independent, the awareness of women's rights in the seventies caused me to wonder if my lack of confidence could be cured, and the relationship with my husband brought back to life, through some of the new philosophy. Realistically, working outside the home would threaten our traditional male-female roles and would complicate the issue of control. But the lure of a job opportunity made me feel more confident and less concerned about my sexual appeal and other traditional gauges of my self worth.

Even though I was fearful about speaking out, knowing it could lead to another fight, I had to risk the backlash. "Phil, I have an opportunity to work with a woman in her interior design studio. She's seen the work I've done here and asked if it would be possible for me to work a few hours a week."

"Well, how do you think you would manage?" Phil asked.

"I'm not sure."

It seemed like months before Phil finally came around. "Connie, if you can be here when the boys get home from school by three, have dinner on the table by six, and don't need any help with the house, it's okay for you to work outside the home."

A position as an interior designer was like the first brushstroke on a blank canvas. The intuitive spontaneous energy from other designers felt like the soul of the world knocking at my heart. I didn't aspire to be a great designer; I merely wanted a chance to express myself.

One day while working at the studio, I overheard another designer. "I'm so lucky to have a husband that supports me in whatever makes me happy."

Another woman answered, "Yes, and I used to wonder why women didn't get what they wanted. But it's simple. You get what you expect. It has to do with how you feel about yourself. When a woman feels burdened enough in a relationship, she'll give it up."

I left the studio that evening with a cramping sensation in my stomach. Arriving home later than usual, I pulled into the garage and imagined Phil and the boys having fun after school, and then later, having dinner together.

Coming in through the back door, I walked into the kitchen where my three handsome guys sat at the counter joshing one another. Aside from the eye-opening comments I overheard at work, I was still reeling from the thrill of a productive day, and couldn't remember when I had been so happy and excited to come home to my family.

Suddenly, without warning, Phil lashed out. "Well, Connie, it must be nice to be gone from eight o'clock in the morning until eight o'clock at night!"

My energy dropped. Thoughts sizzled with rage. It was rare that I was gone from home for more than a few hours. *Why couldn't he understand the importance of my doing something creative in addition to parenting and housekeeping?* I wasn't asking to turn my children over to a babysitter or even a daycare center. Neither did I want to compete with my husband in a full-time career. I simply needed to feel like a winner again.

Shortly thereafter, I watched him prepare for a raft trip down the Colorado River through the Grand Canyon. Proudly organizing his gear and excited about his new camera, he announced the trip was exclusively for men.

"When am I going to have a vacation?" I asked, feeling that I deserved equal benefits.

"You don't need a vacation," he sternly replied.

Once again, I acquiesced.

Two weeks later, he returned from his exclusive male adventure looking calm and relaxed, yet invigorated by his white-water experience. When he excitedly began talking about his conversations with women writers and photographers who were part of a *National Geographic Project*, I stuffed my angry thoughts.

In the days that followed, I took care of family duties with an attitude of indifference. I acted with a seemingly blind devotion, without a desire to continue being someone's wife.

My heart was heavy when I scheduled an appointment with my minister. Feeling disillusioned over the vows *to love and to cherish, till death do us part,* I trusted that the Reverend Fred Venable could put them in perspective.

Sitting in his office, he said, "Connie, the vows are part of the dream that two people can make it for a lifetime. Granted, not all dreams come true."

After I told him about the problems in our marriage, he said our situation would require more time than he could give. My thoughts raced as he thumbed through his file to find a phone number for another professional. The idea of long-term intervention was alarming.

Later in the week, I told Phil I had visited our minister and talked about our marriage, and that he agreed there was a need for counseling. He also said our situation would require more time than he could give. Phil seemed surprised, but agreed to meet with the professional counselors Fred had recommended.

Over the next few months, we met once a week with a man and woman team who patiently listened to our selfish needs and our mutual feelings of abandonment. Sadly, however, our professionals lacked the skills to effectively alter our attitudes or patterns of behavior. As a last resort, they suggested we spend more time together. Phil and I agreed to make dinner reservations at a restaurant called The Dock.

On that particular evening, Phil drove his car from the airport immediately after his flight, while I drove the van from home. I allowed plenty of time to reach the restaurant, which was located off the Yale Exit. Somehow I missed the exit and went to the Evans Exit, which meant I had to go back to Yale.

Arriving at the restaurant almost fifteen minutes late, I pulled into the parking lot and found a space close to the entrance. After locking the van, I started toward the front door and noticed three men walking ahead of me. Since we arrived at the entrance at the same time, one of them held the door and we walked in together.

Standing inside the doorway, allowing time to adjust to the darkness, one gentleman asked, "Are you meeting someone?"

"I guess my date isn't here yet," I said.

"Well, if he doesn't show, you're welcome to join us. We'll be in the back room."

We all laughed, as if it might happen.

After they walked away, Phil came forward from the lounge. He must have been watching, but made no mention of the other guys.

Sitting at the bar and nervously stirring my rum and tonic, I hoped he would tell me how great I looked. He didn't. But then, I failed to boost his ego as well.

After we were ushered into the dining room, my anticipation of a romantic evening of wine and prime rib faded. Our polite conversation reflected the obligations of a long-expired contract rather than an intimate exchange. Sadly, we had not learned to communicate in a way that contributed to a potentially strong and fulfilling relationship. After fourteen years of marriage we had *grown apart,* which, in retrospect, was a condition caused by an accumulation of harmful acts against each other, and even ourselves. The result was a mutual desire to seek relief, and ultimately, a new beginning.

During our months of counseling, the professionals had not been able to help us confess our harmful behaviors, a confession that would have relieved our guilt and eased the tension. Without that, our dinner at The Dock was an exercise in futility.

After dinner, Phil suggested that he take the van home and I drive the car. We arrived at the house about the same time, and while we were standing in the kitchen together, he angrily threw a business card on the counter next to me.

"Connie, here's the phone number your boyfriend left on the windshield of the van," he shouted.

"What!?"

"Yes, this is a card from your friend Don at the Safari Motel on Evans. I guess that explains why you were late, why you missed the Yale Exit and had to go to Evans before arriving at the restaurant."

Staring at the business card in front of me, I saw a handwritten note with a phone number that read, "Call Don at..."

"Phil, I don't even know this man. Neither do I know anything about the Safari Motel on Evans."

The incident not only added to the tension of our relationship, but it became another notch on Phil's tally of my wrong doings. Certainly it fueled his lack of trust. After that, he insisted I leave a phone number so he could confirm my evening design appointments.

Nearly a month later, while driving into the city on the freeway, I still wondered how a total stranger could leave a number on my windshield and expect me to call. As conflicting emotions gnawed on my psyche, I was distracted from the traffic in front of me.

Suddenly, I realized the cars directly ahead were slowing to thirty-miles-per-hour and merging into a single lane. Since I was going fifty-miles-per-hour, I couldn't possibly slow down soon enough. Somehow I had to avoid hitting the car ahead of me. Quickly wrenching the steering wheel as far to the left as I could, I almost cleared that car. But when my right front bumper caught his left rear bumper, the car in front of me was forced into the vehicle ahead of him, which back-flipped into the air and landed upside down on the roof of my car.

The impact threw me onto the floor of the passenger side of my car. But even with the roof bashed in and splintered glass in my mouth and my shirt, as well as through my hair, I escaped with only a drop of blood on my forehead.

As a screaming siren approached the scene, passengers and drivers from the other cars slowly emerged—thankfully uninjured. I uttered whispers of relief.

A policeman walked up to my car. "Ma'am, it's a good thing you hit the car in front of you. Nothing else could have prevented you from becoming a victim of a fatal head-on collision as you crossed the median into oncoming traffic. You are extremely lucky. Now that you've survived, you need to call someone and have your car towed. Is there somewhere I can take you?"

"I work at a design studio just a few blocks away."

"Good. I'll drive you there."

When Sarah saw me coming into the studio accompanied by a patrolman, she looked puzzled.

"Sarah, I've just had an accident."

"You look like you could use a drink," she said, motioning for me to follow her.

After thanking the patrolman, I joined Sarah in the back room. As I sat with a cigarette in one hand and a glass of straight bourbon in the other, I was unable to even think about Phil's reaction. He was out of town now, but when he came home, I couldn't escape giving him the harsh news.

Sitting at home for nearly a week and without a car, I faced the fact that I had married for security and had lived with a man who was emotionally unavailable. From the books I had read, I had learned that my own fear of being unlovable and unworthy had unconsciously drawn me to someone who could not reciprocate love. The situation had become more intolerable as my own deteriorating self-worth kept me entangled with inappropriate and damaging behaviors.

While sitting on the sofa in our upstairs study, I was finally able to admit the seriousness of the accident. I said to myself, *Look, young lady, if you don't get it together, you're not going to be around much longer.*

Our next counseling appointment was scheduled for later that week. While Phil planned to drive our van directly from the airport after his flight, I had to borrow a neighbor's car. At this time, Phil didn't know about my accident, and I dreaded the confrontation.

At the counselor's office Phil and I sat side by side, facing our two therapists. One of them said, "Connie, you look like you've had a long week."

"Yes."

"Would you like to tell us about it?"

"Well, I totaled the family car this week."

"You did what?" Phil exclaimed.

"I totaled the car. It's been towed to the junk yard."

After a long pause he turned to me. "Are you all right?"

"Yes." After that my body felt surprisingly numb, my mind calm. In that moment I realized how feelings could change, viewpoints can fluctuate, and bodies can feel different, all in the space of a few seconds. Suddenly I was more willing to let go of my fantasy of security and get to the bottom of the false perceptions and a crumbling sense of self. Perhaps the accident had served as a turning point.

Later in the day, we joined forces as a family to view the wreckage at the junk yard. Phil and the boys curiously, yet humorously, inspected the mangled vehicle. Everyone agreed it was a miracle I survived without injury.

After that sobering experience, I surprisingly realized a greater affinity for my husband, as if the incident had actually happened to bring about a change. It was inevitable, however, that we would disagree over a new car. Even though he wanted a station wagon that reflected a family image, he finally agreed to my choice of a more sporty-looking model.

After allowing time for the trauma of the accident to fade, our counselors suggested an extended vacation, which they hoped would encourage us to pursue the more positive aspects of our relationship.

I loved the idea of an African safari, but Phil's choice was Hong Kong. At this point, I cheerfully agreed to any kind of vacation.

Weeks later, we boarded a flight on Continental Air Micronesia that would take us from Hawaii to Guam, and then to Hong Kong. On our flight to Hong Kong, Phil noticed a handsome Japanese couple sitting across the aisle with a glow of excitement and enviable affection. When the flight attendant told us they were on their honeymoon, Phil laughed. "Looking at those kids makes our fourteen years of marriage seem like a long time."

I said, "It's not so long when you think of being married for fifty years. But with the problems we've had in fourteen years, I don't know whether we'll make it to our fiftieth wedding anniversary."

"I don't either," Phil answered.

When our plane banked sharply over the water for landing in Hong Kong, I wondered whether the influence of Chinese silks, exotic perfumes, and jade could provide the impetus for us to repair our broken relationship and make a fresh start.

The evening was late when we checked into our hotel, but the idea of a new beginning in this romantic setting was enticing. Standing in the bathroom after a quick shower, I felt unusually sensuous as I massaged my body with oil and perfume. While preparing to model a new black negligee, I heard my husband's voice coming from the darkened bedroom. "I hope you're planning to come to bed soon because I need some sex."

My body went numb. The reflection in the mirror was the image of a woman who appeared not to have any real value, not even as a wife. My husband and I had vowed to remain together *till death do us part*. But did either of us still care? Legally, we were still married, but had we drifted too far apart to reconcile the life that was lost in living?

After years of obligation, I had determined one thing: For a man to get a woman into bed for a true sexual experience, the decision had to be hers. On this night, instead of obediently going to bed, I should have pranced out of the room and down the hallway, wearing the new black negligee that I was later accused of purchasing for my boyfriend.

As I fell asleep that night, the chill of the air coming across the water and through the open window reminded me of the coldness of our sex life.

Later that week, as we walked along the streets of Hong Kong, Phil made several references to the way Chinese women take care of their men.

"See the way the woman follows after him?"

I ignored his comments.

He persisted, "That makes you angry, doesn't it?"

"It makes me angry that you have to keep bringing it up. Is chivalry dead?"

"Yes," he said.

At a street-side cafe, Phil continued the conversation about marriage. "A man likes to buy things for his wife. He wants her to look nice, especially if he feels she really likes *him* rather than the things he provides. A man willingly puts up with a lot if his wife treats him like a king. Many times I feel you don't appreciate me. That's when I cut down on your spending allowance."

"Do you ever think there might be someone else with whom you could better relate?" I asked.

"Oh, sometimes. But then, I figure she'd have worse faults than yours."

As I wandered among the shops that brimmed with temptation, and strolled through open markets stocked with fresh fish and exotic produce, I wondered how long we would find fault with one another, allowing our negative thoughts to dominate our relationship. Would we ever be able to laugh about our differences and honor the uniqueness in each other?

That evening, over chopsticks and Peking duck, I was shocked at the straightforward manner in which Phil brought up the subject of divorce.

"Connie, we ought to be able to settle out of court."

"How?" I jokingly asked.

"Well, what are your demands?"

I unthinkingly quipped, "The house, the furniture and $50,000. But none of that really matters. What's most important is the welfare of our children."

"I agree," Phil answered.

"How would you feel if I came home one day and told you I was leaving and taking the boys with me?" I asked.

"I'd tear you limb from limb."

"That wouldn't solve anything," I replied, wondering exactly what he meant.

"No, it wouldn't solve anything," Phil said. "But if that were to happen, I don't know whether I would ever recover."

Nothing more was said about divorce. As I strolled along the streets of Hong Kong, I realized again that both of us had married an image, a person we thought would fulfill our expectations, someone to whom we could say it all without having to say anything. But clueless about communication skills, we clung to the conventional idea that faith, hope, and love would sustain us.

Nearing the end of our stay in Hong Kong, we purchased tickets for the London Philharmonic, hoping to find mutual pleasure in hearing some of the world's greatest musicians. Sadly, during intermission, we hardly had anything to say.

Returning home, I couldn't help wondering if our suburban way of life, tightly wrapped in security, was any different than a culture of twenty thousand people who had resigned themselves to living on one acre in Hong Kong.

However lonely and detached Phil and I might have felt, the most insulting part of our marriage was the subject of sex. It seemed too laden with guilt to deserve an honest discussion—or at least nothing more than Phil's accusations. To make matters worse, Phil's doctors had recently warned him of early signs of a heart attack or stroke. Fearful of losing his job as a pilot, he blamed me for his condition. "Connie, if I have a heart attack, it's your fault."

Attempting to avoid a confrontation, I tried to convince myself that I was not responsible for his physical or emotional condition. While he was on another trip, I lay awake in bed with muffled tears, knowing my feelings would be the same when he returned. I was beginning to come to the conclusion that if all I wanted was the kind of security offered by a marriage that valued a man's experience more than a woman's, I would have to be willing to sacrifice my own well-being. Did I really want to do this?

I began to understand how women might use an adulterous affair to cope with an unhappy marriage, but I also knew that a relationship outside my marriage would only serve as a substitute for healing the real issues. However, while searching for friendship and acceptance, perhaps even love, I was vulnerable to anyone who demonstrated compassion or support—a young good-looking guy at a car dealership, the polite manners of a stranger who offered to help me load carpet samples into my car, even a well-meaning friend who suggested my marriage was a dead-end street.

Phil later surprised me by announcing that he was going to see Dr. Lamott, a well-known therapist at the Marriage Enrichment Center. Thinking that he wanted to move in a new direction, I agreed to join him.

The following week, in my first session with Dr. Lamott, I learned the truth of Phil's visit. He had come to ask Dr. Lamott to prepare him for a divorce, a divorce he said he didn't want, but felt was inevitable. In that visit, Phil also detailed my character and bad behaviors.

"If she's as bad as you say she is, why don't *you* want the divorce?" Dr. Lamott had asked, without getting an answer.

A week later, Phil and I went for a joint session. Attempting to get at the root of our differences, Dr. Lamott asked specific questions. "If there were an ideal person for you, what would they say? How would they act?

Phil's ideal person was someone who would look up to him, give him recognition, and show him affection. There was no mention of someone strong enough to take responsibility for her own happiness.

My ideal person wasn't so different, except he would be able to acknowledge a job well done rather than kill my spirit with degrading remarks. Most of all, my ideal man would inspire me to become a better person, and a woman who was not afraid to be herself.

Dr. Lamott then asked a second question. "What in each of you would enable the other person to want to be all those things?" Phil's only comment was, "I would be able to respond." No mention of his own traits that could contribute to making our marriage better.

I silently gasped. *Respond to what? Everything I initiate? What about YOUR ability to start the ball rolling and assume part of the load?* As these thoughts echoed in my mind I couldn't find the words with which to make a rebuttal, so I remained silent.

Suddenly, it all looked hopeless. Painful memories from

the past came screaming into the present—the hideous negligence that resulted in a brain-injured child, irreversible damage to my body, problems with our second child, and the emotional abuse of an insensitive spouse.

The painful aftermath of that session with Dr. Lamott erased any degree of compassion I felt for my husband, and totally diminished my desire to find a solution.

Driving home alone, I felt there was no way to turn the clock back. Shouldering a mounting sense of failed purpose and a desperate need for support, I called my friend Joan. Coincidentally, Phil and I had recently helped her move out of her home after her pilot-husband surprised her with divorce papers and a new love.

When she arrived at the house, we chatted about children's activities, her new residence, and the challenge of starting law school, something she had always dreamed about. Still fragile from her divorce, she told me a story about a man with a professional career who had left his wife and two children for a woman of lesser status.

"How could he do it?" she asked. "He was a real nice guy." I thought to myself, *I know how he did it. He just didn't give a damn about what people thought. He had the courage to move past traditional views and risk the possibility of society's stigma.*

17
TORN BY TRADITION

As a woman brought up in the forties and fifties, I thought I would be a wife and mother and live happily ever after. Everything about my upbringing reinforced my expectations of being supported and protected by someone else until the day I died. But during the seventies, like thousands of other women, I began to uncover the lie in this premise.

It was during this time that feminists began to show us that, throughout history, marriage had been a form of slavery. For centuries men had organized their families, their homes, and all of their relationships to accommodate their authority. The women in these marriages too often sacrificed themselves for everyone else, receiving no support for their own needs. In the seventies, we were just beginning to realize that perhaps it was our ongoing desire for approval, our fear of being deserted, that made us so willing to sacrifice.

It would take time for me to apply this information to my own life, learning how to translate my dependency needs into a workable plan, for myself and my family. All I knew, right now, was that I was not getting what I needed in my marriage, or the fulfillment I craved in my life. For me, and for countless other women, all the traditional tokens of appreciation—the Mother's day flowers, the holiday dinners, the occasional trips to exotic places—didn't always compensate for the loneliness and insecurity we felt when we denied ourselves what we really wanted.

When I took the vows of marriage at the altar, I promised to *love, honor, and obey,* but I didn't promise to live in bondage with someone so desperate for comfort and reassurance that

I feared constant reprimand; I didn't promise to subjugate my own identity to become the self-denying partner. But, if I decided that it was impossible to honor the commitment *till death do us part,* every member of my family would suffer, as well as the successful image we portrayed.

In those dark moments when I no longer cared about being home or picking up my children at a neighbor's house, I fantasized about an accident. It would be easy in the mountains of Colorado. I could just disappear and leave no trace, wondering if my absence would make any difference.

My depression deepened when Phil's words replayed a thousand times a day. *"If you take these children, I'll tear you limb from limb."* I was terrified of his threats, still not knowing that his misdirected anger was simply a statement of his own fears and uncertainties.

All I needed was a road map, a way out of the trap of low self-worth that had been holding my life together, waiting for things to change, waiting for the last straw. Because of the conversations that had taken place in Hong Kong, Phil's inflexible views, and then our recent counseling session, it seemed inevitable that our marriage was doomed.

While attempting to sort out plans for my future, I was obsessed with thoughts of my children and their welfare, especially wanting them to have a feeling of a unified home. Even though parents who stayed together often represented only an illusion of teamwork, society still honored them for their longevity. There seemed to be no recognition of the negative consequences of two people living together with destructive communication, or the damage of unspoken hostility toward each other.

With extreme ambivalence about *my* future, and a dreadful fear of existing on my own, I further agonized over where I might live and how I would support myself. After looking at apartment complexes and seeing what was affordable, I shuddered at the thought of a tiny one-bedroom apartment with laundry facilities in the basement and loud music blaring from the hallways.

I was paralyzed by the thought of creating enough income to support myself, especially since my limited teaching experience (one semester of kindergarten in Kansas City and a few months of preschool in North Carolina) hardly provided the qualifications to get a teaching position. Besides, after fourteen years of marriage, my teaching certificate had expired. Minimal earnings from a part-time job as an interior designer would certainly not be enough to provide adequate support for my children, or even myself.

Perhaps with additional education, I could combine my knowledge about disability with a degree in Guidance and Counseling, or acquire the necessary credentials in the field of Social Work. With the idea of creating potential income, I applied to the University of Denver for acceptance into their graduate program and was told that the attainment of a Master's Degree would require an entrance exam.

Within a matter of days, and despite the fact that I had no work experience, or even recent intellectual stimulus, I bravely sat in the college auditorium surrounded by much younger students. The pressure of meeting the requirements for a well-known and respected school such as the University of Denver nearly overwhelmed me.

After two hours of a shockingly difficult exam, I walked outside to a cloudy day, and then drove home to wait for what I hoped would be my ticket to the outside world.

Weeks slithered by before I was notified the test scores were available. Driving toward the university to meet with a counselor, I felt sexy, independent, and powerful. As I hurried from the parking lot to the education building, my steps felt lighter. Even while wondering how long it might take to recuperate from a divorce and shattered illusions, I was proud that I had survived my past without alcohol, drugs, or extra-marital affairs.

Seated in the counselor's office, I anxiously waited as he scanned a list of names on the desk in front of him. Trusting that I could also survive the challenge of graduate school, I sat with anticipation. Finally, the counselor looked at me and said, "Connie, I'm sorry to report you did not pass the entrance exam. Unfortunately, that is a requirement for graduate school."

My heart sank. Visions of emancipation momentarily dimmed. Thoughts darted back to the idea of a life of servitude. But desperate to be admitted, I quickly recovered and said, "My college grades were good. Doesn't that count for something?"

The counselor agreed to have my transcript sent from Kansas State University to the University of Denver.

Meanwhile, waiting and hoping to be admitted to graduate school, I prepared for a possible move. I began to organize the house by cleaning every closet and drawer. I stocked the freezer with enough food for a month and thoroughly cleaned all the rooms. As I purchased new kitchen utensils, dishes, and some linens, and stashed them under the bed in our master bedroom, a surge of new energy moved through me.

The search for a new residence looked dismal until, quite unexpectedly, I discovered a lovely three-story building that was handsomely landscaped with large pine trees and a circle drive. Inside the foyer, mirrored walls reflected a graceful winding staircase. When I inquired about a one-bedroom apartment, the manager showed me a unit on the first floor, a poolside location with lush flowering plants and tall shade trees. From the sliding glass panels of the living room, the view was a picture of solitude. A canopy of blue skies dotted with white puffy clouds stretched beyond the pool to a country scene that included a barn and a few horses in the corral.

In this new environment, only fifteen minutes from where I now lived, I could finally achieve some independence. In this tranquil space, I could live without fear.

Driving home, I gained the strength to separate from long held family convictions and cultural beliefs. Naturally there would be a price to pay, as I would soon discover.

Meanwhile, I was still in suspense about my acceptance into graduate school. Finally, I received the phone call I'd been waiting for! The university had agreed to my enrollment, but with specific conditions. Due to the low scores on my entrance exam, I would be admitted as a special student, and would be required to maintain a B average.

After receiving news of my acceptance, I was thankful I has already scheduled another appointment with Dr. Lamott to further examine the possibilities of a resolution with Phil, or the consequences of a separation. While waiting in the reception area, I thumbed through one of the professional magazines and discovered an article about women who felt persecuted, unloved, and unfulfilled as a result of a harsh, authoritative culture. One example was a woman whose father was a domineering patriarch who ruled with unquestioned authority and total financial control. Another father was emotionally absent. In both cases these women had chosen husbands very much like their father, then later tried to gain control by blindly sacrificing their own identity. Ultimately, feeling overburdened by excessive responsibility and recurring thoughts of incompetence, their behaviors were often irrational with threats of suicide and feelings of rage directed toward themselves, their children, or their husbands. The article concluded by stating that when these women began to take responsibility, and focused their creative energies in a new direction, they also left their marriages.

Shocked by the similarity of the woman in the article and my own situation, I barely heard Dr. Lamott's hello.

Once again, in the privacy of his office, our conversation settled on the subject of custody. Just recently Phil's jarring threats were, *"Connie, you can choose divorce if you want, but you cannot and will not take these children from me. I will fight you in court for custody."*

I didn't know much about court except that it was a place where lawyers intend to win, a place where questions in a deposition are designed to obtain damaging facts about the other party which could be read back in trial. I was certain

Phil would use the shoplifting incident and the car accident to challenge my fitness as the custodial parent. Our marraiage counselor had not even addressed the idea of joint custody, and in a legal system where parents become enemies and the truth is impossible, I feared the judgment a court might make.

In most divorce settlements, the mother was considered the custodial parent and was typically granted alimony and child support. In our case, however, a custody dispute could result in a confusing, frightening experience for our children and a financial cost that could be equivalent to their college education.

As this concern was uppermost in my thoughts, Dr. Lamott returned to the sensitive issue of custody. "Connie, after fourteen years of giving everything to your family, what about going to graduate school to do something for yourself, something you badly need and deserve? Do you not think Phil would be a good father? Do you not feel that he is capable of providing stability for the boys?"

I answered, "Yes, Phil is a good father."

In an earlier conversation, Dr. Lamott had urged me to consider the security that our suburban neighborhood could provide, such as outstanding recreational programs, a progressive school system, and open backyards with close friends and playmates. The alternative was for me to assume responsibility for two active boys, while facing the challenge of graduate school, creating a career, and coping with the inevitable financial struggle.

But when I tried to imagine Thane and Mark returning each day to a home without their mother, and sleeping in their newly decorated bedrooms, I could hardly contain my emotions. Who would make their meals, take them to school, contact their teachers, wash their clothes, and help with their homework? In our culture, a conscientious mother, motivated by compassion and love, typically plays the primary role of loving, nurturing, and training her children for adulthood. In fact, the role of rearing children may be the most important job in the world. Unfortunately, it's not something you can put on a resume.

The session with Dr. Lamott ended on a note of ambivalence, prompting me to ask myself: *Am I entitled to leave the marriage for my own survival? Do I have a right to take the boys away from their neighborhood and their father? But if I had custody, what could I give them? How would I pay the bills?*

Later that week, I consulted with a woman attorney regarding my rights. I was told that if I left the marriage and the boys stayed with their father, I could expect no financial support. She was convincing enough that I didn't seek additional counsel.

As time went on, my rage toward my husband grew. I knew revenge wasn't the answer, but like so many times in the past when I felt I couldn't do anything right, I wanted to scream at him, *If you think I'm doing such a lousy job, why don't you try it?*

In an attempt to gain more information and do the right thing for my children, I read a book titled *Beyond the Best Interests of the Child*, by Goldstein, Freud and Solnit. The authors dared to go beyond old formulas and advocated solutions they considered to be the least detrimental to the child's development. Because of a child's confused loyalty to parents who no longer loved each other, the authors suggested continuity of care by a primary parent. The custodial parent would have complete control of visitation rights and whatever else affected the child's happiness. Most important, the authors agreed custody should be given to the parent who could offer the most security, which ultimately meant the greatest degree of stability.

While Phil could most likely provide more stability, I felt I could provide a strong parent image, even as a part-time parent, and maintain a great relationship with my children. My greatest concern was preventing the boys, at the ages of six and ten, from having to choose between their parents. I couldn't be sure that Phil would share that concern.

One Sunday morning, as an overcast sky reflected my somber mood, I slipped into a pew in the balcony of the church that Phil and I had attended for several years. Encumbered by a sense of duty and obligation, I hoped the sermon would get me through another week.

As the pipe organ swelled and the soloist sang *Bridge Over Troubled Waters*, tears streamed down my cheeks, tears that had been locked inside for many years.

The minister's timely message was titled *The Little Tree.* The parable described a potted tree that was lovingly cared for inside a beautiful home, until he grew weary of being on display. When he began to look outside for new possibilities, he imagined himself growing into a magnificent oak tree. On the other hand, he feared he might become just a cluster of shrubs, known only for their thorny branches.

Just as soon as he was convinced that he was capable of growing into an oak tree, he saw the colored leaves on other oak trees wither and die with the change of seasons, their stately limbs broken by the ice storms. As much as he longed to create a new life, his dreams were tormented by uncertainty and conflicting images. Finally, terrified of what might happen if he were rooted outdoors, the little tree chose.

As members of the congregation filed past the minister, they insisted on knowing what the little tree decided to do. The minister responded by asking, "What do *you* think he chose?"

At home, even before finalizing our divorce and custody issues, I grieved for the loss of a complete family, and for the pleasures of marriage itself. Already I felt the dishonor, the humiliation, and the uneasiness of not belonging to someone. One thing was certain: there would be no trumpets to herald the shameful decision of relinquishing custody of three children.

A short time later, in a joint session, Phil and I joined Dr. Lamott in his office to mediate a settlement. Again, without discussing the possibility of joint custody, it was decided Phil would have primary custody as well as the right to make all major decisions regarding their upbringing. He would be the sole financial provider and the primary emotional support for Chris, Thane, and Mark. Even as I agreed to the arrangements, I questioned inwardly how the boys could receive adequate emotional support when I had experienced the lack for so long. My visitation rights included every other weekend, most school vacations, and a month in the summer, although our days together would be limited because of my having to work full time.

After decisions were finalized and documented, I started to leave the room. Phil stood and faced me, as if to provoke a final confrontation. "Connie, you have deprived us of so much. You have deprived us of a mother, a housekeeper, and a cook." His perception of me as a family servant was chilling and revealing, causing another wound that might never heal.

With astonishing composure, I said, "That's interesting you didn't mention wife...friend...or lover."

A stunned silence followed me toward the door.

Outside, I felt a warm breeze. What almost happened to me must surely happen to other women. Out of fear and guilt, we stay in a place of insanity rather than inspiration. I wondered how a society wallowing in wealth could continue to victimize women. But sadly, when a woman *is* victimized, it's easy for her to think she deserves it.

On so many occasions, I had resisted seeing what was going on. My husband had continued to foster and reinforce the idea that my unhappiness was caused by a flaw in my character. When I finally recognized the damaging impact of this man's emotional needs, and realized it wouldn't allow for a solution that would meet both of our needs, I knew I had to leave. Somehow I had to recover from the collapse of ambition, doubts of sexual desirability, and failing sense of self-worth that had been enhanced by this relationship.

When Phil and I returned to the house, we agreed I would be the one to break the news. Mark was playing outside with his friends. Thane was upstairs in his bedroom.

Walking into his room to relay the news, I quietly began, "Thane, your dad and I have been trying to become better friends and we're still working on that. Right now I'm going to live in an apartment close by. You and Mark will live here with your dad."

Even as I said the words, I couldn't remember hurting anyone like this. Standing in the shadow of truth, I prayed that someday my ten-year-old son would understand.

"Can I go out and play now?" Thane asked, as he seemed to be fighting tears.

In the remaining silence, I wished things could be different, fulfilling all the hopes and aspirations of a loving family. Surprisingly, I felt compassion for my husband, respecting his right to have more children if he wanted, and to enjoy a relationship that would validate him in the way he needed. Even so, my heart was breaking.

18
THE LIES THAT BIND

Over the years I had listened to well-intentioned authority figures such as parents, teachers, ministers, and friends, who had influenced me in so many ways. Naturally they wanted me to be happy and conform to acceptable behavior. Now faced with the breakup of my marriage, I feared that none of them would comprehend my actions or reasons, let alone encourage me to follow a path that felt right to me.

The first reply to news of our separation was a letter from my mother-in-law, written while on vacation in the Caribbean. Her response, and others, would be the test of my strength against the disapproval from friends and family.

Dear Connie,

Words completely fail to express my feelings about this complex situation. I trust and pray daily all the problems can be worked out or accepted, that a change of habits, attitudes and feelings can prevail. It is difficult, and nearly impossible, for me to write this. I want you to know we still love you dearly and trust that two intelligent people will arrive at a workable agreement.

Just remember that no marriage escapes some heartbreak and pitfalls. Communication and faith in each other are the two factors of a successful marriage. Walk together and talk together. Only then will there be peace.

Much love,
Lillie

I was appreciative of her letter and the very special relationship we had always enjoyed. She was undoubtedly the best mother-in-law and loving grandmother. Phil, on the other hand, issued another brow beating remark.

One day while I was working in the kitchen preparing for my upcoming move, he dropped it like a bomb. "Connie, if I had known our marriage was going to turn out like this, I would have had more fun on trips."

I retorted, "What you do on trips is between you and God. And if you didn't have enough fun while you were gone, it's your own fault."

Weeks later, as I piled clothes and a few items of furniture into our empty dining room, I was surprised by another bombshell. "Connie, you can go to graduate school. You can work outside the home. You can do anything you want and still live in this house."

His words were seductive, and momentarily convincing, but sounded more like an attempt to avoid abandonment.

I don't recall where Thane and Mark were on the day the moving van arrived. Regardless, I knew they wouldn't understand how necessary it was for me to save myself and begin to weave the broken threads of my life together and, at the same time, consider their security.

As I backed out of the driveway in the sporty car Phil had agreed to purchase, highlights of the last few years flashed before me. The exterior of the house had been painted with a more dramatic color scheme, and our front yard had a large, newly planted pinon pine. I had designed a handsome deck for our back yard, and Phil had constructed it, even though later, he angrily accused me of having all the talent in the family.

Aside from leaving a beautiful home and backyard friendships, I was giving up the security of a senior airline captain's income. Unknown to others, I had already lost something far more valuable — trust, appreciation, and self-worth. It would be up to me to reclaim those things.

Naturally, there would be speculation among the neighbors about an affair. Since I was leaving, I was the one accused of having an affair. In weeks to come, and the gossip swirled, I would be reminded of Phil's false accusations about my infidelity. I would also be reminded of how incredibly painful it was to live as a target of his complaints, a victim of accusations, and generalizations of wrongdoings. Whenever I had doubt about the wisdom of my decision to leave, I would reflect on times when my husband frequently resorted to anger or jealousy if I wasn't available when he needed me, or times he used oppressive behavior to control the money. When I thought of how easy it was for women like me to trade their esteem and intellect for promises of enduring protection and love, I would reaffirm my decision to leave.

One day, soon after I had moved into my apartment, a friend from church unexpectedly showed up. Standing in the living room and looking out across the pool at the peaceful surroundings, she said, "Connie, do you know what you're doing? Do you know where you're going?"

It was impossible, and frankly unnecessary, to explain how I had ceased to exist as a compassionate and loving person, and needed a new agenda to lower the volume of discord in my life.

"No, I don't know where I'm going," I finally said. "But does it really matter?"

After she left, and I glimpsed another life that floated somewhere in the distance, I felt as if everyone would be waiting and watching my every move. To counter my self-doubts, I knew I would have to rely on my own resources, namely my intuition—a simple, but powerful, *knowingness* that I was headed in a positive direction.

On a Monday morning, I received a letter from another woman from my church, one whose friendship I enjoyed.

Dear Connie,
You have been in my thoughts and prayers lately. In our Sunday morning group, you had mentioned escalating marriage problems. There isn't any one solution to our

problems, except to know that we are often painfully, and sometimes slowly, led to the place we need to be. The hardest part is having the courage to change. You told me once about your students in the "Great Books" class at the high school, and how their parents thought you had it all together. It does seem like the case.

You may be going through some tough times, but I see that you have a steadfast desire to conquer your problems. Just know that when life ceases to be a challenge, we begin to die. But when we acknowledge God and ask him to guide our steps, he is always there. We only need to see ourselves as the capable spiritual being that we already are, and know that we are capable of doing anything we choose.

Peace and love,
Barbara

Now that I had been accepted into graduate school, I had to focus on getting through the next twelve months. Sitting down with a guidance counselor at the University of Denver, I designed my curriculum with courses from three fields of education: Guidance and Counseling, Education, and Social Work.

Soon after entering the academic world, I began to realize other benefits besides education. Occasionally sharing coffee with a couple of men my age, I was actually surprised I could enjoy warm and intellectual conversations without a fear of being criticized. In my classes, I met women who were also detached, women like myself who needed to discover who they were before they got involved with someone else.

It was hard to believe that at the age of thirty-four I was separated from my children and living alone for the first time. Without work experience or a great deal of intellectual stimulus during my fourteen years of marriage, it was nearly unthinkable that I was attempting to get through graduate school while trying to pay rent on a one-bedroom apartment.

In the school of social work, the curriculum included a

course called *Parents of Disabled Children*. We studied the grief process and how it affects the family. We looked at the painful process of dealing with unrealized expectations, as well as the inevitable theological questions that parents ask. It was interesting to learn that when parents are able to alternate between the role of a grief-stricken mourner and that of a supporter, the marriage had a better chance of survival. Studies indicated that when one partner refused to talk to the other and didn't seek professional help for the marriage, the chances of divorce were also greater.

Even though at times I felt qualified to teach the course, I sat in class many days consumed with anger, knowing that this important information could have helped my marriage. It wasn't until now that I fully understood how the debilitating emotions of anger and guilt that accompany a child's disability, and the collapse of mutual support, can add unbearable stress to a relationship, especially when the relationship is encumbered by other insecurities.

In other graduate classes, I studied the concept of freedom and how it related to the sociological changes of the seventies. Freedom of thought was an idea that was advocated by the philosophers Kierkegaard and Nietzsche. Some of my professors referred to them as true prophets because they predicted the *Age of Emptiness*, a time during which society would shift from a conventional belief in God and traditional religion to an increase in self-examination and pursuit of one's own knowledge.

During this time of loneliness and anxiety, the philosophers had predicted an increased awareness of spiritual freedom, and a more diminished role of authority models represented by priests and other patriarchal figures. Rigid rules would no longer define a person's reality and determine their values. It would be the end of a period where parents could responsibly condition a child through physical punishment while saying, "I'm doing this because I love you." Relationships between men and women would be defined by more equality. This period was an opportunity for people to make thoughtful choices about the way they wanted to live, while at the same time, re-examining their selfish desires and irregular behaviors.

As these new ideas intrigued me, I had a desire to explore other philosophies that had imprisoned the minds of our society. For the moment, extensive reading assignments and term papers obscured everything else in my life, but with the completion of each assignment, I became more confident of my capabilities. Knowing that I could take on new endeavors without buckling under the stress made me feel stronger.

To support my new independence, I needed to find a job. Unfortunately, the school of Guidance and Counseling at the University of Denver had neglected to tell me that to use my degree in education, I had to have six years of teaching experience. So, instead of a position as a guidance counselor in a school system, I took a position as a social worker at Hope Center for the Mentally Retarded. As case supervisor for sixty-seven families, my responsibility was to coordinate financial services and educational programs for the younger students and supervise vocational needs for the older students. I made home visits to parents who sometimes lacked money for food, but loved their children and were grateful for the services we provided.

Six months after I started my new job, I stood in the lobby of the county courthouse, where the barren interior reflected the stagnation of a marriage that was soon to be terminated. I had declined an offer from a friend to be with me during the hearing, but was grateful for her support. Unable to find the divorce courtroom and too embarrassed to ask directions, I was relieved to see Phil enter the courthouse. He looked handsome in a camel-colored sport coat, white shirt, and a paisley tie I had given him. Surprisingly, I felt affection for him. He stopped to say hello, and then with an attitude of friendship, we walked upstairs together as if we were headed to a business meeting.

In the courtroom on the second floor, we sat on a wooden bench next to each other and without attorneys. Seeing him without his wedding band reminded me of how frequently I had seen him without it. When I questioned him he quipped, "It's uncomfortable; it gets in the way of things."

Waiting for the judge to arrive, I could only speculate that the woman attorney I had previously consulted had not wanted to take the case because a simple uncontested divorce was not as lucrative as one involving an affluent husband accused of infidelity, or a massive property settlement. Presumably, she wasn't willing to fight for the principles of right and wrong, or my fourteen years of dogged responsibility. I wasn't emotionally prepared to roll up my sleeves and do battle, so I decided not to use the help of an attorney.

When the judge entered the courtroom, he called the court to order and asked us to take the oath, solemnly swearing to tell the truth and nothing but the truth.

The judge continued, "The parties in the above entitled action do hereby stipulate their marriage is irretrievably broken and there is no reasonable prospect they will reconcile their differences. Is that true?"

For a moment, I analyzed the statement I was about to swear as true. Irretrievably broken? Perhaps in the strictest sense, it was not. Was there reasonable prospect for reconciliation? Not right now, perhaps never.

Because of the no-fault law in the state of Colorado, which required no reason, or blame fixing for dissolution of a marriage, divorce may have been too easy. But we were like thousands of other couples whose marriage seemed destroyed beyond repair before we realized the need for help.

As per the divorce decree we both replied to the judge's questions, "Yes."

Phil turned to me and said, "Well, you finally got what you wanted."

In reality, what I got was a court-issued license to return to society without my children and without any means of support—no questions asked. On the surface, it appeared that two adults had settled equitably according to marital property law, and had worked out a fair and responsible solution for custody.

The truth is that months before, and without legal advice regarding pension benefits, work experience, or contribution of time and care to the family, I had agreed to a settlement of $10,000 to cover my tuition for graduate school. It was meager compensation for the last fourteen years of setting up and managing our nine residences, acting as a physical therapist, an elementary education teacher, a behavior-modification specialist, lawn maintenance crew, housekeeper and cook, family chauffeur, social secretary, and a time management expert—all without time off. The sum of $10,000 amounted to less than $800 a year, only $66 a month, or $16 a week—for dedication, and sometimes back-breaking responsibilities for a family of five.

Besides a few pieces of furniture, we agreed I would keep the car and receive equity of a few thousand dollars from the home in which we had lived less than three years. Our marriage counselor had insisted that I also leave a fund of $10,000 intact for the benefit of the children. It was the only savings we had, but with projected high-interest rates over the next twenty years, I would have the satisfaction of having generously contributed to my sons' college educations.

Although the division of assets may have been scrupulously equal to fifty percent of what we had (except for all of our savings), it was in no way equitable. After all, my husband's earning potential would continue to be his greatest asset. While I inherited a future of financial gloom, his security as a senior airline captain would allow him to marry again, build a home on a golf course, and travel to exotic places.

Nevertheless, the divorce was final. Even though the reality of economics hadn't fully registered, I had my freedom. And, at a huge sacrifice, I had provided what I thought was security for my children.

At ten o'clock that night, in a state of unreal exhilaration, I set the rhythm on my Kimball organ to a fast Dixieland beat and pressed the foot pedal to full volume. When I was nearly finished playing *The Saints Go Marching In*, I heard a loud knock on my door. Startled by the interruption, I opened the door.

"Connie, I have some complaints from neighbors in the building. Do you know what time it is?"

What could I say except, "I'm sorry."

It wasn't long before my friend Linda, whom I had first met at the suburban ice rink when Mark and I took lessons, agreed to meet for lunch in Cherry Creek.

Moments after I arrived at the restaurant, Linda, looking chic in her usual East Coast style, joined me in the lobby. Even before we were seated, she asked, "Connie, have you seen the Littleton newspaper?"

"No," I said, wondering why she asked.

"I think you might want to take a look at it. There's an article about Phil and the boys—and a great picture."

Jolted by the news, I didn't remember much of our conversation over lunch. Just a vague recollection of how mothers unquestioningly sacrifice for their families and receive little recognition for their contributions.

After Linda and I hugged each other goodbye, I drove to Littleton, plunked a quarter into the machine for the last copy of the *Littleton Independent* and sat down on a nearby bench. Quickly turning the pages, I suddenly stopped. Linda was right. It was a handsome picture taken in the mountains with a half page article that included some of the following excerpts:

Four years ago, it was not as common as it is today for a father to have custody of his children. But what sets this father apart is his determination that his sons not be left alone during the day while he works. In the beginning, Wright attempted to do the washing, cleaning, cooking, and housework while working two jobs. Even though the responsibility was overwhelming, he felt that hiring a housekeeper was a luxury. At the time of this writing, however, Wright has just gone through his fifth housekeeper. He sympathizes with single parents who can't afford to have someone in the home, especially single women who may have an income problem.

He does acknowledge that a housekeeper could never be a substitute mother for his sons whose own mother lives in Denver. He admits that maybe his sons are missing out on the motherly love and devotion found in a two-parent home, but nevertheless, wants them to feel a solid home environment. He stressed it was important to find someone who understands what a child needs: a gentle sense of discipline and loving warmth, someone with a happy family background, someone who is willing to be home to welcome his sons and listen to their joys and fears. He says home should be a place of relationships and family meals.

Wright does the grocery shopping and leaves notes for the housekeeper to remind her of any appointments for the boys. During the day, she does the housecleaning and starts dinner. When he returns home, he completes dinner. Thane and Mark clean up the kitchen after dinner and do their chores on Saturday, stripping their beds and handling the laundry.

I was angered by his new family values which now seemed to include communication, loving relationships, a well-qualified mother figure, and shared household duties. The most difficult part for me to accept was his willingness to whole-heartedly back the housekeeper, even though in my own conversations with them, I discovered that they too, considered him a task master.

The day after reading the article I went to see my minister. I asked if he thought it was appropriate for me to request equal time with the newspaper.

"Do you really need that?" he asked.

"No! I don't."

But I struggled with the need for revenge. My expectations of a shared family life had been shattered beyond anything I could have imagined. I had read that a loss of a spouse by desertion was more devastating than loss by a death. And even though I was the one who had left my husband, in reality, I had been emotionally deserted years ago.

I would relive the events of divorce a hundred times and endure the shame of my failure to hold a marriage together, even for the sake of my children.

Even though I was busy with graduate school, I was lonely; I missed hearing from friends. Before the divorce, I had organized the neighborhood kids for a Christmas caroling event and was elected president of the parent-teacher organization. Now, where was the support when I needed it? Where was my next-door neighbor, Betty, with whom I had shared so much, and my friend Joan, who gave encouragement to continue my writing? Was everyone just too busy to pick up the phone?

I knew it wasn't that easy for them. My divorce undoubtedly reminded them of issues in their own partnerships. Perhaps some of them felt they needed to side with Phil since he lived in the neighborhood. Perhaps others were still trying to make sense out of what had happened.

Several months after I moved into my apartment, I received crayon drawings from Mark. Every picture was a colorful two-story house with a chimney, a tree in front of the house, and a sidewalk that led to the front door. It was as if he wanted me to have a house, or was telling me to come home.

There were many hopeless moments when I felt I couldn't hold on. Some days I moved through life like a mere shadow, with a grave sense of unreality mixed with numbing feelings of uncertainty, anger, and grief. Even in the comfort of a new space, I was fearful of punishment. One night while sleeping, I dreamed I was running down a long hallway, looking for an escape through one of the openings. But each door closed in front of me and prevented escape. The sound of an airplane flying low over the apartment suddenly awakened me. For a moment I imagined it was my husband.

I wondered how long it would take to feel released from the injustice and begin to experience the freedom of a new life. To strengthen my intention that I was going to make it, I used the back of my door to display quotations from famous philosophers. Each one was neatly typed and mounted on

Mark's Crayon Drawings of Houses
Sent to his Mom - Age 7

black paper. Eileen Caddy, author of *God Spoke To Me*, wrote that we should not dwell on the past but use it to illustrate a point and move on. Shakti Gawain, author of *Creative Visualization*, stated that every moment of our life is infinitely creative and that the universe is an endless and abundant flow.

More than anything, I wanted to know I could create whatever I wanted. My deepest desire was to live as a confident, creative human being—without feeling compelled to live up to an image someone else had created for me. The idea was exciting, if only I could rid my mind of ambivalence and guilt.

Since I was living alone, going to graduate school, and struggling to pay my rent, my bare-bones existence necessitated that Thane and Mark bring their own money for a movie, or other entertainment when they came to visit. Mostly, we enjoyed simple pleasures. Sometimes we strolled down my quiet street past large elm trees to visit the horses in the corral. On other days we walked to the park and tossed breadcrumbs to the ducks, then spread our picnic lunch on a blanket. At night we sprawled on the floor of my living room to play games.

While my children were still young and vulnerable at the ages of eight and eleven (Mark just had his eighth birthday), I was determined to show them the love they needed. It would be difficult enough for them to ignore the gossip of peers, and cope with society's issues regarding divorced parents. I could only imagine how the harsh and unthinkingly cruel remarks by others could be hurtful and misleading.

One night, while driving them back home, Mark, sitting in the front seat next to me, spoke up saying, "I love DAD this much," spreading his arms wide. "And I love you THIS much, because you left," bringing his arms closer together. His words, expressed in his most honest and eloquent manner, penetrated like a knife. Somehow, I managed to stay calm.

"Mark, I'm glad you love Dad, because he really loves you. And guess what? I'm going to love you forever and ever because you are the most important thing in the world to me."

I could feel Thane listening from the back seat. Looking over my shoulder, I said, "You are both special to me."

After I parked in front of their house, I got out and hugged each of them goodnight. As they walked to their house and closed the front door behind them, tears I had forgotten how to cry ran down my cheeks. In previous months, I had been unable to cry in front of my sons, or even my husband, but now, I cried for all of them — for the failed expectations of a wonderful marriage, and for the times that could have been so cherished. I wept for love and for an understanding of God's purpose.

Inevitably, my sons would ask me why. Someday I would tell them all about it. They were too young now to understand how their parents' differing values, seeded in deep insecurities, gave a grim prognosis for maintaining a marriage. If only I had thought to write a simple and truthful statement in words they could understand.

That weekend, during one of the worst snowstorms I could remember, with the streets becoming more treacherous by the hour, my friend Joan knocked on my apartment door. What a thrill it was to see her! After a warm hug, she handed me an illustrated book of poetry written by Susan Polis Schutz, entitled *I Want to Laugh, I Want to Cry.* Only another woman who knew the pain of divorce could understand this gift of encouragement and love.

19

A LONG, LONG
WAY FROM HOME

The transition from my handsomely furnished two-story brick home in suburbia to a one-bedroom apartment was, for me, the epitome of emancipation. A brown leather chair, a brass and glass coffee table, and a theater-style organ added warm and dignified touches to an otherwise austere space. The patio table in the dining area wasn't exactly aesthetic, but it gave me a place to study. When I could afford them, my new living space would include a mattress and frame for a bed, a dresser for my clothes, and a proper desk for my typewriter.

Just to be able to pay my rent, I had taken a job as a hostess at a family restaurant called Crestwood. Occasionally, with barely enough earnings from the job, I stopped to buy fresh flowers before returning home to shut the door on the rest of the world, and collapse into my own quiet space. The French call it *"the private life, a rich, abundant and consciously cultivated private life."* I was grateful to the French.

During those moments alone, I often thought of Chris. Perhaps our lives were not so different after all. His needing to leave home to accommodate his needs and rights, and to become his own person, seemed a close parallel to my own needs. He, too, had been forced to expand his awareness and discover new, viable strengths.

When times were exceedingly tough, with another car accident or an excess of speeding tickets, which required going to court to get my license reinstated, I was tempted to give up the notion of independence and self-responsibility.

The idea of meeting another successful man could eliminate the necessity of having to explore my own life. The status and material achievements, which were often benefits of marriage, could also hinder a greater understanding of myself and replace the joy of hard-earned personal accomplishments. However, for most attractive and intelligent women like myself, marriage was still considered a worthwhile goal. Right now though, marriage wasn't an option.

The last three months of graduate school, with assignments in calculus and never-ending deadlines for term papers, were nearly impossible. The days and weeks without time to see the boys made it difficult for me to concentrate. I wondered how they were coping with their fears, their anger, and feelings of betrayal. If only they knew that in my most discouraging moments, they were my source of inspiration, an incentive for me to pull myself together and complete my homework.

A paper for Educational Sociology was three weeks late. I worried it would affect my status as a special student, which required that I maintain a B average. I had to get high grades on term papers to offset the lower grades in other classes.

Finally, one Sunday afternoon, slumped over piles of research accumulated weeks before, I started to organize my ideas. After shutting out interference from all other sources, I began to concentrate with every ounce of intention, as if my life depended on it. When I finished typing late that evening, I couldn't imagine anything that could give me the same gratification as the completion of this paper titled:

Contrasting Existentialism with the Nature of Human Society
As Seen By
George Herbert Mead and Implications On Education

A week later, my instructor returned the paper and announced in front of the class that he would like a copy.

I said, "It can't be *my* paper."

"You are Connie Wright, are you not?"

"Yes."

As he handed the assignment back to me, he said, "You undertook a most sophisticated analysis. It's one of the best papers I've seen. I applaud your thoughtfulness and would like a copy for my files." He gave me a grade of A-plus!

Besides the grades and credentials I was striving for, I was also learning to express my own viewpoints through my writing—without catering to authority figures who told me how to view my own experiences.

A week later, I proudly turned in another paper titled:

WHERE IS THE LIFE THAT WAS LOST IN LIVING?
Sociological Aspects of Culture and Marriage:
The Construction of Reality in Relation to the Adjustment Process
Faced by Parents of Handicapped Children

My professor said, "Well done. You have developed a most thoughtful, sensitive, and insightful paper on the problems of parents of retarded children. You have written telling observations that make for provocative reading."

I was thrilled to receive another high mark of A-plus! Encouraged by my performance, especially during the hardship of living apart from my children, I felt as if I could make it to the end of the quarter. However, a month before final exams, the Department of Education told me I would be tested exclusively on material from the school of Guidance and Counseling when, in fact, my curriculum included courses from three different fields: Guidance and Counseling, Social Work, and Education.

Feeling a sense of panic, I began to study with other students and tried to memorize notes from courses I hadn't taken.

A few weeks later, those who were hoping to graduate gathered in a small room on campus for the written exam. Graduation would be determined by a score of Pass or Fail—based on four essays written within the four-hour period. After I turned in my exam, I left the room and tried to prepare for news that, as far as I was concerned, could be equated to failure.

Even though the intellectual exposure and a sense of

increased aliveness from the association with other students had provided a counterpoint to earlier feelings of emptiness, I needed something more. I needed my diploma!

Fourteen days later, when I was given a handsome leather-bound diploma from the University of Denver for a Master of Arts degree in education, I realized it was MY strength and MY persistence that had gotten me through the year—and I wanted MY name on that piece of paper.

The following morning I contacted an attorney to have my name changed back to my maiden name. I happily paid the university ten dollars to receive a new diploma with the name, *Constance Kay Morgan*.

Now that graduate school was over, my focus was to expand my role beyond that of being a mother, without feeling guilty. In the past, I had never given myself permission to be a fallible, imperfect human being. I never felt I could have good days and bad, or even a contrary opinion. For sure, no one told me I had to resolve certain painful issues in my own life before I had anything to give to any one else.

The tension that existed between my insecurities and my more charismatic nature looked as if it might take center stage for the rest of my life. The one thing I could count on to bolster my spirits was spending time with Thane and Mark at their house when Phil was out of town.

One Saturday morning, I walked in the back door and was surprised to see a three-layer chocolate cake sitting on the butcher block in the center of the kitchen. "That is some cake!" I exclaimed.

The proud expressions on their faces convinced me they had made it especially for Mom. Later, as I walked back across the kitchen, wearing jeans and a red ski jacket, Thane, at the observant age of twelve (he just had a birthday), announced. "There's a new chick in town. Her name is Connie Morgan."

"Don't call me a chick," I demanded.

"And Mom, you really do have a cute ass."

"Thane!"

I knew that I felt more alive and energetic and it showed.

I even remembered how other men used to call me a foxy lady. On certain days, I still longed for an affectionate kiss on the cheek, a lingering look from across the table, a quiet conversation in which words hardly mattered, or someone to snuggle with in the back seat of a taxi. When I was ready, I knew it would happen.

Another morning, I was invited for breakfast at Thane and Mark's home, again when Phil was gone. Walking into the back door, I heard music in the background and noticed the table set with placemats and cotton napkins with napkin rings, a style our family had always enjoyed. As I was seated and ready to be served, I smiled at their orderly ways and was surprised at their preparations. Mark had made possum honey bread; Thane cooked cream of wheat and fixed scrambled eggs.

During breakfast the boys told me about the new household routine, how they carried dishes to the sink, then loaded them into the dishwasher, swept the floor, changed the sheets on their beds each week, and did laundry on Saturday mornings. While I was happy to learn their dad was teaching them good work ethics, I couldn't help wondering how family cooperation might have made a difference when I lived there.

A few weeks later, I picked them up at their house to go ice-skating at the neighborhood rink where Mark and I had taken lessons. Our time together on the weekends didn't fit the picture of the healthy family with two proud parents affectionately watching their children perform, but it was a creative time that typically brought us closer together. During those weekends, I was determined that my sons would realize how much I loved them, and that my love had nothing to do with name-brand shoes, trendy clothes, the newest games, or a more prestigious home.

As we skated around the rink one of the boys excitedly yelled, "Mom, remember that fancy stop you learned?"

"Yes!" I shouted, as I circled the ice once more. But when I prepared to stop, my blades tangled, which catapulted me into the air. The full weight of my body hit the ice, landing squarely on my tailbone. Paralyzed by fear and shock, I remained motionless for a long time.

As the rink supervisor finally skated toward me, he asked, "Are you all right?"

"I don't know."

"Can you get up?"

"I'm not sure."

Thane and Mark stood watching with their friends as I was carried into the manager's office and gingerly placed on a padded table. After one emergency crew was unable to determine a possible spinal cord injury, they called an ambulance with a paramedic. While I was stretched out in the back of the ambulance en route to the hospital, my worst fear was that of being unable to work.

Inside the emergency room, the examination, thankfully, revealed only a cracked tailbone. However, I was given strict orders for complete bed rest.

Since Phil was gone on a trip, Thane and Mark insisted that I recover at their house. After they gave me permission to take over the master bedroom, I snuggled into the king-size bed, cushioned by lots of pillows. My spirits were soon lifted by the thoughtful gestures of my sons and their neighborhood friends. Mark brought flowers from their yard, and Thane gave me a hand-made card showing an ice skater with her skates in the air. I felt like the woman on the television show, *Queen For A Day*.

My accident proved to be a much-needed respite from my position of social worker. It also gave me time to reassess my life. While working at Hope Center, I realized how my job in the field of disability had challenged me to go beyond the circle of my conventional friendships, crossing barriers of social, racial, and economic strata. For the first time since my exposure to the culture of Greenwich Village, and the life-changing influence of Los Angeles, I was free to mingle with a more unorthodox group of people, whose free-spirited behavior was a sharp contrast to my conservative middle-class views. When I gave myself permission to break free from the rules which had been instilled since childhood, I felt a sense of exhilaration—a woman who had earned her right of passage.

And now, after my four-year-term as a social worker, with exposure to different viewpoints and the benefit of service to others, I wondered if a more altruistic way of life might be the way to real happiness.

20

IN THE VALLEY
OF THE SHADOW

It was one thing to assume responsibility for creating a new life for myself while unraveling the fibers of dependency, but the day-to-day effort required to achieve that life was a rude awakening. While I was forced to confront the uncertainty of a career, I was also forced to confront another area of my life.

I still lived in the haunting shadow of the obstetric injury that I suffered when Chris was born, an injury that terminated the enjoyable lovemaking I had with my husband. As with most women, being sexually fulfilled was as important to my own happiness as the satisfaction I gave to my husband. No one ever knew the truth of what had gone wrong until Dr. Kegel, back in Los Angeles, had told me it was caused by the episiotomy, and there was no way to correct it. By that time, of course, my marriage had more than suffered. A sense of myself as a woman had died. I had even begun to question my sanity.

Living as a single woman, I had become more aware of how women's bodies and sexual performance in a male-dominated culture have been a source of anxiety for men as well as for women. The idea that desirable women serve men seemed largely responsible for getting women into sexual situations that not only didn't serve *their* needs, but often resulted in frustration, anger, or guilt—all adversely affecting their health in some way.

During those years after Chris' birth, I naively thought my lack of sexual desire was the price for having had a baby, for being a woman. And then, while still working as a social worker, I began to have problems with incontinence. The doctor I usually saw within the scope of my medical plan referred me to a surgeon who said he could surgically rebuild that all-important PC muscle. By grafting muscle from one part of my body to the vaginal area where the PC muscle was missing, he was confident he could restore me to normal. For convenience, he would perform a hysterectomy. To relieve incontinence problems, he would suture the bladder to the pelvic bone.

Initially, I was fearful of such an extensive surgery, but I was elated to think that someone could reverse the obstetric injury and restore a healthy body. I was reluctant, however, to have a huge scar on my abdomen, so I was excited to learn it could be done through a vaginal procedure.

Having lived most of my married life with accusations about sexuality and the absence of sexual pleasure, I felt a profound sadness in knowing that now, after a painful divorce, I might have a normal body.

As a single woman risking a comprehensive surgery, I asked myself, *What's the purpose, to please another man?* Even a successful outcome couldn't make up for the past. If only to defy the criminal negligence that had occurred fifteen years ago, I decided to take the risk and feel like a complete woman.

Months later, when the surgery was performed without an outward incision, it was hard for me to imagine that the obstetric injury had actually been remedied, but I was assured the procedure was a success. On the second day after surgery, my parents left to go on vacation. Lacking strength after the surgery, and not fully understanding the intricacies of the procedure, I was happy when Phil and the boys came to visit. With their encouragement and arm-in-arm support, I made the long walk down the hallway, just as the doctor had insisted.

By midnight on the third day, I was too weak to even lift my head off the pillow. I rang for the nurse and she immediately called the doctor.

When he arrived, he looked at the chart and began to criticize me for taking too much medication. As if I *knew* what I was taking! He left the room, and when he returned, he asked if there was anyone who could give blood. I told him my parents had gone on vacation and that no one else was available.

The following morning, Reverend Richard Evans, the associate minister from my church, came to visit. He said, "I hope they decide what to do with you before they let you die." I knew he wouldn't joke about something like that. As we talked, I remembered I had donated blood through the church a few years ago.

Later in the day, when it seemed clear that my body wasn't going to recover without blood transfusions and anti-biotics, several technicians worked feverishly to find veins large enough to accept transfusions. As hours passed, the possibility of death hit me hard. Thankfully, the persistence of dedicated technicians paid off.

As the days wore on, friends from work brought healthy food to boost my delayed recovery. Two weeks later, I was still trying to regain my strength. Joseph, the new man in my life (whose wife had recently died of cancer), sat with Phil in my hospital room, both of them taking turns preparing my food and feeding me. I barely remembered their presence, but I was grateful that someone cared.

After I was finally released from the hospital, I stayed with Cleo Taplin, a friend from my church, who turned her master bedroom into my recovery room until I was able to get back on my feet. I was thrilled when Phil and the boys stopped by to help revive my sense of humor. Weeks later, when Joseph took me out to a movie, I began to feel like a real person. When I slowly regained my strength, I prepared evening meals for Cleo and her teenage daughter.

As time went by and I knew the surgery was successful, I still suffered from negative feelings associated with that area of my body. As part of my recovery, I sought help through therapy and learned that when a woman has sex she doesn't want, or engages in sex that is traumatic to the tissues, the lubrication that normally comes with sexual desire is not present. This, coupled with the friction of intercourse, causes pain. When tissue trauma is combined with a feeling of emotional violation, even the immune system can be adversely affected, and this makes the healing more difficult.

I learned that many women, single or married, are conflicted between needing to be loved and desiring sexual pleasure, but wanting to say no to intercourse. When a woman stays in a relationship with someone she doesn't respect, or even like, due to the possible loss of financial security or a fear of becoming single, she might as well be a prostitute.

Clinically speaking, any treatment for a chronic problem is considered unsuccessful if the emotional aspects of the problem are unknown, or remain unsolved. I was beginning to realize that I could be one of those women who had been cured physically, but still suffered from the emotional trauma of the episiotomy during Chris' birth, the pain of intercourse, and my recent surgery.

I had attempted to handle the emotional scars through traditional counseling, but it wasn't until I did a highly supervised *purification program* that I learned how toxic chemicals such as anesthesia, cold remedies and pain medications, even pollution from the air and preservatives from our food, can accumulate in the fatty tissues of the body and cause recurring problems. During stress or fatigue, these toxic substances enter the bloodstream and restimulate the mental pictures which were recorded at the time the substances entered the body. By doing this program, which took three to four hours a day for approximately twenty-four days (in my case), and consisted of a daily sauna and nutritional supplements, I was able to get rid of the accumulated impurities. Even more important, after completing the purification process, I no longer experienced the anxiety and emotional pain previously associated with that area of my body.

It was an amazing part of my recovery, one that I never would have thought possible. But now, I could look at that aspect of my life as a positive step toward healing the past.

Weeks after the sauna program, while sitting in a reception area waiting to see my dentist, I saw a magazine article titled *The Agony of Being Single*. A woman who prided herself on being independent and unafraid to be alone, was asking the editor if her desire to be alone meant she had a problem. She considered herself open-minded and well informed. She enjoyed male companionship, but loathed the idea of having to answer to a man. She cringed when she heard other women asking their boyfriends for permission to do something, but envied the fact they had a relationship.

The author suggested she had a problem, only because she didn't know whether she wanted to be alone or in a relationship. He wrote that if she really wanted a relationship, she should find one that wasn't so restrictive.

After perusing the article, I realized that we live in a society which continues to reinforce the myth that being without a partner is equivalent to being lonely and incomplete. It was no wonder that single people like myself often feel there is something wrong with them, or that they are missing out. In actuality, a feeling of loneliness merely indicates that we have disconnected from our source of creativity; we have simply forgotten how to share our uniqueness.

Of course when one is single, there is a tendency to over-romanticize the concept of being a couple. When the mystique of phone calls and candlelight dinners cease to provide the necessary stimulus for being together, a couple is often left with the exhausting issues of communication and control, which create barriers to a loving relationship.

As a single woman, I began making decisions that reflected *my* values and assumed responsibility for areas of *my* life in which I had previously depended on others. Instead of hiding behind someone I thought was stronger and wiser, I used this opportunity to develop a relationship with myself. With my own sense of well-being as a priority, I began to emerge from the valley of the shadow.

.

21
UNDER THE OAK TREE

With another year of unforeseen adventures, autumn passed quickly. Days of boredom, sadness, and illness evaporated into furious wind-whipped days of snow. The mountain areas were rapidly accumulating a solid base for the ski season.

One glorious sunny weekend, Thane and Mark invited me to go skiing at Winter Park Resort. Apparently, they thought Mom was an expert skier because they took me to an area known as Mary Jane, the section of the mountain with black-diamond slopes — the most difficult ones. On a challenging run called Outhouse, I was forced to live up to their expectations. With my knees tucked to my chin and my mind keenly focused on staying alive, I made it to the bottom without falling. While they cheered, I thanked my lucky stars I hadn't landed in the hospital.

Another weekend we decided to go skiing at the popular re-sort of Copper Mountain. On the first run of the day, I opted for an intermediate slope and the boys headed for a black-diamond slope. While I waited for them midway down the mountain, I noticed that a cute and younger looking guy was watching me. Finally, he came over and said, "Would you like to ski together?"

Though I was flattered, I was apprehensive about how well he might ski, but I quickly accepted the challenge. "Well, sure."

After a lively conversation on the chair lift, and brisk runs through fresh powder, I was elated that this charming and handsome guy had discovered me on the side of the mountain. While we enjoyed the rest of the afternoon together,

Thane and Mark called, "Hi, Mom!" from the chairlift as they passed overhead, or waved as they skied past.

In the months that followed, my new boyfriend, Bruce, and I slurped ice cream in his red sports car, listened to music as raindrops danced on the windshield, competed on the tennis court, laughed over cups of cappuccino, and shared good times editing chapters of my manuscript. During late night phone calls, we debated spiritual issues and other intellectual topics. This good-looking guy with a great sense of humor was exactly what I needed.

Eight months later, when my affair with this gifted eighteen-year-old college student ended, I had beautiful memories of fun and laughter, and wanted to let him know how special he was. I wrote him the following letter.

Dear Bruce,

You are such a beautiful person, and because of our friendship, I have learned to live each day to the fullest. Because of you, I have learned how to turn an ordinary day into one of beauty and excitement. I want to thank you for the special person that you are, and for those happy times I will always carry with me.

Sincerely,
Connie

Months after that, when I had finally begun to appreciate the opportunities that can come with a willingness to risk everything for one's integrity, I received an unexpected phone call.

A woman on the other end of the line told me that Chris had been selected as one of the first forty-nine residents to live at the *United Cerebral Palsy* facility in Chatsworth, California, which was forty-seven miles north of Los Angeles. His placement was possible only because of participation by parents, families, and friends whose goal was to provide the best services in the country for these children.

It seemed like yesterday when I joined other committed parents to raise funds to purchase this five-acre site in Chatsworth Park. We had created a video narrated by Rod Serling. It opened with scenes of rolling hills and rock cliffs near the Santa Susanna Mountains, and then dimmed to a silhouette of a two-hundred-year-old oak tree with rays of the sunset filtering through its branches.

With our video promotion, audiences were easily inspired to help create an environment where our kids could live with dignity and grace. Perhaps dignity was the most significant contribution we could make to these children with a debilitating condition.

And now I looked forward to my first visit to the new residential facility in Chatsworth, and naturally the chance to see Chris again. During the Continental flight from Denver I tried to sleep, but without success. As I anticipated seeing my son, I realized that the emotional pain from our separation several years ago was still present.

As the captain announced our arrival in Burbank, I worried about having to rent a car and drive myself to the school, but my thoughts were centered mostly on Chris. What would he look like? Would he recognize me?

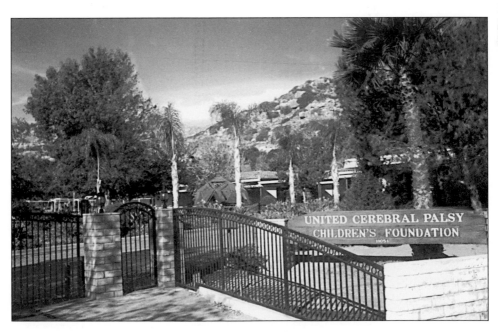

Five-acre Residential Facility
Chatsworth, California

During the drive across the Santa Susanna Mountains, I felt an unexplainable impulse that caused me to turn onto a dirt road that headed into the hills. I stopped the car near a clump of trees next to an open space. After lying in the sun for a long time, I came to terms with what I was feeling. Still vulnerable to emotions of guilt and sadness, and sometimes disbelief, it was nearly impossible for me to place love and resignation side by side.

I hoped that after this reunion with my son I could feel a new purpose and move forward with confidence, perhaps even recover some of the happiness I deserved.

Two hours later, my car eased onto the grounds of *United Cerebral Palsy Foundation* in Chatsworth. As I passed through a wrought iron gate, I was awestruck with the beauty of grounds that were handsomely landscaped with tropical vegetation, winding paths, benches, and gazebos.

Inside the main building, I announced my arrival at the front desk.

"Hello, I'm Chris Wright's mother. I'm here to visit for a few days."

"Oh yes, he's been waiting for you. We'll let him know you're here."

When he was wheeled out to meet me, I noticed that his hair was longer than I had seen, but he looked good. When the technician parked his wheelchair next to me, I gently touched his arm and quietly said, "Hi, Chris, this is your mom."

He looked at me long and hard, then he clasped his hands together and formed a puzzled frown. He waited and listened with a quiet discernment before he responded, using his intuition, as he always did.

After moments of private contemplation, he squealed and kicked his heels against the footrest of his wheelchair. It was still his way of showing recognition and excitement.

Shortly thereafter, one of the staff members eagerly suggested, "Chris, give your mother a hug."

He awkwardly reached forward and put his arms around my neck. I melted.

The staff person then insisted, "Chris, give your mom a kiss."

He gently placed his mouth on my cheek. My heart stopped. I had waited so many years for this. I simply glowed!!

The following day, I watched as another technician encouraged Chris to walk between the parallel bars. Believing that someday he could walk on his own, they were dedicated to teaching him balance. But even though his brain was capable of telling him how to put one foot in front of the other, he was never able to stand upright without losing his balance. Over time, I was forced to accept the reality that he would never walk.

As I strolled through the park-like grounds with Chris in his wheelchair, the sound of birds singing in the trees reminded me of the times when Chris and I walked down the mountain road to the mailbox on the General's estate.

We stopped at a wooden bench that circled the big oak tree which had been featured in our video and later appeared on a brochure with this caption: *Each tree an act of God, each growing differently, each adjusting to its own environment. Each human life is a responsible pilgrimage.*

Standing across from the construction site of six spanish-style villas, my dream was for Chris to live in one of the villas. I wanted him to have his own place with roommates like other young men, so it was a happy moment when I learned that his name had been placed on the list to live in the villa shown in the photograph.

As we sat under the oak tree, I felt Chris looking at me in a scrutinizing, almost intimidating, manner. In recent years, friends had helped me explore spiritual ideas that were different from my earlier views. And now, during these moments when we communicated in silence, I wondered if Chris and I had been together before this lifetime, and were connected in this masterpiece of humanity for a deeper spiritual purpose. Even though Chris communicated with noisy and abrupt sounds, he often used his deep brown eyes to convey feelings and words he could never speak or write. It was as if he was silently steering me in a direction I had been longing to go.

Chris learning to walk between the parallel bars.
United Cerebral Palsy Foundation

The Newport House
A Spanish-style villa where **Chris** became a resident.
United Cerebral Palsy Foundation — Chatsworth, California

As we continued walking, a sweet breeze followed us, then suddenly, surrounded by the lush vegetation and the history of massive red rocks tucked into the hills above us, I realized an intense calm and soon got lost in nature's hypnotic spell.

During my three-day visit, I was invited to stay with Dr. Caro Hatcher, who lived in small cottage on the grounds. With two doctorate degrees, the status of honorary dean of a woman's college, and publications that had gained national recognition, Dr. Hatcher had, over the years, helped me understand the endless stages of adjustment which parents endure. We talked until the wee hours of the morning about the challenges of infancy, the hope of younger years, the adolescent stage, the reality of adulthood, and finally, independent living. "Connie," she said, "the most natural thing a child will ever do is leave home, but most children don't leave home at the age of eight as Chris did. It is one of the most tormenting decisions a parent will ever make."

With each stage of my son's development, I endured the loss of unfulfilled expectations, and felt the challenge of overcoming my anger and jealousy toward others whose lives seemed so perfect. During those times, I was forced to dig deeper to find inner resources.

Late in the evening on the last day, I went to the dormitory to see if Chris was sleeping. As I quietly slipped into the darkened room and tiptoed toward his bed, he appeared to be the only one still awake. Perhaps he knew I was coming.

Kneeling on the floor next to his bed, I peered into the beauty of his soul. With his shining brown eyes and dimpled cheeks, Chris had always encouraged me to live the virtues he had in his life: joy and enthusiasm when good things happen, a curiosity that finds adventure in simple pleasures, a courage that rises from defeat and tries even harder.

As we interacted in total silence, our solitude was complex and divine, as if he understood the dichotomy of love and pain. If there was anything I could say with certainty that he would understand, I would tell him that whatever seemed wrong, whatever had caused him pain, I had deeply cared and tried to understand him. He would always be my son and I wanted him to be proud of me.

As I wrapped my arms around him, my heart shattered. I started to cry. For so many years, I had wanted things to be different. In the past, the inability to reconcile the discrepancy between the way I wanted things to be and the way things were had caused me to suffer. I simply hadn't been willing to look beyond my son's physical limitations and see that inside, he was completely whole. In spite of his inability to walk or talk, he was a child who had forced me to pay attention to things that others take for granted. Through my increased understanding of the bigger picture, I now had a new interpretation of the perfect life.

After a most incredible time together, I slowly moved away. Without saying goodbye, I walked back through the shadows. Outside, I was finally able to release the tears I hadn't wanted Chris to see.

The next morning, Dr. Hatcher talked about a man named Bill Pringle who had come to the school to work as a volunteer. On that first afternoon, a busload of students arrived home from their classes. When Bill saw them, he wasn't sure he could handle it. In fact, the next day he told Dr. Hatcher he didn't plan to stay on.

"Try it for one week," she said.

After two weeks, Bill not only went on salary, but he surprisingly discovered that through the use of affection and a sense of humor, he could communicate with the majority of students. In spite of his initial resistance to the older boys, he was particularly drawn to Chris. He said it was Chris' ability to discern the genuineness in others that caused him to want to spend time with him.

A bachelor father with children of his own, Bill began taking Chris home. He said his younger kids, age eight and eleven, fell crazy in love with their new friend. Without the wheelchair in sight, he said Chris and his three teenagers looked like four normal kids watching television. When they went to Knott's Berry Farm, Bill took Chris on the log ride. When Chris became frightened and was unable to verbalize his fear, he started punching Bill. After hearing this, I could only empathize with the pain he must have felt in not being able to speak.

Over time, the bond that developed between them demonstrated Chris' ability to form deep attachments, but it also created a problem. At the end of each school day, when Chris realized Bill had left the building, he was devastated. Even when Bill tried to leave more discreetly through another exit, Chris knew when he was gone. He reacted with noisy and uncontrollable outbursts, making it difficult for the night technician to do his job.

The following day I met Terri Manno, an eighteen-year-old college graduate who was now a teacher's aide. She told me how she had fallen in love with Chris during the school Easter program. "He was such a ham," she said, "but it was his aliveness and simple honesty, that deeply affected me. I had never met anyone who made such a lasting impression.

Just being with him and feeling his unconditional love helped me through my parents' divorce."

The next morning, while preparing to leave, I learned of a young woman named Eileen Steeg, with whom Chris had also developed a deep and affectionate relationship. Like any protective mother, I felt threatened by another special person who had become attached to my son. I was told that because of Eileen's busy schedule of classes, it wouldn't be possible to meet her before I left, but I was given her address.

As I boarded a flight in Santa Monica to return home, my life seemed like a book with many chapters. As the next chapter began to unfold, feelings of grief mingled with relief. I buckled the seatbelt, closed my eyes, and uttered a prayer of gratitude to the dedicated staff and the Master Creator himself. I was finally able to see myself in all of them, and all of them in me.

After I got home, I wrote a letter to Eileen. Weeks later, I still had not heard from her. Perhaps her college studies and work at the school simply didn't allow time to write. Perhaps I would never hear from her, but I trusted a letter would come. One day an envelope with her name in the upper left hand corner showed up in my mailbox. I quickly pulled it out of the pile and held it for a very long time before I opened it.

Dear Ms. Morgan,

I can't thank you enough for your beautiful letter. I was about to go outside to enjoy the sunset when I remembered I hadn't checked my mailbox. I don't know you very well, except through your son and what I have been told. Nevertheless, I feel especially close to you. I'm sure that is because of our common love of God and that special son of yours.

Chris is one of the most beautiful children I have ever met. As a matter of fact, I have never experienced the kind of love I feel for him. I thank God for his bright eyes and his contented smile. The enclosed photograph of the two of us was taken at my parents' home one weekend.

One night I took Chris out to see the full moon. As he sat in his wheelchair, I prayed out loud for him. While I was telling him how special he was and how Jesus loved him, he got this really neat smile on his face. It was like he was saying, "Yeah, I know."

I was so happy when I read the last part of your letter. For as long as I have known Chris, I've had the dream of taking him to Colorado. Please let me know when that is possible.

In His love,
Eileen

I was overjoyed at the prospect of a visit from Chris and Eileen, but there were a few obstacles. A flight to Colorado not only required cooperation from the airlines, but it would require a technician who could lift Chris in and out of the wheelchair, as well as manage the noisy outbursts that could easily paralyze the nerves of innocent bystanders.

It wasn't long, however, before the uncertainties of travel were handled and Chris and Eileen were on board a 747 flight to Denver.

On a brilliant sunlit afternoon in late August, two smiling faces strolled onto the concourse looking like seasoned travelers. Except for Chris not wanting to eat during the flight, the trip had gone without a hitch. Naturally, Chris was apprehensive of his new surroundings, but with Eileen's reassuring ways he soon reverted to his more gregarious personality.

They spent the first few days at Phil's house before we gathered to celebrate Chris' twelfth birthday. We had the usual cake and ice cream and helped Chris blow out the candles but, for me, the laughter of my three beautiful sons and their rowdy interaction was the highlight of the afternoon.

Later in the week, Chris and Eileen piled into my one-bedroom apartment. Like old friends reunited after years of separation, the two of us chattered endlessly while preparing dinner in my tiny kitchen. The next morning after breakfast, we packed a lunch and walked miles, taking turns pushing Chris in his wheelchair. We finally arrived at the park where Chris delighted in making friends with ducks that dared come close.

Throughout the week, I was intrigued with the way Eileen continued to give instructions to Chris, knowing that he understood exactly what she was asking him to do. When he responded in his garbled and well-intentioned sounds, she interpreted his sounds as a language of love. Through their interaction, I was reminded that brain injury has nothing to do with intelligence, but rather one's *inability* to express intelligence.

Eileen later explained that when Chris had outbursts of rage, it was his way of striking out at a world he didn't understand, a world that didn't always take time to understand him.

Chris is captivated by the ducks during his visit to Denver, Colorado.

On our last night together, my neighbor stayed with Chris while Eileen and I went to see the movie *You Light Up My Life.*

Driving back home, I said, "Eileen, after separation from my family and letting go of a secure lifestyle and the material things that always seemed so important, I feel I have nothing left to lose. However, my family will always be my family, a source of inspiration and love. As far as the symbols of success, I guess they can always be replaced."

"Yes, I've learned that one of the hardest things is to surrender to the uncertainty of life, not knowing what lies ahead except that which we are willing to create for ouselves. What bothers me most are religious people who consider divorce or a disabled child as some kind of punishment, and react to others in that situation with a pious attitude. Their lack of knowledge and awareness often creates more guilt for parents."

After getting to bed late that night, the alarm went off much too early. Except for urging Chris to eat his breakfast, conversation was minimal. After clearing the dishes, we packed the suitcases, readied Chris for the trip, loaded the gear into my Honda, and headed for the airport.

As we waited for the final boarding call, I felt thankful for so many things. Chris, with his good looks and gregarious nature, would always be able to reach out for the attention he needed — not caring whether it was from his mother and father, or his brothers. His intense brown eyes would always discern the integrity of others. And most important, he would always be able to use his smile to show acceptance and approval.

Finally, with a tearful hug goodbye, and the reality of another separation, I felt a tenderness unlike anything I had ever experienced in the language of emotion.

Chris and Eileen soon disappeared down the ramp for their return flight to Los Angeles. As tears trickled down my cheeks, it was clear to me that through Chris, the greatest teacher I could have asked for, I had finally discovered what was missing in my own life — the *real* me. I had perhaps even discovered the life I was born to live. My previous life, with all the trappings of success, had looked great on the outside, but didn't feel so good on the inside. I was depressed and unfulfilled, yet unable to justify my feelings.

Now, I was on my way to understanding that I was here to honor my deeper insight, and to use my imagination in ways I never thought possible. It could be that I was learning what I had known for a long time; I just wasn't aware that I already knew it.

A few weeks later, a letter from Eileen not only brightened my week, but renewed my sense of purpose and further inspired me to celebrate each new day.

Dear Connie,

Just a note to let you know I had a wonderful Thanksgiving. I brought Chris to my parents' house. He has really worked his way into the hearts of my family, especially my dad. I got Chris some new clothes. He is growing up so fast and is as happy as ever.

Peace and love,
Eileen

22

RAINDROPS ON MY SOUL

Relaxing in the living room of my apartment one evening, I gazed past the open patio door and across the satiny waters of the pool, to a sky tinged with vibrant pinks and lavenders. As the horses in the distance became black silhouettes against a darkening gray-blue sky, my last fourteen years took on a new perspective. During a time when love and marriage were supposed to provide a sense of security, I felt that, in many respects, I had survived all by myself.

In the seventies, women were beginning to get a sense that freedom was more rewarding than chasing a crippling sense of security. We were told we had the right to choose what was important to us. We were encouraged to discover our own values, viewpoints, and passions. Perhaps even realizing for the first time that the values we claimed as our own had been inherited from earlier authority figures. The challenge was to separate ourselves from the image of the good wife, the good mother, or even the virtuous daughter, to discover who we really were, without a fear of disapproval.

Observations made during my younger years had convinced me that boys were more adventurous and had opportunities not readily available to girls. Later in life, when the boys appeared naturally self-sufficient, no one was surprised. Women typically ventured out on their own for a while, going away to school, perhaps traveling or working, even making good money, but eventually a male savior rescued them from the anxiety of being on their own.

By now, my life had been altered so completely and publicly that, in a way, I was already free. No longer hiding behind the walls of illusion, it seemed I had nothing left to give up but fear. When I compared my life to others, who smugly and unthinkingly attributed their success to personal goodness and morality, I thought there might actually be something liberating about failure and humiliation.

Underneath a desire for independence, I still longed for the security I knew as a child, snuggled into bed knowing I was protected from the wind whistling in the trees, safe from the coyotes howling in the distance, and the owl hooting close to my upstairs bedroom. This desire to be protected might always be there, but undoubtedly with a different perspective.

In spite of having manifested many changes, I still had difficulty getting past my feelings of incompetence. While at times I was resentful I had to leave home and learn new skills to take care of myself, I longed to find a mentor who, at least, could offer some down-to-earth techniques that could help me become more effective in areas of my life.

Don Krill, who had been one of my professors at the University of Denver, invited me to a meeting which was actually a workshop designed to promote the self-help program known as *est*, or Erhard Seminar Trainings. During that particular evening, I heard remarkable stories from graduates of the program who were changing their lives, making decisions to leave their marriages or to stay, connecting with parents they hadn't seen in years, and getting better jobs. The results convinced me that an investment of two weekends for a relatively inexpensive program was a good idea.

On that first Friday evening the doors opened exactly at seven o'clock. As I was seated in a room that would hold at least two hundred people, I wondered if this was just one more mind-expanding movement, or whether it was possible to learn how to manifest change in less than sixty hours.

Addressing more than a hundred people, the trainer wasted no time getting down to business. He stated that to break through barriers that could inhibit a more productive and effective life, we would have to be willing to look at ourselves from a different viewpoint and examine the unconscious beliefs that kept us going down the same path—blind to the unconscious attitudes and behaviors that kept us obligated to unfulfilling routines.

The most important part of the process was being able to speak about our experiences in a safe environment where we would not be judged. Here we could more easily uncover the fixed ideas and attitudes which unknowingly controlled our life. As people in the group volunteered to stand and share a specific issue or an irregular person in their life, it became apparent that their suffering stemmed not from their situations, but from their inability to handle those situations. Instead of acknowledging *their* cause in the upset, they blamed others.

Many times my thoughts flashed back to a young girl who looked self-assured on the outside, but felt insecure, and sometimes miserable, on the inside. I had done well, at least outwardly, only because I had refused to capitulate to the painful insecurities and confusion that ebbed and flowed during much of my life. It became clear that many of us had created a *masked* identity, which looked good to others and guaranteed approval, when actually we had lost our ability to think for ourselves.

During the second weekend, many people began to admit to a satisfying life that, in reality, wasn't what they wanted. As the truth began to surface, some realized that all they ever wanted was to feel a sense of belonging, to love and to be loved. For myself, I recognized that I had never known how to really communicate and that my lack of knowledge and techniques about communication had contributed to the upsets in my relationships. Perhaps now, things could be different.

The two weekends were over and my four-day transformation was complete. And even though I was reluctant to speculate on what changes might occur in my life, I didn't have to wait long.

After our divorce, Phil and I had avoided face-to-face encounters and had very few telephone conversations, except to talk over concerns about our sons. But one evening, I left a message on his answering service. When he returned my call later that night, I sat up in bed and quickly got to the point.

"Phil, I want to thank you for the contribution you've made to my life and for three beautiful children."

"What?" he asked, puzzled by my acknowledgments.

"And I want you to know that I am responsible for what happened to *me* during our marriage."

"Where did all this come from?" he asked.

In that brief conversation he knew something had changed. And while we weren't close to a relaxed sense of humor or a feeling of playfulness, I felt a new respect for myself that came from knowing I could have a different kind of communication with him.

As I gained a greater awareness of myself, a more playful personality began to emerge. And with that, I began a new lifestyle. I moved to a nicer apartment that overlooked a beautifully landscaped courtyard with winding paths, waterfalls, a large pond, and ducks that wandered about the well-manicured grounds. Amenities such as a glass-enclosed game room offered a place where the boys and I could challenge each other for hours.

A short time later, with a desire to earn more money, I left the field of Social Work. After studying diligently to pass my real estate exam, I joined a small brokerage firm in the affluent area of Cherry Creek. During the first year in residential real estate, my sales exceeded ONE MILLION DOLLARS! It was not only a proud achievement during the seventies, but my success made it possible to purchase my first residence—a two-bedroom townhouse with a fireplace, garage, pool and tennis courts.

The following year, using my commission as a down payment on an FHA loan, I purchased an income property—a cute, but badly rundown duplex, in an indigent part of the city. The area may have been questionable, but I discovered a neighborhood with nice families and an elementary school a few blocks away. I labored nights and weekends to haul trash

Connie with "Mud Designs" and a more playful personality.

out of both units; I supervised workmen who installed new carpet and window coverings; I upgraded the plumbing and electrical. And, after both sides were painted and ready for occupancy, I wrote my first lease agreement.

While I was busy learning about the world of real estate, Phil called to tell me he was getting married to a flight attendant who also worked for Continental. While I was happy for him, I was regretful I could no longer enjoy time with Thane and Mark in their home.

While they were adjusting to a new life, my success in real estate prompted a move to a larger company. After a few months with Coldwell Banker & Company, I wrote a $350,000 contract on a small office building. A week later, I was told that my deal had to be given to the commercial division of the company because it was their department. The loss of a substantial commission and the prestige of a well-written contract felt devastating.

The following month, I met with our managing broker. The meeting was part of our annual sales strategy.

"Do you have your list of goals for the coming year?" he asked.

"No, I don't."

"Why not?"

"I haven't decided whether residential real estate is working for me."

"When will you know?"

"Within ten days."

Before making a decision, I enrolled in another transformational weekend. This time I saw how reasonable attitudes could keep me from moving on to a more fulfilling job, increasing my income, or creating an empowering relationship. The biggest barrier was fear, but with the application of specific exercises during that weekend, even the fear diminished.

Five days later, I resigned from residential real estate, leased my townhouse, moved into an urban row house with interior brick walls and hardwood floors, and launched a career in commercial real estate.

My friends were shocked.

"When did you decide to move?"

"Last Thursday," I answered, feeling proud of my decisiveness.

Only a week earlier, I had called the commercial real estate office of Cushman & Wakefield, requesting permission to stop by with my resume and introduce myself to the managing broker.

My brief appearance, just before noon, turned into an invitation to lunch, another meeting the next day, and a full-time position as leasing associate. As far as I knew, my expedient move into the field of commercial real estate was unprecedented.

At our first Monday morning sales meeting, I sat at a large mahogany conference table with eight men. I was ecstatic at being able to align myself with male superiority and the power and influence that came with it. After two men asked me to join them for lunch, and two others invited me to share a large office space with them, I soon felt like one of the guys.

After six months of working with the managing broker, while learning the market and negotiating contracts, I decided to raise the stakes and work independently within the same company. To generate enough commissions to support myself, I negotiated small, but numerous, transactions with Le Mouton Business Park, which was comprised of a million square feet of historic brick buildings that were being renovated into office and warehouse spaces. I not only survived in the commercial marketplace, but I surpassed some of the men in the office who were holding out for the larger deals.

One day I received a phone call from the owner of the business park. "Morgan," as he liked to call me, "You have leased more square footage in this project than any other broker since the day we opened. Let's have lunch on Monday and talk about your coming to work for me."

On the following Friday, I began my new role as leasing manager of the business park. With the security of a base salary and a potential bonus for my production, I developed a marketing strategy, finalized lease agreements with other realtors for their clients, and coordinated tenant finish requirements with our project architect.

I had my eye on a third real estate property, a condominium in a renovated historic building close to downtown. The potential purchase was an incentive to work toward a $5,000 bonus, which I would need for my down payment at the time of the closing. This would occur in three months and would give me just enough time to lease the required 50,000 square feet of space.

At the end of the three-month period, I was excited to have fulfilled the requirements for my bonus. That is, until my boss decided not to honor our agreement. When I showed him the documentation of signed leases for secured occupancy, he claimed that the tenants needed to have moved into their new space, all within the three-month period.

While standing in his office, I fought back. "Wesley, I've been in the real estate business for a long time. Realtors are paid bonuses based on the property they contract within a specified period, regardless of the move-in date."

"Well, Morgan, this *isn't* a real estate office," he shouted.

"Then maybe you don't need a qualified real estate person for your leasing agent," I retorted, before leaving his office.

I hurried back to my desk and called Gary, the project architect with whom I had developed a close relationship.

After I explained what happened, Gary said, "Connie, when are you going to stop being grateful?"

"What do you mean?" I asked.

"Can't you see Wesley is using your talents while trying to find a way *not* to pay the bonus you've earned?"

My spirits dropped. Obviously Wesley's integrity was not what I expected. Not knowing what else to do, I gathered up the important papers on my desk, stashed them in my briefcase, and took the shortest route home.

The following morning I sat at my desk anticipating the next move. I was startled when Wesley walked in.

"Morgan, let's talk about your termination," he boldly stated.

I stood up and said, "Wesley, you can't fire me because I'm resigning."

While trying to remain calm, I reached into my purse for the resignation letter I had written the night before. My heart pounded. Finally, when I handed the letter to him, he looked at me, and then left the room.

At the end of the day, Wesley's secretary glibly wished me good luck and handed me an envelope, which contained my bonus check for $5,000 and two weeks of severance pay. In spite of having just purchased a condo, a new car, and a fur coat to wear with my jeans and boots (while showing vacant brick buildings during the coldest winter of the decade), I knew I had done the right thing.

Outside, I felt a sense of exhilaration and freedom, like the last day of school, or that glorious first day of summer.

Soon after that, Mark came to stay with me in my new condo. Now pressing into his teen years, he wanted to demonstrate his independence through wearing his hair longer, and even wearing an earring. I could only imagine how his desire to break with family tradition precipitated a struggle against his dad's more conservative views. But while Mark was striving to achieve some degree of reconciliation with his dad, I welcomed his company, and especially enjoyed our walks through downtown Denver, not far from my condo. I was happy to share my son's deep sensitivity during a time when I was trying to sort out some of my own issues. While homework was not Mark's strong suit, he brought a less-privileged student home for dinner, night after night, to help him complete his math assignments so their class would have their party by a certain date—and they did. We both looked forward to the times when Thane would show up in his newly purchased '49 Chevy pickup and take us for a ride.

Naturally, I was concerned about the use of drugs and alcohol, especially when, during the seventies and eighties, my

Mark and **Thane** with their **Mom**
and Thane's '49 Chevy truck.

sons were of critical ages and experimentations were common. With the early use of tobacco, alcohol, and marijuana, the chances of permanent addiction were greater. I could only trust that with enough knowledge and awareness from educational programs at school, and strict supervision at their dad's house, my sons would escape the danger of drugs.

Finally, with my encouragement for Mark to work things out at home, the day came when he told me he wanted to return to live with his dad. The following week, his letter in my mailbox confirmed our deepening relationship.

Dear Mom,
I never got a chance to tell you how much I loved staying with you. You were so loving and understanding. I could talk to you about any problems I had. We had a great time even though we had no money. I learned that you could survive without money as long as there is love. It was hard for me and probably for you when I left, but I had to make a decision. Remember, nothing is forever.

Love,
Mark

After realizing my strengths in the business world, I longed to find someone to curl up with, someone who could effectively interrupt my conversation with a kiss on the cheek, or gently reach for my hand during a movie. I knew I was a spiky, opinionated woman who had learned how to flirt by complimenting that which I found attractive in a man. However, the time just didn't seem right for me to be looking for a relationship.

At home one evening, I received a phone call from Maureen, one of the seminar leaders from the Erhard Training Center.

"Connie, how are you doing since you completed the training?"

"I'm doing much better, but right now I'm recovering from another transition in the work world."

"Okay, let's talk about a relationship," Maureen urged.

"I don't have time to be out looking," I said.

"Connie, it's not about that. All you need to do is make a list of the qualities you desire in this special person, and then determine a deadline for finding him. How about three months?"

"Let's say six months."

"I think three months is long enough," she insisted.

The idea sounded crazy, but I agreed to give it a try. Amazingly, within the next three months, men began to show up at unexpected places, such as the downtown business district in the middle of the afternoon, or a late night phone call from a college friend.

Nearing the end of the three months, however, I had yet to meet the man of my dreams. I began doubting the process. And then, coincidentally, I met someone who was actually dating someone else. During our first meeting, the chemistry between Ron and me was magical. His charming and out-going personality meshed with his aspiration to become a singer. After our first date, we were inseparable. We laughed at silly insignificant things, we sang and danced at a lively inner-city church, we cooked and entertained friends, and we supported each other in a loving partnership.

Less than a year later, Ron and I, along with my sister and brother, planned an elaborate 50th Wedding Anniversary Celebration for my parents and sixty out-of-town guests, all while I recovered from surgery on both feet. The three-day event honored my parents' achievement in turning barren sun-parched plains of western Kansas into a beautiful ranch, as well as their contribution to community and family. It was also a tribute to each of their six brothers and sisters who had all attended Kansas State University in Manhattan, Kansas. The celebration started with a buffet dinner in the wedding suite at the Sheraton Hotel on Friday night, then dinner and entertainment by Ron at the Wellshire Country Club on Saturday night. The weekend festivities concluded on Sunday with a courtyard brunch at my Bristol Cove townhouse.

Larry and **Isabel Morgan** celebrate their **50th Wedding Anniversary** with **Connie**, son **Lyn**, and daughter **Brenda.**

Connie Morgan and **Ron Williams** honor 500 volunteers
at the **United Cerebral Palsy Event**—Los Angeles, California.

Just a few months later, the *United Cerebral Palsy Foundation of Los Angeles* was scheduled to honor nearly five hundred dedicated volunteers. On short notice, I wrote a script for the program, which would correlate with selected lyrics that would be sung by Ron. Through friends in Los Angeles, I found Devon, a teacher and coach at Heschel School in Northridge, who agreed to play piano and sing backup vocal for Ron. We were able to enlist Uan Rasey, first chair trumpet with MGM studios for thirty-five years, whose talent pulled it all together. The script was interspersed with the lyrics from each of these stirring songs: *Could You Believe in a Dream; We're in This Love Together; I Just Called To Say I Love You; You Are Flesh of My Flesh.* The program was an expression of love for those special volunteers who understood that people with disabilities are also capable of developing useful skills. These dedicated volunteers were individuals who recognized that everyone, regardless of their disability, has some contribution to make to society.

As a final tribute, the audience joined in singing the words spelled out on a banner entitled *You Are The World*, lyrics that were written by my nephew, Brian Kolb. Misty eyes from the audience were proof of the empowerment that comes from the recognition of service and love.

Back in Denver, I managed to maintain an optimistic attitude while working two part-time jobs. One day, a former real estate associate told me about a project being developed by John W. Galbreath & Company.

I knew that working for the twenty-fifth largest hotel and office developer in North America was an opportunity to play a key role in the downtown real estate market. *One Civic Center Plaza*, a proposed 600,000 square-foot office tower, would make a striking architectural statement near landmark surroundings of the State Capitol and the Brown Palace Hotel. With a sophisticated concept and unrestricted views of the mountains, it would demonstrate a style that showed respect for the people and the city it would affect. It was slated to be the most prestigious project in downtown Denver.

Months after submitting a resume, I was called for an interview. After nervously waiting in a confining reception area, I was ushered down the hall to a large office. After I was seated in a Queen Anne chair in front of a handsome mahogany writing desk, the marketing director, Tony Cantagallo, walked in and warmly introduced himself. After an exchange of questions, the issue of compensation came up. When it seemed that I was being considered for the job, I boldly requested a salary of $35,000 plus commission.

"Are you worth that much?" Tony abruptly asked, causing me to wonder if they were prepared to pay a top-notch salary in addition to a good commission structure.

My heart stopped. I didn't know what to say.

Tony eased the tension by suggesting we meet for lunch at the Petroleum Club the next day.

After the interview, I quickly called a friend who was a savvy business consultant and had a great sense of humor.

"Patrick, I need your help. Can I meet you after work today?"

"Sure. Five-thirty at the Euro-grille?"

"That would be great."

We chatted over a glass of wine before I brought up my concern about the salary. "Patrick, when Tony asked if I was worth the money that I requested, I didn't know what to say."

"Connie, you dropped the ball. You need to go into the second interview and recover the fumble. You have to bring up the subject of compensation before he does."

I thanked Patrick for his good advice and told him I would let him know the results of my interview.

The next day at the Petroleum Club I waited until after Tony and I had ordered lunch before addressing the issue of money.

"Tony, regarding the salary I requested, you can be assured that because of my initiative, a competitive drive, strong people skills, and sales strategy, I am worth what I requested."

He smiled approvingly. "Well, Connie, after thirty days, if you're happy and we're happy, I will put it in your contract."

The following week, I settled into a private office located on the twenty-third floor of the Great West Tower located at Sixteenth and Broadway. As marketing advisor for *One Civic Center Plaza*, I designed project brochures that expressed a sense of style and tradition and implemented a comprehensive marketing strategy. With a marketing budget, a private secretary, an expense account for entertaining clients, and a rosebud that arrived every week from Ron, I had the necessary support with which to prove my worth.

It wasn't long before I decided to redesign my small generic office to reflect a more professional image. After I repositioned most of the furniture items, I hung a large gold-leaf mirror, brought in a tree, and added a few pieces of quality art. In my new work environment, I was motivated to spend many evenings and weekends working on my client list and marketing program. The goal was to counter the rapidly declining real estate market and make *One Civic Center* the most successful project in Denver.

After three-and-a-half years, *One Civic Center Plaza* was the most successful project in downtown Denver and a wonderful

ONE CIVIC CENTER PLAZA
1560 Broadway—Denver, Colorado

Marketing Associate, **Connie Morgan**, with the President of
Price Waterhouse at the Grand Opening of **ONE CIVIC CENTER PLAZA.**

expression of individuality, heritage, and tradition. A black-tie celebration was held in conjunction with the International Film Festival and was a huge success.

Through Thane and Mark, I learned that Phil (while on strike with Continental Airlines) was working at a geology firm located on the twenty-seventh floor of the same building, only four floors above Galbreath & Co. It was beyond belief how this protected suburban housewife, with no work experience, was now exploring the white male system in the same building as her former husband. Only in my imagination could I have experienced the contrast between the traditional roles of only a few years ago, and the thrill of having my children visit both their parents in the same downtown office building, going to lunch with their dad and slurping ice cream with Mom, all in one afternoon.

As a result of my successful career, I purchased a new townhouse in southeast Denver. The master bedroom suite was a dream. A large second bedroom and bath were perfect for Mark when he came to live with me again. A loft that overlooked the living room gave me enough space for my desk and a sleeper-sofa for Thane's visits. The architectural features included vaulted ceilings and skylights which complemented my newly installed plantation shutters. A brick and wrought iron courtyard off the living room afforded a great view of the mountains.

A purchase of my very own furnishings included a travertine marble table and a luxurious Chinese rug for the dining room, an elegant black sectional sofa, and a handsome Oriental bedroom set with a custom-designed bedspread. I was thrilled to have converted my dreams into reality, when suddenly, the road to success took a sharp turn.

In the wake of changes within the company, Tony, who had inspired my performance from the beginning, had left for a more favorable opportunity. On this day, in the hallway just outside our offices, I overheard a conversation among the other guys in management, including Joe, the other marketing advisor. They were discussing the upcoming selection of their new company cars. My heart sank when I realized I was the only one in management who hadn't been informed about getting a company car.

I calmly returned to my office and decided to approach Rick, a young and aggressive manager with whom I had a cordial business relationship.

Standing in his office, I gathered my courage. "Rick, I'd like to have a conversation about the company cars."

Looking surprised, he said, "Connie, we're not going to have that conversation."

"Rick, if you can show me some justification for Joe having a company car, and my not receiving a car as part of my compensation, we won't need to have that conversation."

"If you're asking me to show you Joe's income, I can't do that," he replied.

"I understand," I said, swallowing the truth.

Joe was married with two children and was a longtime

friend of Rick's, so it didn't take a genius to figure out what was coming next.

At two o'clock on Friday afternoon, just days after I uncovered their secret, Rick walked into my office, closed the door, and sat down in front of the desk.

"Connie, you're no longer part of the team."

As if I had already rehearsed the script, I replied, "Rick, I never was part of the team."

In spite of having achieved dramatic results for the company, I had felt the pain of persecution for several months. Like so many others, financial security had bound me to a place where women were not as highly regarded as men. Regardless of the success of our project, Galbreath & Co. and the other developers were experiencing an economic downturn and reducing their overhead.

Losing my job only *seemed* like the end of the world, but the inevitable feelings of shock, rage, and shame were painful. Perhaps everyone has, at some time or another, experienced sudden termination, received walking papers, or been the victim of downsizing. Nevertheless, I couldn't help noticing that when men lose their jobs, they blame the system or someone else before they blame themselves. Women, on the other hand, feeling the emotional impact from the situation, often think the problem lies with them. It would be a long time before I would learn the truth of that misconception.

23

PRUNING THE ROSEBUSHES

Being fired marked the beginning of a challenging personal odyssey. I wondered how I was going to manage a mortgage payment on my new townhouse, expenses on two other real estate properties, and a car payment. Adding to my stress was the termination of my relationship with Ron.

During our year together, I had experienced a rare kind of intimacy, with affection and tenderness I had not known in fourteen years of marriage. Due to one major unresolved conflict, however, the relationship ended. I thanked God I had known unconditional love—a source of power and creativity that has strengthened the lives of men and women since the beginning of time.

One day a friend stopped by. As we sat talking in the living room, Susan said, "I would give anything if my house looked like this. My husband left five years ago and took all the good art. I can't afford to buy anything new."

I hadn't seen her home, but I said, "Why don't I come over tomorrow and see what I can do?"

"Really? That would be great."

The next day we started rearranging the furniture in her small living room. We moved the sofa to face a large bay window, which gave a distinctive view of the landscape lighting outside. We brought the stereo components from the family room into the living room, which added purpose and enjoyment to the new space. With a few books and minimal accessories, the room took on a feeling of warmth and hospitality.

In the entry hall, we discarded old macramé hangings, dying houseplants, and a broken rattan chair. By applying simple design principles and using only those items consistent in quality, we created a good first impression.

"I had no idea my house could look so good," Susan exclaimed. "It now feels like an interesting person lives here."

The following week I called Bonnie, a friend who lived in a wonderful English Tudor on Ash Street. Still feeling displaced by my recent unemployment, I knew she could give me the emotional boost I needed.

As we stood talking in her living room, she showed me samples of paint for her walls, shades of beige and off-whites that had been suggested by another designer.

"Connie, what do you think?" she asked.

I immediately reacted in disgust. "None of these colors enhance the distinctive crown molding, the wrought-iron staircase, or the beautiful hardwood floors. I thought for a moment, then flippantly asked, "Why don't you do something exciting?"

"Like what?" she retorted.

"If this house were mine, I'd paint a deep avocado green on the crown molding, then add a plum-colored molding two inches below that. The fireplace and shutters on each side should also be painted avocado green."

"Then what color would you use on the walls?" she cautiously inquired.

"A lighter shade of the same green that will blend into the celery-green carpet."

"You don't think that would be too much color?" she asked, hesitantly.

"Well, do you want people to walk in and say, 'It smells like you painted?' Or do you want them to go, 'Wow?'"

Bonnie had always preferred to make a dramatic statement, so within thirty days we had redesigned every room in her home with a more cohesive placement of furniture and art, and painted the walls of each room an exciting bold color. When friends and business associates saw how her home had suddenly come alive and reflected her dynamic personality, I began to get calls for design work — which prompted the idea of a new business.

While change was rapidly occurring in my life, my sons were having their own challenging adventures. Thane had just returned from the back country of Australia, where he hitch-hiked from Melbourne to Perth—six days across the Nullarbor Plain—the same distance as Los Angeles to New York. When he returned home to Colorado, he still questioned whether he should travel or go to college.

After his freshman year he packed up his bike and toured part of Europe. Thankfully, he remembered to use the cards and stamps I sent before he left Athens for Belgrade.

Hi, Mom!
I realized a postcard wasn't enough to address the window of my experience, but where do I start? Too much to tell you about Europe, except there are a lot of people and we're just the same. Don't you know, we're just the same. Right now I'm about halfway around the world on a ferryboat sailing towards the island of Thira, Greece, just north of Crete. A big, round, orange moon just came up over the bow. Nice! When I think of all that I'm seeing and feeling, the magnitude of it all makes me realize how much I have yet to learn. It's as if I live behind a small window and occasionally poke my head out.

Oh yes, if you haven't already, go buy Howard Jones's first album "Human's Lib." Sit down by yourself and listen. Then get his second album "Dream into Action."

Give my love to all,
Thane

By now, his education had reached beyond the university curriculum. With his yearning for adventure and the exposure to other cultures, he later postponed a semester of college to work on a fishing boat in Alaska.

Hi Mom!
I am now sitting in the Ranger Dick's boat after working on
the bait shed and cleaning up the stern of the boat. My bunk
is down in the hull by the engine room. I had to buy a crew
license, ninety dollars, also a raincoat. Bush gave me his old
pants and I patched them tonight. We're going out tomor-
row for three days of fishing. Alaska is really neat with
totally awesome scenery.

Thank you for your moving letter which I read on the plane.
It was great that you and Mark came out to say goodbye. I
am fortunate to have a mother who really cares and is
always there when I need her.

Love you,
Thane

Mark, in his teen years, had decided academics were not a priority. Instead, he developed leadership skills and created enviable relationships. During his elementary years, he was elected student-body president, he excelled in soccer and baseball, and had just returned from soccer competitions in Europe. While he was attending Kent Denver private school during his middle-school years, his passion for lacrosse inspired a team effort toward a winning record.

During the past few summers, he and his friend George had hitchhiked across the country to attend concerts of their favorite music group, Jerry Garcia and The Grateful Dead. It wasn't until Mark invited me to a concert in Denver that I, too, experienced the special relationship between the group and their fans, as well as a rhythm and lyrics which would meld into a spiritual awakening for many of their fans.

I had my own unexpected awakening when, one day, I received a call from George's father. Somewhere in the eastern part of the United States, the boys had hitched a ride in a Volkswagen bus. En route to the concert, flames from the engine in the back of the bus were noticed by a passing motorist, who blared a warning just in time for those on the bus to bail out, narrowly escaping a fatal explosion. After learning that only a backpack was missing, I hung up the phone feeling numb, but mostly thankful.

Even though I had encouraged my sons to use their imagination and think for themselves, I had to also accept that a mother's fear was unavoidable. Happily I received a letter from Mark shortly thereafter.

Dear Mom,
I am listening to music written and sung from the heart while thinking of you. I'm just beginning to see that a mother's love will never end. Just remember that through the years, as we shine our light on fears and tears, we will all be free, and someday life will be so beautiful.

Love,
Mark

Both of my sons, in their unique and introspective ways, were good at expressing themselves with words, so I particularly loved getting their poems and letters. I had a special concern for Mark, since he was younger at the time of our divorce. But even with the pain of an early separation from his mom, I hoped that, over the years, he would understand how much I loved him, and even the sacrifice I had made.

Later that year, Mark traveled to Mexico to live for a few weeks with a family. After he returned with conversational Spanish, I asked him how I could give my Hispanic tenants a three-day notice prior to eviction. He said, "It's easy Mom. Just knock on the door and say, *Tres dias, adios!*"

It worked! Three days later, even though they demanded a return of their deposit when they hadn't paid their rent, they moved and left the place immaculate.

Thane had recently graduated from the University of Colorado, and then he spent time traveling to Thailand, China, and Hong Kong. After three months in Taipei, one of the most densely populated and highly polluted cities in the world, he gave up his study of Mandarin and a pursuit of international business for his passion of cycling.

When he returned home to Colorado, he took a short-term position as the technical director for a two-day bicycle event called *Ride the Range.* I agreed to solicit vendors to feed the hundreds of expected riders, and I felt good about my contribution. But not long after that, Thane posed a larger challenge. "You *are* going to ride, aren't you?"

Taken aback by his question, I snapped, "Of course I'm going to ride!"

Over the next few weeks, Thane's girlfriend, Megan, helped me purchase a Trek bike, a helmet, special shoes, a wind jacket, leg warmers, water bottles, gloves, upgraded pedals, and a more comfortable seat.

When Thane took me out for my first training ride, I received basic instructions on how to position my body on the bike, how to stop at the traffic lights, and how to push off with my pedal. He then insisted that I ride *every day.* I had only two months to train for a ride that would cover one hundred eighty-five miles in two days.

During my intensive training, friends encouraged thirty-mile endurance rides by offering invitations for breakfast and lunch. While Thane insisted that the two-day event was only a recreational ride, he was my most relentless supporter.

Dear Mom,
It's Thursday night. I'm writing this in bed. I want to express thoughts I have about you and the art of the bicycle, so simple, yet complicated, functional, measured, consistent and machined yet, utterly personal. It's not something you buy into like a club. It's an art form to be learned and appreciated. The art of pedaling in circles is to feel from the heart, from the soul, to feel in touch with the whole, common theme in cycling - consistency.

You must give of yourself, your heart, your tired legs and your mind to ride, ride, ride. I fear you will never realize the high that comes from the bike as it will be just another fleeting infatuation.

But for now, you've signed on for the ride, so do it! Make it hurt. Feel the sweat drip off your chin, feel the lactic acid build up. Push it! Whatever you do, don't let this art escape you.

With love,
Your mentor

It was a quiet Sunday morning, several weeks before the event. I had gotten up early for a two-hour ride to a friend's poolside townhouse located in Bristol Cove, just around the cul-de-sac where I had formerly lived. During a phone call that morning, my friend Terry had insisted I could make the trip in less time. Halfway to his townhouse, I attempted to shave thirty minutes off my time by taking another route. That resulted in a sandy dead-end trail. Brushing aside the frustration and mental fatigue, I rallied in knowing I was now on a wide, quiet street with almost no traffic. As I rode, I thought of the empowering relationships I had enjoyed with men such as Terry, a millionaire with an international business, and Don, a news anchor who worked for NBC in New York City. For many reasons, a serious relationship with them was never in the cards.

As fatigue began to penetrate my thoughts, I was relieved to know that Bristol Cove was only a few blocks away. Suddenly, in the midst of the morning calm, a car blared from behind. When I twisted to see what was happening, my bike sharply hit the curb, throwing me three feet onto the sidewalk. My bike landed on the grass between the curb and the sidewalk. I glanced up in time to see a carload of teenagers laughing as they drove down the street. My left arm was killing me, but I managed to make it to the entrance of the complex that circled around to Terry's place.

Walking the bike and feeling completely exasperated, I stumbled onto his front lawn. Terry greeted me with a grimacing, "What happened to you?"

As I told him about the accident, I realized it was actually caused by diverting from my well-planned route to a less predictable one, attempting to accommodate *his* expectations of a shorter ride. I secretly vowed not to make that mistake again. After Terry gave me medication to diminish the throbbing pain in my right arm, the sight of a brunch with homemade muffins, fresh-squeezed orange juice, and asparagus omelet brightened my day. As we sat on his brick courtyard facing the pool, I could finally laugh about the incident.

Later that evening, with recurring pain in my right arm, I drove myself to the emergency room. X-rays showed a severely bruised bone, which would be painful for some time.

After giving myself a few days to rebuild my confidence, I intensified the level of my training by going to the gym several times a week. Additionally, I began running nine flights of stairs in an office building, and was finally able to do that three times in succession.

One week later, while standing in the hallway on the second floor of a high-rise apartment building, I waited for an elevator to take me to the lobby. As other people gathered, anxious to catch the same elevator, I decided to take the stairs.

After the first hurried step, the heel of my shoe apparently caught in the cuff of my slacks, causing me to tumble headfirst down the flight of concrete steps. As I tried to hold onto the handrail, I felt a burning sensation on the palms of my hands, and the impact of my face hitting the concrete wall.

When I landed at the bottom, I prayed the manager's office was close to the stairs. And it was. After I knocked on his door and waited in the living room, unknowingly dripping blood on the white carpet, he telephoned a doctor. Surprisingly, there was nothing to do except let my face heal on its own.

Once again, with dampened spirits and a gash on my cheekbone, I wondered if two accidents so close to the morning of the event might be a warning to cancel.

In need of emotional support, I called my son, Mark, who had trained under several great chefs and was now a cook at Strings, a popular five-star restaurant near downtown.

Connie participates in **Ride the Range,**
a two-day charity bike event covering 185 miles.

"Mom, come on down. I have some time before the dinner crowd arrives. We'll go across the street to Acappellas and have a drink." I was grateful for his gentle way of consoling my spirit; it helped me not to lose faith.

I had given myself permission to withdraw from the ride, even as late as the morning of the event. But when the alarm went off at five-thirty that morning, I readied my equipment, gorged on pasta for the energy-boosting carbohydrates, and drove to the Interlocken Business Park at the north edge of the Denver-Boulder metro area.

After parking and unloading my bike, I followed the signs to the starting point. Most of the 450 riders had started earlier and at different times. As I headed out I was glad to know there were others just ahead of me. After riding nearly forty miles, which put me halfway between Denver and Fort Collins, I suddenly realized I was all alone, with no other riders in sight. Pedaling through open farm country, I felt refreshed by the virgin smells of an occasional barnyard and hay fields along the way. As I rode I began to imagine I was the most important person in the world, not in a selfish or self-centered way; it was just a feeling of floating free.

At the next rest stop, someone told me that Thane and his dad were riding in the lead van. Since Thane had been hired as the technical director to plan the route for the two-day ride, he needed to be in front of the group, so I never saw him. I tried not to think about anything except riding, but I couldn't help wondering how it might feel to see Phil again.

Suddenly, when a thunderstorm threatened, I pushed harder to reach the next shelter. As I came to a stop under the wooden structure just minutes before the downpour, I heard cheers for *"Thane's mom."*

On the second day, with the wind spitting in my face, I put forth a punishing effort for the worst part of the ride — the uphill climb to Horsetooth Reservoir and Carter Lake, then another steep incline to the lunch stop. I was surprised to see

Thane and Phil standing there, waiting for me to arrive.

Noting my Alfa Romeo bike shirt, Phil said, "You look sharp. Did you ride all day yesterday?"

"Yes, I did."

"Connie, why don't you ride in the lead van with Thane? I'll take your bike."

"No, I'm going to finish."

Phil shocked me when he borrowed a bike and rode with me. I wanted to hug him for his support.

As the afternoon wore on, dark clouds moved in and another thunderstorm hovered. I was grateful for Megan, who rode nearly thirty miles from Boulder to meet me for the final and hardest phase of the ride.

Determined to make it to the finish line, I exerted energy I didn't know I had. As I rounded the final uphill curve, relief and exhaustion merged with exhilarating sounds of a country and western band, and the sweet smell of barbecue. When I rode across the finish line and my feet touched the ground, Thane wrapped his arms around me with a hug I will always remember.

As if I needed more excitement and challenge in my summer, Thane and Mark initiated a camping trip that would begin at the mining town of Minturn, Colorado, and would take us to timberline. On the first day, with the sun already high in the sky, each of us carried our own packs and began hiking at a steady, but relaxed pace, unconcerned about time or distance. However, when a group of four-wheelers caught up with us and offered a ride, we gladly accepted. After bumping along in an open jeep for several miles, the trail forked and we parted company.

Once again on foot, we passed century-old mining shacks. Accompanied by the fresh scent of pine and clusters of willowy aspens, silence was a consoling companion, and allowed time for reflection. Even though all my life people had seen me as strong and capable, and somehow less vulnerable to the insecurities that affected others, I always felt I had to prove myself. Today was no exception.

Connie climbs **Grays Peak** in Colorado, her first 14,000 foot peak, during the summer of 1989.

When we finally reached timberline, I stood in disbelief at a lake nestled into the top of a mountain with gently sloping snow-capped peaks on three sides. Thane and Mark, smiling with proud accomplishment, began to clear rocks from an area near the lake to assemble our tent.

Before the sun slipped behind the peaks, they gathered dry timber for a campfire, just in time for a dinner of buffalo burgers, baked beans, and s'mores (melted chocolate and marshmallows between graham crackers). After brushing our teeth in the stream, we crashed in our sleeping bags inside the tent. I was thrilled they had brought a camping pillow for Mom.

Two days later, we hiked along the ridge above the river, and then realized that the quickest way back to our car was to cross the river. Walking the log plank was no big deal for Thane and Mark, but to me, it looked fatal. After successfully traversing the waters while carrying a thirty-pound pack on my back, I was beginning to get a glimpse of the spontaneous and uninhibited being that was the real me, and it felt great.

Later that summer, Thane suggested I climb my first 14,000 foot peak. When I hesitated, he quickly insisted that we only needed to hike part way to the top.

On the day of the climb to *Grays Peak*, we reached a point where I thought I couldn't go any farther — that is, until Thane told me this was the point at which his girlfriend had stopped. Not wanting to be outdone, I vowed to continue, and couldn't help noticing how the people on the trail above us looked like tiny specks against the mountain.

When we considered going all the way to the top, we evaluated our food and clothing, and decided we could safely manage it. At the higher elevation, the warm sunny day suddenly turned to snow and poor visibility. Finally, in the midst of blizzard conditions, we reached the summit and were happy to share hot chocolate with other brave souls.

The summer ended quietly in celebration of my birthday, with red roses and chocolate mousse topped with fresh raspberries from Mark and his girlfriend, Careen.

Even though positive changes had occurred in my life, the work scene was still irregular and unpredictable. Primarily, I lacked organizational structure and a marketing plan that would help publicize my business. In spite of knowing I had the ability and potential for interior design, feelings of incompetence and uncertainty about running a successful business hindered my financial stability. I continued to spend evenings and weekends working on my book-length manuscript, but of course, that didn't contribute to my income.

When the Pacific Northwest was promoted as an ideal place to live, I used this opportunity to fulfill my dream of living by the water, and I flew to Seattle. On the last day of my trip, I saw a *FOR RENT* sign near the water in the village of Kirkland. As I walked into a newly renovated, two-bedroom condominium at Washington Shores, overlooking Lake Washington, I knew it was the place for me.

When it was time to fly back to Denver, the manager of the complex thrust a set of lease papers in my hand and said, "Here, fill these out on the plane and mail them back to me."

Back in Denver, it was remarkable how the place on the lake perfectly matched the desired features I had jotted down on a list and taped to my refrigerator. This process was exactly as described in the book *You Can Have It All*, written by Arnold Patent.

To have money for the move, I reluctantly sold my black Oriental bedroom suite, the marble dining table and upholstered chairs, as well as my handsome black sectional sofa. Letting go of the costly pieces I had purchased over the last five years was difficult, but after all, I was trading things for what I hoped would be an exciting new adventure.

A wonderful acknowledgment of my relocation came from a long-time friend.

Dear Connie,
Gosh, that bike ride must have jarred something loose! Well done! I should think your sons would be proud of you. And now your move to Seattle. There is always good news and bad news about a major move. But, if you can do a bike ride like that, you can do anything! I will be watching you in Seattle.

Love,
Alan

When I drove out of Denver, waving to my sons through the sunroof of my Honda, I felt incredibly brave. As I traveled, the changing colors and textures of the rugged terrain became my most intimate companions. When daylight faded into evening, warnings from friends about the dangers of a woman traveling alone momentarily dampened my courage. But the willingness to take that illogical, artistic license to experience life was exhilarating.

While a moving company transported the furnishings I didn't sell, I carried my most prized possessions such as the Ginori china from Italy, my typewriter, the boys' baby books, college scrapbooks, and of course, my manuscript, in the trunk of my car.

After arriving in Kirkland with $500 in the bank, and without the security of a job or friends, I reveled in the idea of only one kind of success: that of being able to spend my life however I wanted. The condo I had leased was in the final stages of renovation. During the day, I supervised workmen. At night, I slept on a pile of blankets in the master bedroom. Ten days later, my furnishings arrived.

From both bedrooms of my condo, the seemingly barren scene of a wooden pier overlooking the rippled waters of Lake Washington was so incredibly peaceful, it was impossible to think of being lonely. Sitting at my typewriter, I was wonderfully content to work until late at night, even into the early morning.

In the past, I had been accustomed to expressing only those thoughts and feelings that were appropriate and safe, but all that began to change. I knew there were other women who had the same feelings of being used up, taking care of everyone except themselves, and could benefit from the truth of my experiences.

While others around me were sailing, going to movies, or enjoying Thanksgiving dinner, I was completely fulfilled by my writing. At times it seemed like a lonely way to live, perhaps even an escape, but it was exciting to be absorbed in something I loved.

During the holiday season, I missed the closeness of family and friends. My brother Lyn and his wife Joanne were hosting a family reunion in Vail for my parents, my sister Brenda and her family, and Thane and Mark. In the absence of family and friends, it was comforting to know that Helen Roll, whom I had met years ago in Denver, lived on Diamond Point. The island was some distance away and was only accessible by ferry, so when I found her letter in my mailbox, I smiled.

Connie's view of the pier on **Lake Washington**
Kirkland, Washington - 1989

Dearest Connie,
Hope you're not having second thoughts about living in an area which is so wet during the winter. Of course the excessive moisture makes for a gorgeous, lush country in the spring and summer, as well as a beautiful fall. You will need time to become acclimated to conditions here. You are to be complimented on making this move by yourself. You have our prayers that everything will work out beautifully. What a joy to share the countryside together.
Take care and God bless you!

Much love,
Helen

One evening after dinner, I heard an unexpected knock on my door. "Hello, I'm Mary Lord. We met at the mailbox. I'm having a cocktail party at my place tomorrow night. I would like for you to come."

"Thank you, I'd love to come," I said, pleased that our brief conversation in the foyer was possibly the beginning of a new friendship.

"Great! I live at the end of the hall on the first floor overlooking the lake. Guests will probably start arriving around eight o'clock."

Standing in her living room, which overlooked the shimmering waters that seemed to reflect the entire universe, I once again felt a strong connection with a higher power, and knew I was where I needed to be. As I mingled among the guests engaged in conversation, I was introduced to Nancy Bradley. Before the evening was over, we had covered the dynamics of the creative process, discussed the woes of perfectionism, and the issue of procrastination. I was flattered when she offered to look at my manuscript.

After spending weeks poring over the chapters, her exceptional insight confirmed the direction of my writing, but also substantiated the need for a total rewrite. From then on, our conversations, whether biking in the rain on Mother's Day, touring a winery, or attending a lecture at the university, always turned to the subject of *the book*.

Some Saturday nights, I walked into the village of Kirkland to browse through the bookstore or stop for a bowl of Bouillabaisse with delicious chunks of fresh seafood, served with the best French bread. The route along the lake was a peaceful scene with weeping willows against a sultry sky, one that nurtured my soul. On this particular evening, it felt good to be at my typewriter writing to my friend Megan.

Dear Megan,

If you were here, we could sit by the water or chat in a nearby coffee house. The number of books per capita is much higher here in Seattle, as well as writers, published authors, bookstores, frame shops, and art galleries.

I encourage anyone to consider a major move, just to discover who they are in a new environment. It has forced me to create relationships beyond those which were simply comfortable and convenient. It has shown me that I am capable of surviving anywhere.

You mentioned some of the confusing issues in your relationship. At the singles group I attended last night, the speaker focused on the topic of sex. He emphasized that the warmth and pleasure of sexual chemistry can be exhilarating and powerful. But he re-affirmed that what most of us want and need is a feeling of security, which only comes from knowing that someone is truly in love with us, and can nurture us with kindness and sensitivity.

He stated that sex has absolutely nothing to do with building a strong relationship. It can promise involvement without delivering anything. To build a strong relationship, two people must have a common purpose and straightforward communication.

Well, my friend, it's a big job to get free of our selfish needs and hold out for the reality of love. Tomorrow is Sunday, with another new church to explore, and a coffee date with two male friends. Must go get my clothes out of the dryer and do some more writing.

I love you,
Connie

Weeping willows against a sultry sky along **Lake Washington**
Kirkland, Washington - 1989

In order to assuage my loneliness when I wasn't working or writing, I went to museums or movies in the University District. One day I had lunch at an outdoor cafe with a new friend from my hometown in Kansas. Through my sister, I had learned that Berdene lived in a suburb of Seattle and owned an antique shop on Beach Drive Southwest. While she talked of her challenges with real estate ventures and the antique business, I excitedly told her about my part-time job at Archie's bakery-cafe in downtown Kirkland, where I was blissfully happy learning how to prepare lattés, cappuccino, bacon-cheddar biscuits, peach macaroons, and a variety of muffins, blueberry oat bran being one of my favorites.

When I wasn't working at the cafe, I promoted my interior design concept, *Using What You Already Have*, and generated clients through realtors as well as new acquaintances. Without realizing that creating a career of my own required intensive effort, I managed to survive against the odds of being new in town, and also organized a seminar for women at a leading community college. During this event, I explored the creative process and used the philosophy, *We are never truly happy unless we are following our passion*. With the support of a few close friends in attendance, I felt the power and exhilaration of throwing myself into action without a net, and gave credit to my fiercely determined spirit.

In the meantime, the adventures of my sons were no less exciting than my own. Mark, now twenty-three, still had a passion for the culinary arts. Having discovered cooking as one of the most gratifying art forms, he had become a key figure in the opening of a new Italian restaurant known as Ciao' Baby. As the head cook, he created the daily menu, managed food costs, and handled the payroll.

Thane's recent letter indicated he had just completed a five-day race in Nevada with some of the stages covering more than 100 miles a day. He would then go to Mammoth, California to compete in national mountain bike events. But

Son, **Mark Wright,** helps open the new restaurant **Ciao' Baby.**
Denver, Colorado

Son, **Thane Wright**, competes in the "first"
International Mountain Bike Competition.
Durango, Colorado—Summer of 1990

the grandest moment was the summer of 1990, when, at the age of twenty-seven, he competed with the world's elite in the *first* international mountain bike competition in Durango, Colorado.

Chris, having turned twenty-eight, had just made an appearance on national television. For the last several months, the staff at his school had used a computer with a joystick to teach him how to operate a motorized wheelchair. During the *United Cerebral Palsy Telethon*, he made his way around the big oak tree and down the sidewalk with the proudest smile I had ever seen. But due to the lack of state funding and Chris' inability to safely operate a motorized chair, the idea of his independence was short-lived.

Christmas had arrived all too quickly. And with the sentiments of the season it was easy to want to be with someone special. I had a few dates with a seductive and good-looking guy who seemed a viable prospect, but when he confessed he had a girlfriend back in Ohio, I ended the relationship.

When I had trouble shaking the vulnerability to unavailable men, I again experienced the familiar isolation and self-pity. When I was convinced I hadn't really sprung loose from the dependency trap, I decided to meet with a counselor to get a new perspective. She immediately asked, "What was it about this relationship that was so special to you?"

I said, "I was happy, I felt more creative, more sensuous, and more attractive."

"Connie," she pleaded, "whatever you felt with him is what you need to create for yourself. Too often, we look to someone else to fill the void that exists within ourselves. It's easy to get involved in a romance when, realistically, a healthy self-worth is what contributes to a successful relationship.

"Every situation is perfect for the next step of your spiritual journey. It sounds like you're ready to read some of the mystics, perhaps *Man's Eternal Quest* by Yogananda. His wisdom won't magically protect you from all the disappointments, angst, and grief, which are part of everyone's life, but it will help keep you on track."

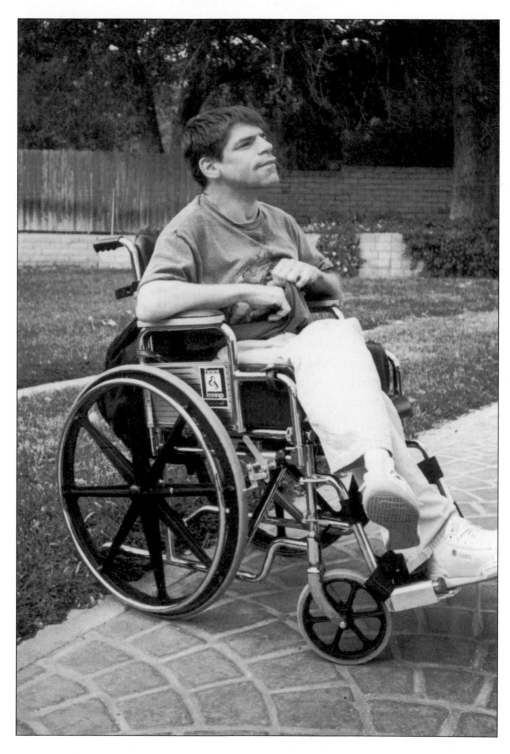

Son, **Christian Wright**, after being featured on
United Cerebral Palsy Telethon.
Los Angeles, California

In growing up, religious practices were a matter of family tradition and also appeared to have a social benefit, even adding to one's status in the community. The teachings from the parables had given me a foundation for discipline and morals. But while scriptural authority promised rewards to the virtuous and conscientious, it seemed that religious people who adhered to the imposed structure and believed in a literal interpretation of the *word of God*, were often quick to judge others who were seemingly disobedient, or had differing philosophical viewpoints. A religious fixation on strict dogma had somehow failed to take into account the possible benefits of my accumulative experiences. Perhaps the most important thing for me to know was that I was in exactly the right place, and doing what I needed to do for my own spiritual journey.

In some ways, the religion of my youth had failed me. It resembled a report card that graded me for my performance, rather than showing me how to get rid of everything that was not me, everything that distorted or diluted the person I really wanted to be. Later in life, when I rebelled internally against personal losses and injuries, my questions were never fully satisfied by theological explanations. Rather than seeing loss as an opportunity, I was often trapped in some of the old beliefs, the most harmful of which was the idea of punishment. *If you got sick or were born with a disability, it was payment for something you deserved.*

After reading Yogananda's work, I saw how I could use my knowledge and experience from all of my lifetimes and tap into the deeper part of my soul, the *real* source of power and creativity. This would not only give me peace and comfort, but I could possibly experience the fulfillment of a life that I had not yet imagined.

Socrates said, "Know thyself and everything else follows." The Christians asserted, "The truth shall set you free." Perhaps they both meant the same. With an increase in knowledge about myself as a spiritual being, I could actually fulfill the purpose of my existence.

I remembered the story in the New Testament where a woman of adultery was commanded by law to be stoned. When Jesus appeared at the scene, he said, "If there be any man among you who has not sinned, let him be the first to cast the stone." Those who were convicted by their own conscience soon scattered, leaving the woman to discover her true nature, without condemnation.

Grateful for a life chock-full of extraordinary experiences, I began to realize that my experiences had not, in fact, caused my suffering, but rather my perception of them. In reality, my trials were also my greatest triumphs!

As if my life had been perfectly planned, I met Mike McManus, the founder of a program called *Source*, which offered guidance to people who were at a crossroads in their lives. The program was designed to uncover one's deepest passions and get at the real source of their creativity.

The first assignment was to write an autobiography that reflected on memorable experiences from childhood, special people who played a significant role in my life, and meaningful geographical places, sights, sounds, touches, and smells.

Through this comprehensive written exercise, I discovered certain curiosities and strengths that had been there all my life. I saw that since childhood I had an unquenchable thirst for knowledge and beauty.

When I wrote a description of my ideal career, it became clear that I would create my own design company, which would transform home and office environments into more aesthetic and functional spaces. It would also include writing about the highest state of spiritual awareness, and teaching others how to fulfill their life purpose. The most difficult part of the process was being willing *not to know* how it would all come together. I was assured, however, that with enough intention and perseverance, the appropriate resources would find *me*.

After completing this program, I felt as if I had reconciled part of my torment, the uncertainty about who I was. The

Connie enjoys the freedom to live her life with fewer restraints.

question now, was how to reconcile my desire for freedom with my need for roots and stability. How could I actually put down roots at a time when the ground seemed to shift daily beneath my feet?

Not long after that, while driving through Bellevue en route to Seattle, I saw a sign on the sidewalk that said *FREE PERSONALITY TEST*. I turned sharply across the yellow line and pulled into the parking lot next to the building.

I went inside to ask about the test. Technically, it was known as the Oxford Capacity Analysis and was composed of two hundred questions to which I could answer yes, no, or maybe. My answers would measure my strengths and weaknesses in ten different areas. Because the personality test was an indication of *my* perceptions rather than someone else's opinion, the test would help me understand myself better.

The scores were effectively displayed on a specially prepared graph and showed areas of my life that were working very well. Other areas fell below the normal range. For the most part, my scores indicated a pattern that had been working against me most of my life. It was a condition of stress that resulted from continuous degrading and discrediting by physical or verbal attacks. Over time, this had been counter-productive to my efforts and good intentions.

I always thought people just had stress and coped the best way they could. I hadn't considered there might be an identifiable source, but now I understood why I often felt helpless to change things, why I sometimes made incorrect assessments of people and situations. Even the glass-door incident, the car accidents, the shoplifting episode, and even illnesses, were part of a pattern of suppression. The cause of this pattern, which stemmed from an underlying and unknown source, would eventually be identified.

In addition to doing the personality profile, I signed up for a series of life improvement courses and thirty hours of individual counseling known as *auditing*. I was told that the counselor, referred to as an *auditor*, was trained to ask questions specifically designed to pinpoint problem areas. The process would be non-judgmental and non-invalidating, making it easier for me to confront and handle those areas that were keeping me from maximizing my natural abilities.

After weeks of being helped to unravel and review those painful incidents in my life (emotional or physical), I discovered that I could actually eliminate the unwanted emotions and irregular behaviors which stemmed from those experiences. As I continued with the auditing process, the sorrow and sadness associated with things in my past gradually lifted, and I slowly began to overcome my lack of confidence.

Through this process, I began to feel that I was in control of my own happiness. It was one of the biggest successes of my life. I owe a debt of gratitude to L. Ron Hubbard for dedication to his research, which resulted in these phenomenal counseling procedures. I now felt that I could enjoy the freedom to break into the professional and artistic scene and live with fewer restraints.

24
SEASON OF RENEWAL

In retrospect, I had always been creating, but had needed to withdraw from the distractions of life in order to rediscover who I really was, and to reclaim my ability to make things happen the way I wanted. Now with a clear sense of my chosen path, I was ready to move back to Denver where my two sons lived and where I still owned three properties. Due to the declining economy of the early eighties, my downtown condominium had gone into foreclosure. My larger townhouse was leased to a woman attorney, and the duplex was occupied by two families on a long-term lease. A third property, an eight-hundred-square-foot townhouse, had just been vacated. It would be the perfect place to live.

Sitting behind the wheel of a rented U-Haul and pulling my car across the country alone was a bold way for a woman to travel, but it was affordable. After several days on the road through a raging snowstorm in parts of Idaho and Wyoming, I excitedly approached the sign in the distance that read *WELCOME TO COLORADO*.

Entering the outskirts of the city and driving across town to my vacant townhouse, I eagerly anticipated the idea of re-creating my life and a new business. I knew it wasn't going to be easy, but with strong convictions and a strategy comprised of small, deliberate steps, I hoped I could make it happen before the elusive dream burned out.

I had barely unpacked when a brown envelope arrived from Nancy in Seattle. She had sent a newspaper article from *The Seattle Times* which showed *before* and *after* photographs of a living room that had been transformed by two interior designers, using only the client's existing furnishings. The dramatic new look had required only a few hours and minimal expense.

Knowing it was the same concept I had been using in design, I immediately saw how it could be promoted in Denver. The article prompted me to make inquiries. I finally located someone at *The Denver Post* with whom I scheduled an appointment.

A few weeks later, I sat across the desk from Cynthia Pasquale, a staff writer for the section of the newspaper entitled *Colorado Living Homestyle*. I explained that my approach to interior design was to show people how they could achieve dramatic results in a home or office — *Using What They Already Have.*

I handed her the article from *The Seattle Times,* which illustrated the same idea. As she scanned the article and nodded with interest, I quickly pulled out photographs of my work. She smiled and said, "Very nice." Then she paused and continued, "In all honesty, Connie, I can't guarantee how long the *Homestyle* section will remain part of our paper. And even if *The Post* decides to do an article on this idea, it might not be published for a couple of months."

I assured her that if the newspaper could present a concept of interior design that was not only affordable, but feasible with *any size space* and *any kind of furnishings,* they would be making a tremendous contribution to their readers.

"Connie, if we publish the story, I would require new pictures taken by our photographer. After he photographs the rooms, I will interview you and the homeowner."

I left her office, determined to find rooms that, after the process of rearrangement, would photograph well. After several weeks, the work was done and Cynthia and her photographers completed their portion of the assignment.

It was Friday morning, December 29, 1990, a week after Christmas — nearly a month since I had talked with Cynthia at *The Denver Post.* When the telephone rang, I rolled over and glanced at the clock radio next to my bed. Who could be calling me at seven-fifteen in the morning?

When I picked up the phone I heard a woman's voice. "Hello, I'm calling for Connie Morgan."

"Uh-uh, this is she," I mumbled.

"Perhaps I have the wrong number. I'm looking for the designer, Connie Morgan."

I quickly sat up in bed.

"This is Connie Morgan."

"Yes, I'd like to schedule an appointment."

"Let me get your name and number and I'll call you back." I quickly reached for a pen and paper next to my bed.

As soon as I hung up the phone, it rang again.

"Hello."

"I'm calling for Connie Morgan who does interior design. Perhaps I have the wrong number."

"This is Connie Morgan. Let me take your phone number and I'll call you right back."

As I scrambled for my robe and scurried into the bathroom, the phone continued to ring. Before getting into the shower, I took another call. The woman said, "Hello, I'm calling about the newspaper article."

"When did you see it?" I asked, swallowing hard.

"It was in *The Denver Post* this morning."

"Let me take your name and number. I'll call you back."

Instead of taking a shower, I hurriedly threw on my jeans and flew down the stairs and out the front door toward the newspaper stand. Breathlessly, I dropped a quarter into the machine and anxiously pulled out a copy of *The Denver Post*. I hurriedly thumbed through the first section of the paper, then I stopped short. Oh my God! Featured on the front page of the *Colorado Living Homestyle* section was a full-page article and pictures with a headline that read:

BREAKING THE RULES OF DESIGN
CONNIE MORGAN MAKES DARING DECISIVE MOVES

The *before* picture of a townhouse living room illustrated the effects of an ill-arranged and non-functional space with boring

BEFORE: A non-functional boring space;
neutral sofas, walls and carpet; art hung too high.
Featured in *The Denver Post*

neutral-colored sofas, walls, and carpet. The art was hung too high, and bookshelves in front of the windows obscured the view of a beautiful lake and evergreen trees outside.

The *after* picture dramatically showed how existing furnishings were repositioned into a more functional and aesthetic style, and walls painted a Wedgwood Blue.

Author Cynthia Pasquale wrote, "If you're thinking about redecorating a room or two in your home, remember that you have enough. You don't need to go out and buy more stuff. You can have a warm and luxurious feeling without forking over a big chunk of your salary.

"It's a simple theory really, but one that most people fail to put into practice. That's when Connie Morgan takes over. She waltzes into a room, stands with her hands on her hips, squints with a critical eye, and then jumps into action. She moves the small pieces of furniture out of the room and takes the pictures off the walls. In other words, she starts with a clean canvas. In a matter of hours, the room is transformed

AFTER: A more cohesive, aesthetic room with walls painted
Wedgwood Blue and furniture repositioned.
Featured in *The Denver Post*

into a living space that is orderly and well balanced with a
look of total harmony.

"Even though people are not trained in the technology of
interior design, Morgan says everyone has the innate ability
to *recognize* beauty and order. But because of a lack of
exposure and training, they are often fearful of using bold
color, especially in small spaces."

On that unforgettable Friday morning, I received thirty
phone calls in the first half hour and forty more calls within
the next hour. Unprepared to do business, I called a friend
who agreed to design client-information forms, invoices, and
business cards.

My first design job started that afternoon. I completed
three more homes by the weekend. My calendar was booked
for the next six months. Whether my clients lived in a sparsely furnished studio apartment, a two-bedroom condo, a
three thousand square-foot-home, or simply needed a more
professional look in their office, I could promise results.

BEFORE: A home office with no color;
small pieces of art and a challenging wall space.
Featured in *BusinessWeek Magazine*

Now that I was no longer wearing an anonymous face, my earlier frustrations had been turned into a new and fulfilling purpose.

Since I was making good money, I remodeled my kitchen with new Formica cabinets, matching countertops, and wood floors. I transformed my bathroom by removing the outdated tub, adding a large shower, new cabinets, and a tile floor. The rich taupe-colored walls and carpet were coordinated with matching wood blinds on the windows which visually enlarged a relatively small space.

As referrals came from a rapidly growing clientele, I became known as the designer who could *Change Rooms* and *Change Lives*.

Over the next few years, I was honored to have my work published in other newspapers and magazines: *Expressions,*

AFTER: A more functional and exciting work area;
dramatic use of color on walls and floor; added artifacts and plants.
Featured in *BusinessWeek Magazine*

BusinessWeek Magazine, Colorado Homes and Lifestyles, Alpine Living, The Boulder Camera, and 5280 Magazine.

Since I used the concept, *Making the Most of What You Already Have,* my work was extremely physical at times. But from my long-standing practice of nutrition and exercise, I prided myself on having high energy. I was therefore shocked, and frightened, when suddenly I was barely able to get up in the morning, and was forced to sleep in the middle of the day.

When my symptoms continued, I drove myself to the emergency room at two o'clock in the morning, trusting that a doctor's prescription would take care of the problem. However, as days wore on, my condition worsened.

After being at home for nearly a month and unable to work, my friend John, whom I had met during the *est* training, invited me to a farewell dinner given in the honor of a man who was leaving for South America to practice a new therapy.

"Yes, if you're driving, I'd love to go," I replied, excited to get out of the house.

At the restaurant, I sat opposite the guest of honor who began sharing the amazing results of a simple hands-on therapy. When I inquired further, with the thought of helping Chris, he gave me the name and phone number of a woman who was conducting a seminar in the Denver area.

Two weeks later another friend, Maria, whom I had also known since the *est* training, drove me to the two-day seminar to hear about this new *Bio-Magnetics* technique. On the first day, Nancy, our supervisor, explained how the *light-touch* procedure addressed specific points on the body and opened the nerve endings to increase the flow of electrical magnetic energy. In this way, the body was able to utilize its own natural healing ability. Then, one by one, she examined the color and texture of our skin and asked questions about our medical history.

On the second day, another woman spoke about her debilitating fatigue and inability to care for her family. It was then that I began to fear the worst. I immediately went to the supervisor and said, "Nancy, I think I have *Chronic Fatigue Syndrome*. My symptoms are exactly what she just described."

"Yes, you do," she said.

"How do you know?"

"When I examined your body yesterday and noted your earlier history of mononucleosis, which affects the immune system, I was certain of your condition. Because some people don't want to be helped, even in spite of their symptoms, we prefer that *they* originate their concerns."

"What can I do about it?"

"I'll give you the telephone number for Kathy Gale, a woman in Denver who is a Bio-Magnetic practitioner. She is trained to perform the technique that addresses the

Chronic Fatigue virus. The treatment, however, must be performed every day within the same hour and must be done for seven days."

Desperate to recover my energy, I called to schedule an appointment. On Monday morning at eight-thirty, Kathy began with the simple hands-on treatment, which took less than fifteen minutes. "In theory," she said "the virus duplicates every twenty-four hours. When the energy in the body is altered by this procedure during that same period, the virus is unable to reproduce."

Every day, after Kathy's Bio-Magnetics technique, I felt a slight increase in energy. After the seventh day I knew the virus was gone. Within a few weeks, I resumed my usual activities.

Naturally, when I told friends and family what had happened, some of them were skeptical. But when I heard how others who had been given the diagnosis of *Chronic Fatigue Syndrome* and forced to limit their work schedules, or give up their work entirely, I was thankful to have found a cure. It was a condition that reportedly could be a disease of the brain and spinal column rather than the immune system, and was NOT curable with antibiotics.

After getting back to a normal schedule, I began to promote my interior design business by conducting design seminars, using a slide show with photographs of my work. As word spread about a design concept that could transform average and ordinary spaces, I traveled to Seattle, Los Angeles, Kansas City, Wyoming, and New Mexico to re-design home and office environments.

Success in my business allowed me to make plans to return to Los Angeles for a luncheon and fashion show sponsored by the Mothers' Auxiliary of *United Cerebral Palsy*, and supported by women's clubs throughout the city who had also worked hard to donate money for our children.

After boarding a flight to Los Angeles International, I eagerly anticipated this annual fund-raising event, and especially looked forward to reconnecting with mothers I had known during those early years.

As I glanced across the crowded ballroom of the Beverly Hilton, I saw faces of women who were wiser because of their sorrow, and stronger because of their hardships. In my mind, they were pillars in the temples of God. In spite of the many interactions at the Auxiliary meetings and fund-raising events, these women had never discussed the causes of brain injury in their children and they had never asked for pity. Instead, they had worked diligently to raise hundreds of thousands of dollars for programs to help their children transcend their difficulties.

Sitting in a room with some of the greatest human beings I would ever know, I was reminded of how a sense of fellowship had been crucial to our survival. One of the mothers whom I had always admired was Maggie, who was sitting across the table from me. She was as beautiful as I had remembered. With her long dark hair and gorgeous smile, she was a picture of perfection. There wasn't a hint of how she had suffered when her son was suddenly disabled and became a resident at the Foundation where Chris lived.

As we talked, she confided for the first time about how it happened. "Connie, I took my two-year-old son to the doctor for a minor problem with his walking. The doctor gave him a medication, which promptly caused a reaction of convulsive seizures. The hospital put him on a respirator for twenty-four hours. After that, he survived with a normal mind, but regrettably, was completely paralyzed except for movement in one hand.

"I was in shock for five years. Our marriage fell into shambles. My husband withdrew from any meaningful communication and was unable to give any moral support. As long as he had meals on time, clean laundry, and undisturbed comfort in front of the television, he got through the day."

Maggie's story reminded me of the phenomenal strength that was required to live with the uncertainty of a disabled child, and to walk that special path laden with emotional land mines.

Maggie introduced me to Karen, who also had a son with cerebral palsy. She told me how a family emergency had occurred and how she had no one to keep her ten-year-old son. As a last resort, her doctor suggested she put him in an institution until she returned. Desperate, she finally consented. Karen told how, when she returned two weeks later, her doctor insisted she leave her son there.

"No way!" she protested.

"But look at him," he said. "He's laughing and interacting with other children which he wasn't doing before."

Karen couldn't deny what she saw. Again, she reluctantly agreed to leave him. But as time went on, her all-consuming guilt led to thoughts of suicide. Even though she was physically free, she felt condemned. Without the responsibility of her son, or a husband to take care of, she felt worthless.

"My neighbors told me to get a job, go to work. The turning point was realizing people cared about me, and knowing that my son was happy. "

Looking back on those early years, I saw that our lives were based on fear — fear of rejection by society, and even our family. Most of all, it was the fear of rejection from our husbands. It was easy to interpret their emotional withdrawal as some sort of punishment. If we stayed with our husbands, we often had to conceal the painful and inappropriate emotions linked to the unbearable responsibility we felt for our child, as well as the relationship. While husbands acted out their feelings of inadequacy and guilt by withdrawing or attacking their wives, the women used part-time jobs or community involvement as a way to escape. Many marriages were simply held together by financial security, or bound by religious sacrament, leaving little opportunity for personal growth and honest communication.

After hearing the stories of other mothers, I was even more indebted to the *United Cerebral Palsy Foundation*, who had not only given me a life, but had given my son an opportunity to become his own person. When I saw Chris during that visit, I was overjoyed just to be with him, and grateful to see that his energetic spirit was still alive.

After returning to Denver, I read about another woman who had experienced an unhappy marriage. Suffocated by the expectations of being a wife, she went to her attorney to begin divorce proceedings. He suggested that while the legal documents were being prepared during the next several months, she should use every imaginable strategy to romance her husband. Once he was happy, she could then serve the appropriate papers.

Months later, she returned to the attorney's office. When he handed over the divorce papers, she said, "I won't be needing them. We're getting ready to leave on our second honeymoon."

It was a good story, that is if she didn't confuse the longevity of a marriage with real satisfaction, and that she was willing to consider the possibility of recurring behavior.

As for myself, I wasn't willing to ignore what I had learned about a woman's hidden fear of independence. Neither was I willing to continue being subservient for the sake of status and a more comfortable lifestyle.

On the other hand, I was learning that nearly all problems and all types of suffering are possible to overcome, if only we are committed to finding a solution. But as long as we remain a victim of our own inner conflicts, and are willing to live with false information and perceptions that are not true, we will always be vulnerable to decisions that don't serve our best interests.

Realizing how frequently I had lashed out at others because of my perceived inadequacy, I was proud to know I had made some progress toward understanding those earlier behaviors.

Unfortunately, it took another devastating incident to show me that I had more to learn. A friend had referred me to an accountant whose new computer system was purported to enhance the management of small businesses. During our first meeting, we reviewed the services I needed: a depreciation schedule for three real estate properties, a monthly accounting system for my design business, and completion of yearly taxes. Before we concluded the meeting, I trusted that he understood I was an entrepreneur with a limited budget.

A month later, sitting in his office, he spoke in generalities about the work he had done, and handed me an invoice for $4,000. Stunned by the disproportionate figure, I felt trapped in a tangled web of deceit and betrayal. I grabbed my briefcase, stormed out of his office, and slammed the French doors behind me.

Enraged and confused as to whose responsibility this was, I hurried down the stairs and out the door to the parking lot, and then managed to drive home without speeding. Once inside my comfortable space, I realized the need to align with people who were capable of reason and trust, and could help me make appropriate choices.

I picked up the phone to get a number for the same group I had worked with in Seattle, a group of highly trained staff who had the capabilities to resolve any kind of upset or conflict.

"Yes, I have three numbers," the operator said. "Which one do you want?"

"Whatever looks like a main number," I pleaded.

When I dialed and a friendly voice answered, I shared my ordeal and was immediately given the name and phone number of a woman accountant who could help resolve the situation.

On Monday morning, Paula and I drove to the scene of the crime. Sitting side by side in wooden armless chairs, we faced the accountant who sat in a tall leather chair behind his desk. During the next half hour, I listened as Paula negotiated the $4,000 invoice to a sum of $2,000 and arranged monthly payments. Then she addressed the issue of communication, the real source of misunderstanding. Unfortunately, there had been no discussion about an hourly charge or a flat fee. I couldn't help thinking the exorbitant fee had something to do with the cost of his new computer system, or his upcoming back surgery.

In retrospect, the handling of the situation was amazingly simple, but the snapped threads of my emotions represented a setback in my reasoning ability. Making a wrong judgment of character caused me to wonder what else I needed to work on, possibly just understanding the warp and woof of life in a way that could make living easier and more predictable.

I had already learned that the inconsistencies in my life didn't indicate that something was wrong with me, only that there were perceptions and feelings that needed to be looked at and handled.

After the good results I had achieved in Seattle, it was comforting to know there was a group in Denver that could help me sort out the confusions, and further eliminate the irrational thoughts which often filtered through my mind.

After weekly auditing, which included a series of specialized processes, I saw that a major barrier in my life was the tendency to act according to the expectations of others, rather than honoring my own values and integrity. When I felt degraded or discredited by the opinions of others, *my* good intentions became less important. I always seemed to be well liked, but I felt I had to be really great in order to get the kind of acknowledgment I craved.

Over the next several years, and with continued hours of one-on-one auditing, I unraveled the causes of my unwanted behaviors and inconsistent productivity. The most incredible part of the experience was seeing that I was more messed up than I thought I was, and realized that it was totally okay. There was no shame in having been messed up, only shame in not having done something about it sooner.

Negative attitudes, emotional upsets, fears, and problems that had existed all my life began to disappear. Gradually, I began to see that I had more potential than anyone had ever given me permission to believe. As I began to feel better about myself, my need for praise and recognition lessened.

With a feeling of relief from unwanted situations, and a new sense of self, I also began to notice that my life was nearly void of accidents and illnesses. Not only did I begin to expand my vision of what else was possible but, I was told I looked lighter and brighter, even younger! The greatest reward, however, was simply knowing that I would no longer be a victim of irrational thoughts and behaviors.

From now on, nothing was more important to me than to separate myself from the threads of life-long conflict, those fixed ideas or considerations I had always thought were valid, and to use my abilities to play a bigger game and accomplish my dreams.

It had been apparent for some time that I needed a larger residence and more space for my home office. I wanted a house with architectural excitement, a park-like setting, and direct access to all parts of the city, as well as an easy escape to the foothills.

For nearly three years, I had searched for an affordable property that would become the home of my dreams. I drove around late at night looking at *FOR SALE* signs. I repeatedly got out of my car to write down the phone numbers of realtors and addresses of properties, only to discover the next day they were well beyond my price range.

In my painstaking search, I had discovered an area called University Park, known for its mature trees, a nine-hole golf course with outdoor pool, neighborhood parks, bike paths, and close proximity to the University of Denver. However, the minimally priced homes of $250,000 during the early nineties exceeded what I could afford.

Determined to have exactly what I wanted, I kept returning to the same neighborhood. One day, I discovered an entire block of renovated, ranch-style patio homes. When I spoke with the developer, he gave me a key to preview the only unsold property on the block. Within minutes after walking through the house and seeing the vaulted ceilings and exceptional windows, hardwood floors, and a master bedroom suite with walk-in closet and bath, I knew this was my home. Walking outside, I stood in the open park-like yard with thirty-foot pines and mature maples, and saw that the property also had a detached two-car garage. To my amazement, the price was $125,000!

I returned to my condo that evening and called a realtor who could help me write a contract for purchase and list my other two properties for sale. As a single woman with an entrepreneurial business, I knew it wouldn't be easy to qualify for a loan.

After being turned down by three lenders, the purchase looked impossible! As days went by, I asked myself, *Is it exactly what I want? If so, how can I get it?* If I were willing to persevere long enough to accomplish my dream of owning this home, it would happen.

While sitting on the chaise lounge in my condo, the telephone interrupted my thoughts. "Ms. Morgan, this is Harry Blackman, the lender you spoke with yesterday. I'm sorry I can't help you with a loan, but I have the name and phone number of a non-conforming lender who has different guidelines than we do."

I thanked him and immediately dialed the number. I was relieved to have scheduled an appointment for the next day.

While waiting patiently in a reception area with a décor of low-budget furniture and cheap silk plants, I was determined to purchase the property of my dreams, one that would give me the satisfaction I craved.

When my name was called, I hurriedly grabbed my briefcase with the necessary loan information, and followed the secretary down the hall. A gentleman in his mid-thirties, dressed in a tie and light blue button-down shirt, introduced himself as Howard Hill from Applewood Mortgage. After he gestured for me to be seated, he scrutinized my financial portfolio, especially noting the equity in properties that I still owned.

Looking up, he said, "Well, Ms. Morgan, since your other two properties are listed for sale, I believe we can secure a second mortgage on those properties until they are sold. If everything goes well, we can close on the loan in ten days."

After signing the preliminary papers, I walked outside feeling like a genius of all time.

While working full-time in my design business, I managed deadlines with electricians, painters, and carpenters. Within two months, I had updated the lighting, added texture to the walls, painted a bold color on ceilings and walls throughout the house, and coordinated furniture items I had purchased and put in storage. The exterior work included construction of a large deck off the living room, installation of new black gutters, and landscaping with lots of evergreen bushes and pinon pines.

During those busy weeks I rewarded myself with small celebrations. Occasionally I stopped for dinner at Bistro Europa, a cozy place with original art on two walls, lace curtains on the windows, and located close to my new residence. At other times I curled up with a cup of tea and a book at bedtime.

After the closing on October 1, 1993, and the actual move by Thanksgiving, I planned an open house for friends and clients. Mark and his kitchen crew, dressed in their white chef coats, organized a cooking station in my basement, prepared wonderful hors d'oeuvres, and served approximately three hundred people. As the guests engaged in conversations about the complex matter of creativity, they not only seemed to recognize the artist within themselves, but discovered mutual friends. For me, it was the recognition that home design, in its purest form, was no different than designing my life. It was an invitation to the sweetness of possibility.

That same year, foregoing my imagined limitations, I sold my nine-year-old Honda Prelude for $2,500—the exact amount I needed for a down payment on a new Honda Civic. By now, it was clear that the time spent working on myself had not only helped me confront the things in my past, but my future as well. Most important, I knew that on this great universal canvas, I could paint whatever my soul desired.

25

A Rose That
Blooms Forever

When my son Mark called late one evening, I was gratified to know he had grown into an artistic young man with many talents. His artwork and poetry, his love for music and guitar, his strengths as an athlete, were all part of his gifts. Through hard work, self-discipline, and an unwavering belief in himself, he had excelled in the culinary field. When he moved to Keystone Resort in Colorado, he joined award-winning chefs at the Alpenglow Stube, a unique and secluded mountaintop setting with exquisite contemporary cuisine. I had gone there recently with friends for a five-course dinner for my birthday. As I watched him create with meticulous attention to detail, I was thrilled he

had found a profession that allowed him to fully express himself. He was later appointed head chef at the Great Northern Tavern in the heart of RiverRun in Keystone. As we said goodbye on the phone, I knew I would always love him for his emotional sensitivity and artistic expression.

A few months later, Thane, who was also living in Keystone Resort, sent me a hand-painted Valentine, an expression of his unique creative energies. With a passion for biking, inspired by a love for the raw beauty of the outdoors, and coupled with strong leadership skills, he had organized cycling events throughout Colorado and the mountain states.

He would soon be leaving to do a 100-mile mountain bike race through the rainforest in the Cascade Mountains of Oregon, a climb of 15,000 vertical feet in less than ten hours. Later, his fierce competitive spirit would lead him to a race in Costa Rica, participating with cyclists from Central America and Europe in a 300-mile race known as the *Route of the Conquistadores.*

In another week, he would be competing in the world's most grueling mountain bike race here in Colorado, appropriately named *Montezuma's Revenge.* It would be a 24-hour race that would take him across ten mountain peaks and approximately 22,000 vertical feet. Thane had done well in the same race several years ago, but this time his mission was to ride in the name of his brother Chris.

In the *Summit Daily News* of Dillon, Colorado, the following items appeared, written by Dan Thomas, sports writer:

Friday, July 14, 2000

HIS BROTHER CHRIS SERVES AS AN INSPIRATION

Montezuma's Revenge is promoted as the toughest challenge a solo cyclist can undertake, but Thane Wright won't be riding alone. The saddle on the bike he will be riding during this 24-hour mountain bike odyssey is big enough to accommodate only one rider, but Thane will be carrying his older brother, Chris, with him. Wright said, "I'm racing the Montezuma's Revenge in Chris' name to honor his spirit and share my love of cycling with him. I want to prompt an increase in awareness about people like Chris, who have also lived a life riding a set of wheels."

Sunday, July 16, 2000

BROTHERHOOD THE WRIGHT STUFF

With a goal to race strong and keep a tight pace, the Wright brothers soared on their night flight with just a bicycle, riding trails which crossed the Continental Divide. Winning the race on a different set of wheels than his brother, Thane delivered his message by covering a distance of 150 miles and climbing 22,000 vertical feet in 24 hours. It was an affirmation of his love for cycling, a microcosm of his spiritual journey—rather than a need for recognition. More significantly, it was a race that was done out of love for his brother.

MONTEZUMA'S REVENGE
Thane Wright crosses the finish line
and delivers his message to his brother **Chris**
by riding 150 miles and 22,000 vertical feet in 24 hours.

Winning this race was a validation of family support and a commitment of team members who not only coached Thane during months of training, but rode with him on every punishing route throughout the day and into the grueling hours of darkness. They cycled over rugged mountain passes in rainy and cold weather, calculated changes in gloves, shoes, jackets and rain gear, as well as the appropriate food intake for reserve energy and maximum endurance.

When the race was over and we reflected on our collective efforts, it was clear that the real adventure is never outside ourselves, but rather an internal odyssey. It's a decision to cycle beyond our crippling circumstances, knowing that we can climb any mountain of our choice. It's the echo of each footstep, the exhilaration of each plateau. It's the knowledge

Celebrating with **Thane**
after he wins the 24-hour race of **MONTEZUMA'S REVENGE**.
Mark, Connie, and **Thane**

Wilderness on Wheels
Connie and **Chris** with friend **Bob Earle**
Conifer, Colorado

that courage and tenacity are half the victory. And finally, it's the realization that it's not too late to become the person we were meant to be.

During my pilgrimage, my three sons had inspired me to look at every moment with the magic of exploration. They were a source of strength that helped pull me out of bondage and move me to the next level of my evolution.

And to them I want to say: Just as the rosebush is awakened by the breath of spring and each rosebud unfolds into its own expression of beauty, the same possibilities exist for your awakening. At certain points in your journey, you will make decisions that influence the rest of your life. Learn to honor your vision, your passions! Listen for what moves you, touches you, makes you want to get up in the morning. Forget your past. It's done. Look at what turns you on in this moment—right now! Your heart's desire will lead you in the way your spirit wants to go. It will be the direction that is the most grounding, the most gratifying, and the most joyous.

Remember that whatever heartbreaking struggle or crisis you encounter, it will be an opportunity to realize your true nature, to discover within yourself a divine power to do the things you never thought possible. Only by living your story and exceeding the limits of who you thought you were, will you experience joy and heartfelt happiness.

I will always love you, not just because you are part of me, but because you are unique and individual expressions of God. You are special. There is no one else like you in the whole world.

In spite of the expectations and standards of a society that had nearly incapacitated me, I was simply amazed at how new information had suddenly become available at the appropriate times. From the beginning, the voice within had cried for a perfect life. Later, the conflict between the delicious security of dependence and independence was huge, only because I had been so unsure of myself. The shackles of patriarchal domin-ation, limiting religious beliefs, and sometimes incapacitating vulnerability had added to the fear of creating a new identity. When the journey seemed vague and even hopeless, I felt as if I were caught in some tough, but translucent, membrane of unconsciousness that would forever hold me captive. That is, until I recognized the need to bulldoze through it and move beyond rigid and regimented patterns.

By being willing to plow through the darkness and con-front the sources of confusion and self-destruction, I had finally discovered the reasons for debilitating emotions and unwanted behaviors. I would no longer live with fixed ideas that were not true, or preconceived ideas that caused me to wander from my self-determined course of action.

Free from the past, I could now direct my energy toward those things that were satisfying, and away from those that were not. Focused on taking responsibility for *all* my actions and a willingness to shape my life, I no longer fooled myself with empty dreams. Instead, my mission was that of seeking a deeper understanding of myself, and the universe.

I not only felt a complete and total relief from the emotional upheaval of my past, but I experienced an immeasurable depth of the God within, a oneness with the *source* that could help me achieve every goal my soul desired.

As I realized a spiritual connection with the entire universe, I was able to surrender to that energizing and intuitive force within and perceive life as a truly joyful experience.

In my pursuit of a perfect life, I never dreamed that my journey would lead me to the one thing that would never deceive me: the rediscovery of *ME*, a woman with abilities far greater than I ever imagined, a woman with courage, perseverance, and creativity, a woman with vision and understanding, a woman whose soul can climb the highest mountain, or sit quietly on a pier overlooking a misty harbor.

Never would I have thought that my trials and tribulations would bring me closer to a realization of my true purpose. In reality, my beloved Chris had shown me how to live the life I came here to live, to walk the path my soul had already chosen.

I hope my story will help you find the truth in your own experiences and discover possibilities you never imagined.

To laugh often and much.

*To win the respect of intelligent people
and the affection of children.*

*To earn the appreciation of honest critics,
and endure the betrayal of false friends.*

To appreciate beauty.

To find the best in others.

*To leave the world a bit better,
whether by a child, a garden patch,
or a redeemed social condition.*

*To know even one life has breathed easier
because you have lived.*

This is to have succeeded.

— RALPH WALDO EMERSON

A woman whose soul can climb the highest mountain,
or sit quietly on a pier overlooking a misty harbor.

Epilogue

Nearly 5,000 babies and infants are diagnosed each year with cerebral palsy. Another estimated 1,500 children of preschool age have related symptoms. Those symptoms can range from poor coordination to speech impairment. Cerebral palsy is NOT inherited. It is NOT a disease, but rather a condition resulting from an injury to the brain, an injury caused by a variety of circumstances. Some are listed here:

Insufficient amount of oxygen to the fetal or newborn brain.

Premature separation of the placenta from the wall of the uterus.

Awkward birth position of the baby.

Labor that is too long or too abrupt.

Interruption of circulation or oxygen supply caused by the umbilical cord.

Blood-type incompatibility between mother and infant.

Infection of the mother with German measles or other viruses in early pregnancy.

Premature birth, low birth weight, or Rh negative.

Brain infection.

Most frequent occurrences: During pregnancy, labor, or delivery.

Common causes of brain injury: A severe blow to the head caused by a car accident, a fall, or child abuse.

The extent of disability in the individual depends on which areas of the brain have been damaged and to what degree. An injury to the brain is *not curable*, but training and therapy can help significantly. The most common conditions seen in cerebral palsy are:

An inability to control motor function and muscle coordination, which affects full body movement.

Muscle tightness or spasms, involuntary movements, disturbance in gait and mobility.

Impairment of sight, hearing, or speech.

Seizures.

Mental retardation.

A disability within a family can easily diminish the joy and self-confidence of any loving, decent human being. It can create a deep sense of unworthiness. Loneliness, isolation, and depression can occur when the connection between family and society breaks down.

United Cerebral Palsy serving Los Angeles, Ventura, and Santa Barbara Counties is one of the largest and most efficient charities in the country, and serves hundreds of adults and children with disabilities. This organization provides comprehensive care for people with severe disabilities, and counseling to help families make appropriate decisions. The primary objective of *United Cerebral Palsy* is to enable these individuals to receive the highest quality of care and training and lead lives of dignity and purpose. *United Cerebral Palsy* does not replace the family. Instead, they become part of the family, bringing energetic love that encourages the child to become as independent as possible.

Whether families are in need of residential services, education, or nursing care, or simply want their child to have a life of joy with friendships and sense of personal achievement, *United Cerebral Palsy* is a force in transforming the lives of families everywhere. For decades, their dedicated staff of physicians, teachers, custodians, bus drivers, cooks, therapists, aides and administrators have poured their hearts and souls into a simple, but powerful idea, the survival of families through the wonderful healing power of love and understanding.

When parents receive this kind of significant support, and are no longer in bondage to any one person, or an imposed lifestyle, they are free to fulfill a new purpose—perhaps even discovering the perfection beneath the tragedy.

www.ucpla.com

818-782-2211

United Cerebral Palsy

6430 Independence Avenue

Woodland Hills, CA 91367

AUTHOR ACKNOWLEDGMENTS

We are all in this world for the purpose of creating.

*The ideas and intuitive powers that come
from a spiritual source
impact our service to others.*

*Those who can help us build on our strengths,
rather than address our weaknesses,
provide a place in which creativity can flourish
It is to those people that I pay tribute.*

With gratitude to Dr. Leroy Netrick, my first writing instructor, for showing me how to use the techniques of writing to share my experience with others.

With love to Nancy Bradley, an artist in Seattle, whose perception and dedication to the direction of this story strengthened my commitment to tell it like it happened.

Thanks to Paul Carr from *Tattered Cover Book Store*, whose enthusiasm for a more comprehensive story on disability provided the impetus for pulling it all together.

With special thanks to Robert Earle, whose willingness to plow through many editions of the manuscript with detailed evaluation was evidence of his love and concern for humanity.

A special appreciation to Erin Smith, whose editorial experience not only enhanced the writing, but led to a definitive cover design and an unforgettable trip to Europe.

I am indebted to Nancy Braan for six weeks of daily telephone conferences, which gave an ethical light to the characters and a more accurate sequence of events.

My appreciation to Ruth Smith from *ABC BOOKS* in Denver, whose editorial direction gave me courage to tell the truth about women's issues as they pertained to me.

With gratitude to Barbara McNichol, whose expedient editing process and dedication to excellence forced my verbs to dance and caused my sentence structures to stay on the right path.

To Nancy Harris, our social worker whose problem-solving applications not only helped our family, but whose contribution to this manuscript will provide insight to other parents and families.

With special appreciation to Norma DeHaan, whose leadership as the administrator of the residential facility in Chatsworth, California, has inspired others to greatness and provided a beautiful place for our children.

I am thankful for the ongoing support of C. E. (Ken) Kennedy, whose professional background in human development and family life at Kansas State University, contributed sensitive insight and confirmed the merits of a story about a family in crisis, and Lois Kennedy for her love and encouragement.

With appreciation to Jerry Barlow for his coffeehouse concerts of Celtic guitar from his album, *Keepsake*, which nurtured my soul during critical stages of editing.

My special thanks to Donald L. Campbell from *Campbell Enterprises*, an irreplaceable computer guy who always knew I was in a jam when I called at eleven-thirty at night.

With gratitude to Rick Wheeler, Music editor of *Music Manuscript Service*, for his exceptional contribution as my data base and software advisor.

To Ty Dillard, my friend and life coach in Ojai, California, whose thorough investigation of the content solidly confirmed the purpose of my soul's journey and taught me to honor the place within me that is disturbing to others.

To my friend and associate editor, Marilyn Imel, in Goodland, Kansas, whose ruthless support helped weave dignity and compassion into the characters and enhanced the drama of the human experience.

With affection and gratitude to Marianna Will for all those evenings sitting on the floor evaluating chapter after chapter, then going out to dinner for an outrageous good time.

Special recognition to Susan Love, Communications Director, *United Cerebral Palsy of Los Angeles*, for her illuminating viewpoints which contributed to the expression of the message.

With gratitude to Anne Wendt, Executive Director Emeritus, *United Cerebral Palsy of Los Angeles*, for her convictions, faith, and hard work toward building a better world for families and their children.

To Stephanie Hill for her elegance of simplicity and artistry in furthering the cover design and original layout.

A special acknowledgment to Becky Sue Asmussen at *Image Graphics* for her standards of excellence in pre-press production and digital refinement.

To Mario Bejarano Caballero in Costa Rica. Even as time passes, I will never forget the colors of the forest and a love which continues to inspire.

To Tony Stubbs from San Diego whose commitment to helping us all return to our Source furthered the divine purpose of this writing.

A special thanks to Marilyn Stoddard, who showered me with love and encouragement throughout the trials and tribulations of this process.

To Zoe Winterburn, *Celebrity Centre of London*, who helped me achieve the freedom to be more of who I really am.

With affection to Pia and Russell Algor for their friendship and encouragement, and especially those provocative late-night conversations.

A special thanks to my friend, Alan Trachsel, for sealskin moccasins and for taking the time to share the back roads of my journey.

To Larry Pease, who embodies the *Humanitarian Award* he received October 2001, for his outstanding service toward individual freedoms.

Thanks to Jan and Lonnie McIntosh for their friendship and support during the uphill climb to the finish.

With much gratitude to Lucy Beckstead, whose editorial ability enlarged the scope of the manuscript and inspired uncompromising excellence.

With love to Camilla Beck, whose guidance as production consultant evoked a huge sigh of relief as we entered the production stage.

My very great appreciation to Connie L. Schmidt and Ron Kaye, literary consultants in Houston, for their razor-sharp conceptual ability and comprehensive review.

I am eternally grateful to Helen Griffith Johnson, an accomplished writer and editor, who walked with me through the entire manuscript.

I am deeply grateful to the hundreds of volunteers in San Antonio, Texas; Lyons, Kansas; and Thousand Oaks, California, who took Chris into their hearts and became part of our family. Your compassion was an expression of the true nature of the human spirit.

The staff at *United Cerebral Palsy of Los Angeles* will be remembered for their extraordinary gifts of service and compassion that strengthened me during one of the great enigmas of my life. Ronald S. Cohen, CEO of *United Cerebral Palsy serving Los Angeles, Ventura, and Santa Barbara Counties*; Anne Wendt, Executive Director Emeritus; Susan Love, Communications Director; Nancy Harris, Director of Client Services; and Mae Stephenson, Director of Client Services.

With deep gratitude to the generous *Volunteer Board of United Cerebral Palsy of Los Angeles*, for their abundance of time and philanthropy which enables families to live with dignity and purpose.

A special thanks to the technicians, therapists, cooks, custodians, bus drivers, and teachers at the *United Cerebral Palsy (Spastic Children's Foundation)* on 105th Street in Los Angeles, the *Chatsworth Residences,* and the *Bledsoe House* in Sylmar, California, where Chris now lives. Thank you for the loving care he could not have received elsewhere.

Much love to John Tejeda, who was Chris' roommate at *Chatsworth Residences,* parents Pat and Louis Tejeda, Rick Riccitelli, Bill Pringle, Eileen Steeg, Bill Coleman, Terri Manno, and Dorothy Thomas. A deep gratitude to staff and others who have strengthened Chris' character and taught him the beauty of trust through unconditional love.

In recognition of countless other beautiful people
whose enriching friendships have inspired me
throughout my journey.

Caro Hatcher, Ph.D.

Vel Peranni

Ray and Lois Seick

Virginia Rupp

Vickie White

Mary Harr

Charlotte Griffin

Betty Allen

Jo Hemple

Sue Daigle

Jan Smith

LaDene Tarabocchia

Ralph Shugaart, MD

Tom Dunn

Anthony Cantagallo

Reverend Richard Evans

Don Williams from NBC

Reverend Fred Venable

David Torbett
Director of Family Enrichment Center

Cleo Taplin

Patrick Allen

Judy Dankenbring

John and Deborah Linebaugh

Joan Gessner

Pat Patterson

Sam Higdon, DDS

Mary Lou Hambright, MSW

George Brantley
Director of Hope Center in Denver

Hazel Hunt

Alice Kacirek

Irene LeBlanc

Carol Gilger

Judy Richards

Ron Hansen

Maria Martinez

Palmina Gover

Dorine Sloan

Shellah Garrett

Reverend Margaret Hankens

Max and Barbara Ward

Barbara Damaschek

Patricia Werner

Errol Hilborn

Dana Scott

John Siepp

Bruce Ostrem

*A special recognition of my family,
whose bonds of a common heritage and
examples of courage will always
remind me of who I am.*

I want to acknowledge and honor my parents, Larry and Isabel Morgan, whose courage and hard work in turning barren, sun-parched plains of western Kansas into a beautiful ranch, have inspired me toward higher creativity.

With gratitude to my brother, Lyn Morgan, who has inspired me through his achievements as a Marine Lieutenant, awarded the *Bronze Star* for heroic combat action in Vietnam, and as the Administrator of the Eagle County Ambulance Service in Colorado.

My affection and appreciation to my beautiful sister, Brenda Kolb, and my brother-in-law, Reverend Jerry Kolb, for their wealth of love and contribution—a special gift to my family and me.

With love to my sister-in-law, Joanne Morgan, for her creative and vibrant energy and commitment to good design, which heightened my inspiration for a beautiful product.

Since the writing of
STAND, WALK, RUN FREE
*has taken nearly as long as living the story,
I may have forgotten someone who has
helped in the process. Nevertheless, I want to
acknowledge all who have helped me on this
extraordinary mission.*

STAND, WALK
RUN FREE

Overcoming Expectations of a Perfect Life

C O N S T A N C E M O R G A N

DESTINED TO BE A BEST SELLER
A rich and memorable story

STAND, WALK, RUN FREE

Overcoming Expectations of a Perfect Life

CONSTANCE MORGAN

ISBN: 0-9715744-0-5

TO ORDER ADDITIONAL COPIES OF THIS BOOK PLEASE USE THIS

SEND TO:

ORDER FORM

NAME _____

ADDRESS _____

_____

CITY _____ STATE _____ ZIP _____

Daytime Phone: _____

E-mail Address: _____

❑ *Check here if you would like an E-mail update from Shallow Creek Press*

SEND ADDITIONAL COPIES TO:

NAME _____

ADDRESS _____

_____

CITY _____ STATE _____ ZIP _____

Daytime Phone: _____

E-mail Address: _____

PLEASE MAKE CHECKS PAYABLE TO:

SHALLOW CREEK PRESS
P.O. Box 100337
Denver, CO 80250

303-758-3707

FOR MULTIPLE BOOK ORDERS or CREDIT CARD ORDERS VISIT US AT

www.conniemorgan.com

QUANTITY **Book Sale Totals**

_____ **@ 24.95 each =** _____

Colorado Residents
Add 3.8% Sales Tax _____

Shipping & Handling
$4.95 for the first book
$2.50 each additional book _____

Sub Total _____

TOTAL SALE _____

For more information please visit our website: **www.conniemorgan.com**
This offer is subject to change without notice.

If more order forms are needed, please photo copy this page.